SUB JUD...

Und...

SHERYL SOPHIA SLEIGH

An Autobiography

First published in 2012 by:
Sheryl Sophia Sleigh

© Copyright 2012
Sheryl Sophia Sleigh

ISBN: 978-0-9551785-1-1

Printed and bound in Great Britain by:
Book Printing UK, Remus House, Coltsfoot Drive, Woodston, Peterborough PE2 9BF

CONTENTS

Also by Sheryl Sophia Sleigh

Sunshine and Shadows

Introduction

I would be no nearer determining my own unique identity without this exhaustive and agonising search from where I have finally gained the knowledge and freedom to hermetically seal the past and realign the future with the things I believe to be an inherent right and privilege for all human beings. I have come to recognise that I possess an instinctive aptitude that allows me to interchange freely within the rigid boundaries of culture, religion, race, prejudices and fear. I characteristically become transmuted by a holy and omnipotent influence directing me into the pathways of individuals whose struggles to freedom are constant echoes of my own. Irrespective of whether a person chooses to sit, stand or walk beside me either in their joy or sorrow, I know faithfully and compellingly that being with them and showing unlimited compassion and care, is undeniably the purpose to which my life has been called.

I believe that a majority of individuals are adequately equipped to overcome every difficulty and conflict that arises within their lives. This begins to manifest when an optimistic view takes place over a damaging and pessimistic one and old modes of behaviour regarding fears and addictions can be confidently relinquished and giving way to inexhaustible possibilities. It would have been impossible to identify what my life was created and destined for without a rigorous excavation from the past to the present, from where I could began to recognise the signs of victory at each demanding stage as I was exultantly released from the hold of oppression and captivity. Everything that was lost, damaged or misplaced in my life demanded a working backwards through a process of cleansing and understanding in order that a new and untarnished pathway may be created forwards and lived guardedly in the present and triumphantly into the future.   Naturally in this process towards transformation, growth and change, I was finally permitted to confidently forgo all my presumptions and prejudices and by so doing increased my autonomy to be patient and considerate towards my friends but especially towards my enemies and to be humble where possible and strong and decisive when necessary. For me, life is not simply an equation of colour, creed and influencing factors to which a person is born but rather a multiplicity of questions and answers; some formulated at the inception of every potential action, whilst others are continuously developed as we become pre-disposed to peripheral dynamics in our everyday interactions with others.   The aim of this book is to ask some of the most disturbing questions and to linger, though only briefly in a number of excruciatingly painful spaces but this time round without the fear of entrapment and failure.

Of course there are a number of measured inquiries to stimulate a robust approach in my chosen methodology and analyses which is merely a malleable apparatus to further highlight the necessity of appropriate questioning without the overbearing urge to provide specific answers. Whilst it is my intention to allow each person to walk alongside me, it is not my imperative to carry anyone through to my own desired conclusions, since, many who participate actively will need to adjudicate at seemingly difficult intersections and will undoubtedly question the integrity of a number of issues. Neither the objectivity nor the subjectivity of each observer is a prerequisite, since each person's overall inferences should develop from a judicious orientation, thus applying the most autonomous submissions. The answers to a number of life's more sinister challenges may be found in these pages and although it has never been my intention to provide 'right' answers, since I believe that there are greater benefits to be gained by asking pertinent questions at appropriate times and from the most direct and authoritative sources. If this happens, then I believe that I have partly fulfilled the purpose of this autobiography. It remains my durable hope that encouragement will be given to all those who have suffered any type of abusive behaviour or a violation of trust from family, friends, institutions or governments and to take courage from the fact that although much of that suffering was borne in silence, that in the end nearly all acts of injustice and wrong-doing will be fully exonerated since, there is always an assurance of victory in every number greater than one.

My Family & I
February 2008

Dedicated to every child who has suffered
at the hands of those entusted with their
CARE

CHAPTER ONE

My Shoes: Not Yours!

I am somewhat indeterminate as to how to begin straightening out the tangle that has been my life spanning over four arduous decades, for within me there is a need to attempt to make sense of the many places and situations in which the years have vituperatively propelled me. Undoubtedly, a number of people may show a deep level of incredulity and begin posing obdurate questions, and one such query which resonate is; "Why should a relatively unknown person such as I choose to write her autobiography?" Naturally, I will endeavour to answer each question with honesty and integrity every step of the way but for the moment I simply ask that wherever possible, that each person suspend their judgements in order that this enormous hiatus be overcome and as each one disarm and forego a number of their assumptions and prejudices, they will enthusiastically walk alongside a woman born, not necessarily to achieve greatness within her own life but born in order that others may become great. Great thinkers, prevaricators, great manipulators, great at despitefully using others, great lovers, friends, preachers, lovers of self and when all else failed, become great imposters. In order to accomplish this, I must first bypass those critical of my lack of visible presence on the 'world stage' and begin by asking the most pertinent question to expedite the continuance of this journey; "Does every human life merit a story to share?" If the answer is yes, then it is for this very reason I have decided to take this exhaustive route since, my life though ordinary at a brief glance, at a deeper level is one that I can only describe as being full of victories and triumph; triumph over a lack of education, victory over poverty, triumph over loss of identity, victory over psychological and physical abuse, triumph over erosion of cultural values and belief systems and an on-going mêlée to move from exclusion [the outside], to inclusion, [the inside].

If however the answer is no, then I simply wish to ask one final question and that is; "Does the mechanics of fame, success and notoriety increases the overall attributes of a previously unknown character that instantly transforms them into highly trustworthy human beings? This has been increasingly apparent in the lives of many young people who, having tasted fame and success for the briefest of moments believe they immediately have stories of triumph over adversity, the likes to which not previously witnessed. I do not wish to compare nor do I wish to compete, for there are always persons lesser and greater than me and I simply have no wish nor desire to deceive myself that I have the transit of Venus or the moon rising perpetually in my life. I am a natural survivor and for every step of my existence I have overcome difficulties which have moulded my character and hermetically sealed those things I place at an equal, if not higher value than life itself. Naturally, I have begun and it is my intention to complete this journey by way of questioning the once unquestionable and reverting back, yet not lingering within some of the most painful spaces of my childhood and observing where necessary and intervening where possible from the relative safety of maturity, wisdom and understanding.

I have seldom begun something that I did not see through to completion for this to me is accredited to a lack of discipline and self-determination and so, if those questions that arises at the start impinges upon my profound belief to relate a credible and authoritative appraisal of my life then, I am once more allowing those influences way outside of my own experiences and culture to continue to determine my self-worth; it would be simply too awful to continue along this disparaging and unproductive pathway.

I wish to be as open as possible but of course, I also wish to be daring, for it has often been in the times where I risked the most that I have reaped the greatest benefits and rewards. I have a particular route in mind but it would be too simple to have everything signposted to highlight the entire journey, instead, I wish for those prepared to accompany me to remain patient as the route I have opted for does not necessarily form a typical chronological pattern since, I don't believe my life could be understood via that approach. It is my intention however, to stir both conscience and values of those who are prepared to participate fully in the life of another, yet at the same time reflects through the folios of their own journey.

I will not be directive neither am I in pursuit for own glory. My singular intention is to be a companion to those determined to ask pertinent questions relating to unresolved issues within their lives but like me, have found it much too painful in previous attempts to navigate alone. If I choose to walk, there are no reasons you should not run ahead of me but should this occur the direction and topography might change beyond recognition, making it necessary to navigate through towards your own conclusion. Should I start to deliberate and scrutinise, you are free to bypass my thinking and develop your own methodology and problem solve. Perhaps your need may simply be to orientate yourself to your own reality and become transmuted from an incapacitating sphere to a dynamic and enabling experience. Should I start to dream, then you can either dream with me or remain awake and work out your own exacting outcomes. If the idea of walking alongside another is too imperious, then it is acceptable that you may simply prefer to walk in front or some distance behind me. So, whether you choose to walk alongside me in my shoes or you simply wish to be an observer each step of the way in your own, our voyage must begin in the place and on the day that I was born.

I was born in the microscopic village of Newcombe Valley, part of the parish of St Elizabeth along the South West coast of Jamaica, on the eight of March nineteen sixty six. I believe my mother was in labour for almost five days. The 'midwife' who brought me safely into the world was Miss. Hilda who was born blind but was miraculously enabled to deliver hundreds of babies during the course of her long and unbelievable life. She was in her ninetieth year when she finally died and delivering babies right up until her final days of mobility. As soon as a woman went into labour, a young child, [whom she had also delivered], would lead her into the home of the expectant mother, returning to collect her when her job there was complete. She never lost a baby during that lengthy period and in contrast to the maternity clinic which opened locally many years later and who had lost a number of infants because they were doing the job for a pay cheque; Miss. Hilda on the other hand did it for love, because it seemed this was the only time she possessed her sight. It seems that there are a number of people in the world alongside us who are fully sighted but are completely blind, [Saul of Tarsus, a typical example of his time] and there are those like Miss. Hilda who are blind but are able to see everything which is essential.

I was apparently a very small baby, the smallest ever seen locally weighing just under four pounds and in true spirit of my culture where the brutal nature of people is very destructive if left unchallenged, I was given the nickname; 'rat' by my educated and highly respected cousins, the Lewis family. I don't believe it was anything to do with the fact that I looked like a rat, [who knows] but it was obvious they must have compared my size at birth to a rat and so it was for many years I was

6

known as rat. My sister Carol decided she hated the nickname as we got older and made a bold decision to change it to 'musmus,' this is an endearing name for a field mouse and so it was, I became a mouse instead of a rat; how utterly delightful! I must stress that I was not in the least offended by being called 'rat' or 'musmus,' everyone in my culture is given a number of nicknames and rat was kind in comparison to some of my peers. To this day, if I don't like something in my life, I simply build an imperceptible wall for defence and nothing which is debilitating is allowed to permeate its boundaries. I have no argument with rats as long as they don't attempt to scale my walls and overwhelm me; I remain oblivious to their existence. Mice on the other hand, are relatively industrious creatures that seem to get along in life by minding their own business.

Although I was given the Christian and middle names of 'Sheryl Sophia' I never enquired from my mother about the origin of the name 'Sheryl', perhaps it was because she never used it to address me; it was always Sophia, Sophie or musmus. I did however asked about the origin of her preferred name for me, 'Sophia' and was told that it was during her time in London she saw a beautiful Italian actress on the television by the name of Sophia Loren and decided that if I was born a girl, I would be given that name.

Admittedly to me, Sophia Loren remains one of the most beautiful women in the world and not just externally. She appears to possess great strength and resolve; characteristics I admire deeply in a handful of women. I have found nothing detrimental about her private life during her long and impressive public career. In my observations of her, she appears to have a deep sense of identity based upon strong family values, which seems to highlight her noticeable dignity and ever present humanity. She married her soul-mate, the one person with whom she felt truly loved and safe and it is obvious even to this day that her love for Carlo Ponti remains undiminished even after his death in January two thousand and seven. He was not only her older and wiser companion; he was her friend, lover, custodian, and father like figure. It was no surprise when she was asked if she would consider marrying again Loren replied "No, never again, it would be impossible to love anyone else." I am not for a moment comparing aspects of my life with Sophia Loren's but simply trying to imagine what her life was like before and during the height of her fame. I am a person who simply observes more readily than I participate and whilst I can never fully imagine what her life has been like at many levels, it certainly does no harm to try and envision her reality from the relative safety and distance of anonymity. The idea that someone like me without a 'public face' in the places with known faces means, I am often granted permission from those whom approval is necessary and it is from this place that my observations of my own life and the lives of those people around me, becomes patently authenticated. I am not for a moment deluding myself that I am the only observer keen on making sense of senseless situations, for a majority of people would sooner observe than participate. Participating requires effort and a disarming of all previous prejudices and presumptions; it also demands a mutuality of respect for others that cannot be ignored. Those who actively participate are far better equipped to make those life changing judgement calls, since they have been respectfully invited to accompany another human being into extremely painful and difficult areas of their lives.

Observers on the whole are generally better problem solvers since they talk less and think a great deal more and there are no real expectations placed upon them and they can determine the pace and speed at which they choose to travel since, they are largely excluded on the 'outside' of almost everything. I can categorically state that the majority of my knowledge is a direct result of being 'exiled' on the outside of many different life experiences but it is from these peripheries that I have meticulously studied both object and subjects and where I have always benefited the most.

To illustrate this thought of observation in greater depth with the view of walking either with another human being in their shoes or alongside them in my own, if permitted to do so, there is a proverb first expressed as a metaphor in Muslim tradition; "To understand a man, try walking a mile in his shoes". It was used by Harper Lee in "To Kill a Mockingbird." I understand the cast and characters are loosely based on the authors' observation of her family and neighbours. Not surprising, it won the Pulitzer Prize and has invariably become a classic of modern American Literature. (Wikipedia) The precursor to this proverb is one that would pose a question that many would not be able to answer since, there are very few who could imagine what the life of someone else is like at a superficial level but at an even deeper level requiring participation; what must it be like to experience the reality of another person? One particular observation common in my every day interaction with a number of people is to never ask two questions when one will suffice but of course, sometimes two is the imperative; becoming the connecting threads that aligns the seams in the garment, making it wearable, tangible and credible. I have a particular dislike for any question that arises merely from a point of curiosity since, if a question is asked to inform, then that information should be used to influence particular outcomes.

This question and answer scenario is evident in every type of person to person relationship but can be best characterized in many of the helping models. Psychotherapy a typical example where a client, having committed himself to the process week after week yet, cannot find a breakthrough because he already hold the solutions he seek and they are not 'out there' but within him. Fear however, [a major disabling factor and which we shall explore in-depth later], restrict his movement from a moderately safety zone to unfamiliar and abysmal new territory. This inability to move through invisible barriers negate the whole effect of the therapeutic process which is likened to one on a road running towards a costly self-determination and having lost one shoe, turns around and risks all to retrieve it. It is better to anticipate the unexpected and to assume that many other 'pioneers' have already traversed this pathway and it is almost a certainty that someone else will have abandoned a shoe somewhere along the way and it is better to keep going and to try on every shoe that is along the way, until the perfect fit is found and continue through the labyrinth towards to a well-earned freedom.

The idea of an observer, enabler or someone who simply stay alongside one whose wish it is to explore deeply painful aspects of self-perception and issues of identity, would be extremely difficult if that helper was to assume that he or she could meritoriously walk in that person's shoes; a position which is fundamentally flawed. A great number of people have given much thought to the idea of; 'walking' in another's shoes but of course, such metaphors seldom sits comfortably with the masses, for very few have an unlimited or compelling imagination concerning the challenging circumstances of others, especially when their present reality paints a vastly different picture.

Of course the ability to assume the position of another person is a matter requiring thought and care since, there are a number of factors outlining the singularity of a person; factors such as culture, creed, individual disposition, belief systems and bedrocks will naturally form a majority of the foundations in which a person functions. The uniqueness of an individual is their way of self-definition, for there must be some incomparable features, besides those ostensible commonalities that separate one person from another. It would be a demoralising thought if I was to be compared against others whose suffering was similar. Even though this may indeed be the case, I am an individual whose coping mechanisms have been developed around a vast array of values, my Christian belief system in particular, where there are constant reminders in the Bible of how one should be in the face of adversity. In Romans 12:12 we are prompted, "Be joyful in hope, patient in affliction, faithful in prayer."

Although I might share culture and many other values with others, my uniqueness as an individual must remain the utmost priority. It is for this very reason I believe it is essential for me when seeking resolutions to issues within my life, to set my own standards and to raise myself above the malicious labels that have been attached to me through a number of biased and familiar perceptions. From the moment I am able to disregard the opinions of others, I begin the process of freeing myself to see the completeness of who I am. For those wishing to define the character of a person who is relatively unknown to them, serves one purpose only; since, if others attempt to define who or what they imagine me to be, they believe they have a right to treat me anyway they choose.

This thought can be better supported by this illustration; imagine someone who, having spent thousands of pounds to remove a person from dire poverty or a similar hardship and to declare at a point in the future that they have some right or ownership over that person. Absurd! Identity is not found in circumstances, [good or bad], in wealth nor position but in the culture and broader associations with particular attachments to religious beliefs and core values. If a person was to be stripped of all their wealth and position, yet held many of the aforementioned attributes, they would still have an irrefutable identity. In our post-modern world where the view of wealth is inextricably linked to identity and if we were to switch that around and empty a man or woman whose distinctiveness was confirmed by the position they held, the car they drove and the salary they drew, they would be utterly lost if they were to forfeit all their material possessions. This is indicative of the dreadful decision taken by a number of men and women who choose to end their lives when their position, status and wealth abate.

The idiosyncratic nature of human beings continues to be in conflict with culture, materialism and identity, for it is from here where many of the deeply held views, orientations and life definitions for many people are drawn. Culture in particular, has a broader spectrum of religious beliefs and core values that has sharply opposing views of materialism; a particularly ruthless principle to aspire towards. Whether a person's identity is hermetically sealed at birth by cultural givens, or that it may indeed be interchangeable as a person matures and becomes predisposed to external factors, are questions that, when explored are able to ascertain the challenges encountered by many individuals who are directly in the line of fire of cross-cultural dynamics.

It is a privilege for me to be with a person and attempt to understand their concerns as they travel along the 'highway' of their misfortunes, in their defeat and disillusionments. This however, demands willingness on my part to be adaptable, trustworthy and to display a readiness to participate when I am invited to and to be an attentive listener when I am not invited into deeply painful and impenetrable spaces. I must also be prepared to relinquish any pursuit of selfish ambitions that may be in direct conflict with the sensitivities of those who depend on me as expediter. Status and kudos are underlying demons, impelling a number of individuals within the centre of those who are hurting. There are so few people who can actually do an ounce of 'good' without the overbearing need to tell the world in advance, during and after the event. For me, this is bordering on crude and Pharisee-like; the Scribes and Pharisees were at their most animated and vocal when they were displaying their 'goodness' overtly but what they were in fact doing, was masking all the darkness that they found unbearable in their private lives. Of course this is representative of all human beings; who in the right mind want to live and never be applauded for excellence? No one!

For some reason, I never consciously insert myself amongst people but a number of individuals habitually attach themselves to me and because of this, I can care secretly and confidently for others without the scrutiny of eyes and ears that simply could never understand the nature of what transpired between me and many strangers.   If someone is hurting, I hold them tenderly with strong arms. I take them close to the centre of my being and whilst this may not be a comfortable situation for many, it nonetheless exacerbates a hideous fear that resides in human beings. It is completely uncharacteristic, unwarranted and ludicrous; for with wisdom, I can safely discern who gain access to my heart without the dread that they may gain direct access into my heart. It is often from this position of openness that I am most able to stand, walk, sit, weep, or just being with another in their anxieties and distress.

I remember a number of years ago travelling back with my companion from St. Martin in the French West Indies. The seat configuration at the front was two, three, two and the row with three seats found me sitting next to a French lady travelling alone to Paris. Some distance into the flight, I began noticing how she would hold onto the seat in front whenever we met unexpected turbulence and when it was at its most severe she was rigid with fear. My heart went out to her and I took her with both hands, without uttering a word and held her close to me. She spoke French and I was grateful I understood some of it but my companion was able to translate some of the more difficult words. I held this lady on and off for the entire journey because I knew she was terrified of flying. This experience was just too unbearable for her alone. When we finally arrived in Paris it was remarkable how she held onto me showing appreciation for the support I had given her.

I have no idea what the fear of flying is like; I simply do not entertain the thought of meeting an untimely end. If I was to meet my end in this or a similar way, it would by no means be an untimely one but determined by a higher authority. I always display gratitude and acceptance in recognition of those things that are incorporated into the human state. These are part of the on-going process from birth through to death that holds us all in a mighty grip and is neither understood by reason nor by logic. So, with this thought in mind, I prefer to live in complete acknowledgement that there are many factors which are non-negotiable and simply cannot be reversed. These include: choosing to be born, choosing one's family, culture, creed, colour, disposition, one's religion, or even choosing to die.

Admittedly, choosing to die has become increasingly problematic in recent years, where many seriously ill people are having to wade through the opposing political, legal, ethical, social, religious and moral dilemmas in order that they may select a time and place of their dying. If it was as simple as having a choice over such fundamentals or the right to choose one's destiny but still, this would not necessarily safeguard the desired outcomes that many may choose. While one may wish they could choose not to die, if this was possible; what are the landmarks and ground-braking revelations that would accompany the fantasy of an eternal life in the physical? The physical body is not self-sustaining and the rigours and demands of living would seriously impinge upon its ability to function under stress and diverse change. This in turn creates additional conflicts as one tries to make the transition from one known state of being to another mainly unknown proliferation.

The impossibility grows thereby since; everything in the world would have to become perfect in order that a notion such as this could exist since, many seemingly unconnected systems are based upon a process of inter-dependency. Day and night for example; one simply would not recognise the inception or completion of the other, if both were not perfectly aligned together. Similarly, the earth would fail to be self-supportive and viable without equal amounts and rain and sunshine. The imperfections would unravel, as the aspect of longevity heralding onto eternity would outsource the natural laws of creation. Man was created for eternal life but sin and its imperfections drastically reduced mankind's foothold into the great unknown dimension of a timeless and space less existence free of constraints and pre-determined laws. There are however, many flaws immersed within the fabric of such a hideous assertion.

The seemingly endless plethora of known and unknown possibilities held in tension against what is feasible and unfeasible could effectively be no different to that of a culture where basic values and norms are exchanged for a concept so diverse, so foreign, that it will struggle for its very survival in the capitalist and westernized cultures. Since its intent is to create such a chasm in the lives and values of other cultures that it would be easier for that culture to make the transition from death to life or day to night. There is however, one thing that I can choose and that is, the direction my life should take; empowering me to become the unbroken vessel central to God's purposes. For when a vessel is whole it is not only fit for its own persistence but is fit for guiding and walking as well as 'carrying' others towards the beginning of their own actualisation and hopes. In all such relationships, the objectivity of being with another is to allow them to reassert their position of value in the wider sense and to dispel a number of myths that either surround or enslave them.

The uniqueness of human beings, their complexity and design, the concepts that are of value to some and meaningless to others, the contrasting experiences and views, the outward shows, the hidden depth, shoes or no shoes, another whose ideals are combative with that of another person cannot be wholly expected to facilitate a journey in darkness. A journey such as this may highlight similarities, as well as explore differences. Judgment calls will undoubtedly be made; conflicting and contrasting views may be met and successfully managed. This is the indisputable reality that all are different. While difference can pose unreasonable and fictitious psychological threats, they should by and large be celebrated and not obliterated, nor should they be ignored, for it is the things that we have in common that allows dialogue but it is unquestionably the variance that make almost every aspect of human relationships stimulating. The pathway to meaningful dialogue must remain open; this can be achieved by a deep and obvious respect of difference. Much of what is perceived as the 'norm' for a variety of people concerning others, are images inaccurately drawn from the typically unhealthy stereotypes which tend to lean towards a number of biases that are steeped in negative undercurrents; culture, religion, ideologies and core beliefs of traditional peoples. These hindrances merely mask the overriding issues needing exploration and the matters that need urgency can become absorbed by those embedded prejudices.

I remember a number of years ago I was in a helping relationship with an elderly lady who had been recently widowed and having spent a number of hours in a soul searching self-diagnosis with her, was rather surprised by her blasé comment towards the end of the third session; "I have some African neighbours and I cannot stand their dark faces and dark hearts but I have to put up with it." I noted her comment and allowed her to continue until there was a natural pause. Of course I probed her on her [Freudian slip] and was surprised that she opted out by saying that I was 'different' and nothing like them but a response like this is far too ambiguous for me, I demand greater clarity when I choose to walk alongside another human being. I was unlikely to be given an in-depth analysis of the exact reasons behind her assertion since, many people who hold grudges and prejudices are seldom aware of their exact nature and orientation. I imagine what she meant to say was; I was different from her neighbours because I was there to empower her and they disempowered her but only because she refused unequivocally to have any type of meaningful dialogue to break through the barriers she had placed between herself and them.

Naturally, I informed her that she had made my position untenable and that I had no alternative than to end our relationship. This was too painful for her and of course, she did not wish for me to leave with thoughts of her as a bigot or something worse. It was only at the point where we disarmed and exposed a number of vulnerabilities by acknowledging our difference that we were able to give mutual respect. I refuse to assume that a person needs to go to a 'foreign destination,' when it is abundantly clear almost at the inception, they desperately need to remain on 'home soil.' The stimulus in this partnership will be the values common to both of us even though this lady appeared to have lived a life within a narrow scope of fractured and out-dated views. Although our cultures were at opposing ends of the spectrum, our commonalties remained intact. This is no surprise, for many post-modern peoples are becoming increasingly fragmented and are clinging daringly to out-dated rhetoric in order that they may continue to assert their sense of purpose and priority in society. Refusing to surrender has dire consequences but to become a slave or a victim to seemingly irretrievable circumstances is not a forgone conclusion. The position from where many references concerning culture and identity are formed can be detrimental to individuals who hold such views and damaging to those of whom such views is held.

The reality of someone like me, from a different culture and another person on the 'outside' who is merely observing my interactions within my own cultural boundaries may suggests hard work, effort and determination to break down any barriers, as the overall appearance seems complicated. Cross-cultural exploration of notable differences cannot be avoided but at all times must be fully valued since, any attempt to highlight variances in microscopic terms may only serve to alienate rather than a bringing together; exacerbate, rather than facilitate the process.

I recall being in the church I attended as a teenager one Easter and the pastor was preaching a sermon on difference and I was amazed that anyone could have preached such nonsense. He declared that each time he looked at his congregation he only saw faces. Not black, white, nor oriental, just faces. After the sermon I emailed him and told him I had never been so insulted by such harmful lies, for he stood defiantly in front of his congregation and dismantled everything which emanates the good of others. Not surprisingly, he still to this day has not replied to my email, which speaks volumes of a leader lacking wisdom, vision and humility. For who in their right mind could stand in front of a group of eighty people; with brown faces, white faces, oriental faces and declared, he only saw faces. When individuals fail to speak to make an impression we remember them by their faces. If they speak, we remember both.

Many of us sadly, are clumsy, infantile and often ignorant of the facts even when they are visible in the empty space beside us. It is often through ignorance that many people are overlooked and consequently develop insecurities. This is a direct result of those who refuse to celebrate their difference, perhaps, due to their own erroneous prejudices or the fear of the political correct evil that has engulfed our nation. I asked him in future to be bold enough to affirm difference, since no right-minded person would walk into a garden and declared they only saw Roses when in fact, it was teeming with Geraniums, Poppies, French Marigolds, Sweet Pea and Lavender; his was an assertion made in complete ignorance. I for one, affirm difference, especially when it teaches me something new and extraordinary. Whilst it must be acknowledged that difference is never the crystallising agent that bring communities together but the things that human beings have in common that dismantle fixed boundaries; principles, beliefs, success, suffering, inequality, fear, poverty and every necessary detail to which each person cling that continue to underpin their identity as they move through the complex maze of life.

I am a very single-minded person and the attitude I embraced at a very early age has become the mechanism that propels me forward each step of my life. I was particularly focussed upon the social and economic benefits of a good education, having witnessed the success of numerous members of my family who were educated both at home and abroad. Education admittedly, is not the overriding factor to success since; I had to become more determined to rise through the barriers of criticism, rejection and prejudices. I found it essential to become resilient and adaptable in order to exact much needed change from those whom approval is necessary. It is my wish to determine my own destiny, as it is with many individuals and in my on-going quest to manoeuvre through a variety of difficulties and conflicts, I am now finding it easier to move more freely amongst a variety of people.

An interesting observation I have made in recent years is that, a number of people who are the most confident amongst us, are often the ones who inspire the most confidence in others. Confidence must not be mistaken for arrogance, arrogant attitudes simply devastate lives, not facilitate them. Confidence grows when people are made to feel worthy and appreciated. For me, there is no greater sense of belonging than when I am amongst my own; those who share same or similar culture, religious orientations and heritage, as there is a sense of belonging which surpasses that of many other known feelings. I am not suggesting for one moment that there are no challenges to overcome in a particular group, for it is often in 'families' where we experience the gravest challenges and battles. Whenever we are enabled to be strong within our own places of comfort and approval, we are then empowered to be everything in whatever groups we must later function.

I have learnt how to be prepared for many of the unexpected actualities in life since, my character has been forged in highly interdependent cultural groups which have allowed me to hear and respond to echoes of personal struggles to freedom that can never be understood by mere observers. There are a number of dynamics at work within specific groups that instantly identifies and combat opposition and hindrances, rejection and prejudices and the silent struggles, similar to robust undercurrents with the potential to submerge everything in its path. There are many people, who like me, fear the erosion of cultural values and loss of identity through; assimilation, media and institutionalised thinking. I believe the way forward is to redefine my core values by reverting back to the place of optimism; the place where the majority of my principles, beliefs and values were founded. Since, it is only from there, that I believe I can revolve back to real meaning and purpose in my life. The most valuable things in life should not be left to mere luck or chance, [like winning the lottery] and because I continued to ignore the warning signs in their infancy, it was almost impossible to avert them in maturity.

This thought could be better supported with this illustration; imagine a great dam which had sprung an undetected leak and gradually over a period of time got bigger. Finally, the pressure becomes too great and the dam breaks, sending gallons of water surging out causing irreparable damage to everything in its path. Of course, this could have been averted but the watchmen during the day had designated this as the responsibility of the watchmen of the night, so in fact, no one was paying the least attention. The surging waters came unexpectedly, sweeping everything away in its might and erasing any opportunity of circumnavigating back to the centre of denotation and optimism.

Cultural Values: Lost in Transition

My optimism was palpable. I had left a world behind which was the only one where I could make sense of everything; however senseless. It was nevertheless the foundation from where my cultural values and identity had been first established. To me, England was as far away as the moon but at least my parents were there and I was certain that, although I had endured a great deal of suffering and distress in their absence, this transition would provide healing and a way forward. I arrived in Manchester on the 8th of December, 1978; a Friday. I remember the stewardess walking with me to the arrivals hall, [I know it's an arrivals hall now in view of the number of times I have passed through as an adult, as I child, it was simply a place where I saw the strangest faces waiting] and guiding me along until I came to the place where I could see my mother and father. Her responsibility to me ended here, my parents were just beginning. I remember the weather was cold, grey and wet; some things never change! I simply braced myself, accepting this was my new life and there was simply no point in looking back.

My home for the next nine years was a Victorian house in Levenshulme which was excruciatingly cold, imposing and unbearable; I hated that house vehemently! The high school I attended was thankfully just a brief walk away and I knew that wherever there was a school, there were teachers and pupils and when this combination meets, there is learning and learning leads to freedom. In view of the fact that my father was very poor at reading and writing, I had to seek extra help from my teachers whenever I could. Furthermore, with my mother being deaf, I knew that the way forward was not going to be easy, nevertheless my mother's excellent reading and writing skills was a blessing to me on numerous occasions.

Throughout my time at school, my attendance record remained unblemished; except on the one occasion where I was suspended for a day over an altercation with another girl but was so disheartened at being excluded that, I spent the entire day at the gates, checking on what I had missed. My friends said I was stupid, I said I was dedicated. My teachers were superstars who allowed me to shine, in particular, Mrs Percival and Mr Pritchard, both ardent for all of us to succeed. Of course there are a number of things I regret deeply during those years; not being kind enough to one or two fellow pupils and the occasions where I could have intervened to assist others but chose not to, due to the fear of being considered, 'uncool.' Although I loved my teachers, I was a pain to a number of them as I was such a high spirited girl and was experiencing a type of freedom I had not known previously and so, kept pushing the boundaries as far as I could. Going to school was the happiest days I knew and although there were many aspects of life in

Manchester I simply could not understand, I nevertheless embraced the firmer principles and discarded the rest. I could not comprehend the way children spoke to adults, regarding them as peers; no demarcation between the two. There were as many children smoking as adults and the use of bad language; was the norm; for them perhaps but never for me! There was such a noticeable lack of discipline and children asserted their rights in every sense, so much so that the adults lost all of theirs. Manchester was a very big city where 'neighbours' were unfriendly and self-absorbed. There was never any hope of getting to know them; if you got a smile that was a miracle and a hello, two miracles in one day! If you did however, managed to get a sixty second conversation at an opportune moment, in the post office or somewhere similar, it was always dominated by the awful weather which was either; too dark, too miserable, too hot, too cold, too wet, or too dry! I could not figure out how there were so many things in Manchester and the world to discuss, yet, people were obsessed with the weather.

I was determined to improve my spoken English and at the same time enhance my social skills; understandably, I would often find myself outside of what was culturally acceptable on numerous occasions. Of course I was excluded and ridiculed at high school initially but from the day Marcia took me under her wings, I never looked back. Marcia stepped forward and agreed with the teachers to take care of me since, we shared the same culture and heritage from our both our parents. Marcia has remained one of my closest friends and we have continued supporting each other for almost thirty-four years. I love this woman dearly. I remember being teased for a number of reasons, which at the time made no sense but did much later on. There were aspects of my approach to others which was seen as unacceptable; wanting to hold hands with the girls I considered as 'good' friends for example, [this is normal in my culture] but was mocked as having sinister motives. They disliked my closeness with the teachers; I was called 'teacher's pet' routinely.

Similarly, at a time when a majority of girls were fanatical about trendy boy bands, once again, I was the 'odd' one out. They would all be competing to collect newspaper clippings for their scrapbooks and my only interest in a celebrity was Roger Moore, aka, James Bond. No one could understand my choice and admittedly, neither could I at the time but I needed to be different. One thing was certain for me and that was the incredulity of Bond's deviant behaviour and even more unbelievable, was the fact that his conduct was state sanctioned;

astonishing! While I did not wish to emulate his behaviour in any way; I would often wonder just how many individuals were able to live 'above the law' in reality and be paid vast sums of money for as little effort as the habitual raising of one eyebrow?

Once more, Marcia came to my rescue and brought me the first magazine clipping of Moore and that was where my scrapbook began. There was a lot of teasing and name calling but that was fine, it was the exclusion that was unbearable. This was a difficult time, especially with the task of fitting into a culture which was so alien to me and as I struggled to find a place to insert myself, it became apparent that, as long as Manchester remained my home, I would struggle into the foreseeable future. This was the beginning of an uphill climb, not only to become accepted by people from my own culture but also those whose culture was way beyond my youthful comprehension.

I was plunged into seemingly opposing lifestyles, where my previous values became so insignificant, they were bordering onto non-existent. As I grappled with the enormity of such vastly contrasting values, I found myself becoming increasingly lost under the weight and forfeiture of my own distinctive cultural values which underpinned the core of my own unique identity. From the moment I arrived in Manchester, I was prepared to insert myself into almost every aspect of the British way life yet, in absence of many of my previously known reference points I was often fearful that my own values were moving further and further away from me. Admittedly as a child, a number of my fundamental values had been previously dismantled or denied, although my belief system remained unmovable. Over the years I have witnessed the demise of numerous friends and associates who simply could never make the transition from one known culture to another. Even those born in Manchester faced many challenges as they attempted a process of assimilation only to be hurled through the revolving door of change.

There were so many who faced enormous hardships in their attempts to assimilate into British cultures which left them bereft of all sense of being and identity. Many became indoctrinated with the erroneous view that a westernised way of living is to be desired over all others aspects of life; this view promulgates a belief in success marked by material possessions: glamour, wealth, educational excellence and life styles which suggest a lack of effort for the most enviable and rewarding careers. I imagine this assimilation process to be like a revolving door which encircles you but as it continues moving, the position where one disembarks must be recognised in advance as a revolving door, by virtue of its functioning, will not stop to allow for re-evaluating a number of viable options.

In this continuum as this allegory suggests, effective monitoring must be done in advance in order to ascertain what is to be gained and what might potentially be lost through this mighty process of conversion. There is a delicate balance of opposing world views and for those who hold values and beliefs in tension against interpretations that are neither accommodating nor particularly helpful. This often challenged the attitude and integrities of individuals, especially within their own communities, where they can appear ambiguous and contracted to outsiders. This can prove increasingly problematic. At this point of potential change, there is a call for a rigorous assessment of one's own inherent values, [I would simply not jump straight into a foreboding body of water since I am a nervous swimmer but would approach cautiously, first testing its depth with one foot, then both]. There is often a hypocritical approach from some participators, who merely wish to assume those aspects that are beneficial by having one foot immersed in one culture and the rest of their body in the preferred one. This is often a major source of conflict since, so many wishes for the kudos and wealth that accompanies the merits and benefits of social accomplishments; human beings will foremost look for the remunerations, rather than the drawbacks and discards the attributes they consider cumbersome or inconsequential.

Subsequently, many people are becoming lost as they negotiate through unknown territories, comparable to deep waters to where there are no accurate measures. In the end, relying heavily upon own instincts, as opposed to making judgements to where there may be few or no valued reference points.   In a brief synopsis of existing trends, where a majority seems to be precariously hinged to the revolving door of culture, there appears to be too great an emphasis placed on what a person has in terms of possessions, rather than the value system to which they have been predisposed from a very young age. I would sooner forfeit all those things which emphasise my life as being 'successful' and to regain my identity as a Christian without the usual derision from those who see it as out-dated and irrelevant in that same society. Yet, these are the direct descendants of the dedicated men and women who brought Christianity to my forebears as missionaries centuries earlier. This has been the most enduring and non-transferable ideology which have absolute priority and permanence within my life. Sadly, for those who continue to hold fast to obscure values from centuries past, there is undoubtedly an on-going struggle for numerous observers but especially those who immerse themselves fully before calculating the consequences and risk involved in the assimilation of something that appears to mask rather than define the identity that so many seek.

The seismic shift within culture globally is both disconcerting and acute; culture is no longer an exclusive right of passage but the titanic wheels turning individuals and communities at will which have become both destructive and intrusive. It advances like a giant magnet drawing people in and pushing them towards obliteration. The magnitude and scale of this shift is not merely sweeping away the outer layers but is eroding the core of many ancient peoples existence. It is a certainty that, for those of us witnessing this phenomenon, there will undoubtedly be a number of questions arising but some may become immobilized into a morbid indifference, while others may simply welcome the opportunity to be empowered to embrace some aspects of the ensuing changes; be it subtle or radical, beneficial or harmful and especially when such changes are from vastly opposing sides of the spectrum and with the potential to exact consequences that may be far reaching.

I recently had a deeply moving conversation with my dear Friend Winifred. We talked in great detail about the shifts within cultural boundaries over the last fifty years and the impact this is having within the lives of a number of people globally. We were particular drawn to parallels within African culture as it merges with European, becoming more anglicised in its manifestation. We contrasted and identified youngsters, whose core beliefs and values were handed down from traditions rooted in Christian values. A notable immersion into western culture has seen an erosion of many such beliefs, where the process of assimilation is constantly breaching the demands of one's own values. Upon reflection, there appears to be a distinct lack of foresight and self-determination from many individuals who seemed to have surrendered much of their motivation and direction to be state managed, influenced and controlled. This process has been done in such a subtle and surreptitious way that many continue under the illusion of being in control. For those driven by the 'machine of greed' and who are pursued by phantoms into wheels of chaos and lack of self-determination, cracks are beginning to appear beneath the veneer of solid traditions where an entire generation will become potentially lost in the obligatory menace of cultural reintegration.

"When in Rome," does not necessarily make a person become a Roman citizen? Very many may find the idea incongruous, just as in the same way a person does not become a brain surgeon, simply because they are visiting a sick friend in a brain trauma unit, nor does it make another an expert at flying passenger aeroplanes because they enter the cockpit to meet the pilots and view the instruments. Walking in the shoes of another is not down to mere luck or chance, it is often by invitation. Whilst one may be completely out of their depth in a situation that seems beyond their understanding, much can still be achieved under the watchful gaze of mutual respect. It is my belief that from a place of respect some bridges can be restored while others can be built to enable brief links to the past and durable ones in the present and going beyond all pre-set limits. For when a durable connection is established, a direction becomes clearer. When one is privileged to see into the world of another and accept what they see, respect differences and encourage growth in spite of the challenges faced, this is the most productive way in which to illuminate a non-corrosive pathway. One simply cannot be an effective enabler or helper if they allow themselves to be informed by any underlying prejudices. One must remain honest, flexible to change and be completely transparent so as to inspire the confidence of those seeking their company on their voyage of recovery and especially where vulnerabilities are decidedly exposed. When these are in place, an environment which is non-threatening becomes the point of safety from where a person can begin to flourish.

Regardless of whether their cultural differences are westernised, Africanised or marginalised they can set about redefining their identity and the essential peculiarities that underpin their lives. In African culture there is particular attention given to forefathers and much of a person's identity can be determined from what their ancestors did in the past; those who had overcome seemingly insurmountable odds to determine futures for the forthcoming generations. This generation in question, cannot relate to the enormity of such sacrifices where everything, including life may have been forfeited for their freedom. There is an acknowledged appreciation of past victories and humiliations but also an exceptional display of a people's enduring strength.

In westernised culture however, ancestors are not given the same amount of acknowledgement in terms of their humiliations defining subsequent generations. Only victories are considered which can create a form of illusion, producing a damaging air of superiority towards others, since all cultures have endured both victories and defeats in every aspect of their lives. Understandably, the emphasis can shift in cultures from strength to weaknesses, pagan to Christian, or other religious orientated values but young lives in any community around the world will invariably suffer the same or similar pressures and effects from their peers and value systems. Given that the idea of wearing the shoes of another is not a comfortable thought, it could be a simple fact that such an idea is not understood or permissible in another's culture or that their semantics cannot accommodate such a thought.

A different approach may be necessary since, what is misunderstood cannot be directed and a suitable method of communication would need to be employed to open up a feasible pathway. If we are to appreciate that loss of identity is not exclusive to one particular culture and the very painful anomalies that we try so much to avoid are in fact, the very ones that shape and define each person's life. This giving of meaning and definition to a person's life and existence should not be undervalued, otherwise many end up feeling resentful and insignificant, since they cannot find a place where they feel a real sense of 'belonging'.

Although I have spent the majority of my life in Great Britain from the age of twelve, in many ways I still have a deep sense of 'not belonging,' of course I bear no ill feelings towards anyone who has deliberately excluded me and it's also worth remembering that I did not choose Great Britain because, as a child I had no choice but I continue to wonder endlessly; would Great Britain have chosen me? Life was granted to all and whilst many may have a view of life as being a 'right', there are still many others, myself included who see life as a privilege and a celebration and thus, spend much of it in thanks and praise to the one who has so graciously bestowed such an incredible gift. No one was placed on earth simply to exist - but to live. The idea of being with another in the place of their disputes, their suffering and in their attempts to halt the erosion of the fabric of their existence; one exemplified facilitator immediately comes to mind.

Exemplified Facilitator

For those of us who bear the marks of suffering and loss of identity, [our Lord Jesus a typical example of immense suffering], through no fault of their own, are to be reminded that whilst little comfort can be derived from supportive voices at the time of great distress and hurting, that suffering has been part of the inherent human condition from which none has escaped; not even the Lord Jesus! In 2 Timothy 1:12 we read; "That is why I am suffering as I am. Yet this is no cause for shame, because I know whom I have believed, and am convinced that he is able to guard what I have entrusted to him until that day." There is no shame in suffering, for if that was the case, every human being would be permanently ashamed for either the cause or the effect of suffering.

Christ was the exemplified facilitator who seldom had to seek those whose identity had merged with foreign gods and pagan ideologies. Those who had forfeited their peace of mind for aspirations through unsavoury means would immediately be restored as they surrendered to Christ in absolute contrition and humility. The spirit of change cannot be effective until there is a willingness to relinquish all the past errors, sins and selfish goals and a spirit of humility takes preference over all previous dispositions.

Humility is the crown with the thorns, it is the dress of 'kings' endowed with wisdom, strength and honour and is self-supporting in every sense. I suspect anyone too proud to wear humility as their inner garment as they insert themselves in the spaces left vacant at the side of others, will remain manifestly naked throughout. I would imagine it a difficult transition for a number of people, especially those from extremely privileged backgrounds, to be congruent with people in their suffering. Since, many would possess a very limited knowledge of different people and the social and economic factors which may or may not have contributed to their current situation. The idea of a prince or princess visiting a drug addicts' clinic and displaying warmth and understanding is acceptable but they are wholly unable to understand the mechanics that hold such people in bondage. They simply have nothing from their own life experiences to measure this against and only one who had endured the same, [a recovering addict], could be completely empathetic to their plight since, they themself have undergone the same process of dependency, withdrawal and recovery. It is for this reason that Christ is much loved; for he is not only the prince of peace, but also the prince of suffering and in view of his own death by crucifixion, no one could refute the claims in Christ's favour as the most compassionate being who has ever lived. If my purpose is one of enabling those in ferocious relationships with people, God, identity, substance addiction and misuse then, everything which is a hindrance must be fully addressed throughout. Anything which is detrimental to human beings is an erosion of identity and in turn leads to poor decisions being made towards future goals and aspirations. It is during such challenging encounters where I believe there is a pressing need for a revision in my thinking; otherwise, I simply cannot aim for a satisfactory conclusion, when the inception was crowded with a host of misaligned predeterminations.

There are stumbling blocks that disempower a number of people throughout their lives; I recognised this from a very early age. Suffering can be attributed to a number of contaminated sources; from families, 'friends' and from association within community groups such as schools and churches. The Christian church in particular may advocate forgiveness and compassion at the heart of its doctrine but are in fact, guilty of being both unforgiving and unloving on a truly reprehensible scale. When the focus of a person becomes misplaced, the ensuing predicaments that follow make the accomplishment of the most straightforward relational disciplines virtually impossible. This could be likened to attempting to drive a car with a blindfold covering both eyes; a crash is definitely the end result. Although I have never attempted to escape from the pressures which life has imposed upon me, as I believe it is from these testing times that my strength becomes most apparent. No one reaches the end of their destination by way of a seamless, uninterrupted passage. In 2 Corinthians 2:17 we are assured that; "Our light and momentary troubles are achieving for us an eternal glory that far outweigh them all." In my struggles to freedom, I have taken courage from a number of inspirational sources, Paul the Apostle, [whose life I shall examine more in-depth later on], was one such character. From these sources, I begin to understand that I have in fact, gained more than mere insight and have also gained an inner strength and resolve from my characteristic struggles to liberty. This occurs when I begin to look beyond the immediacy of the present and focus more daringly into a future to which I have been called in faith.

If it were at all possible to be gifted with sufficient strength to bear the suffering and heartache of everyone that I held in high esteem but of course, this is not possible. I am an inconsequential mortal being, without divinity and possessing little spiritual strength and where the majority of my astuteness has been gained principally from my relationship with the divine. I have often heard it said that the rich do not understand suffering which is merely another way to undermine their wealth. Those who have been gifted with the most; whether possessions or status will invariably suffer the most. Money provides comfort from poverty but poverty only and is no use in emotional anguishes, illnesses and in the death of family and close friends. In recent years I have witnessed some of the most wealthy and privileged in society being eclipsed by addictions and deceptions, often resulting in their untimely and horrific deaths; in misery and isolation.

I pay particular attention to a number of issues which I find mildly amusing occasionally but of course, there is often a hint of sadness attached to my observations. This concerns extremely wealthy people and the vigilance necessary to guard their assets from little thieves as well as the grand dealers and schemers; the rich suffers incredibly, we simply don't see their tears in the press, just their habitual smiling faces on grand yachts and private planes. The rich will invariably hurt more in many ways, since the affection that many of them crave is simply 'not for sale.' There was a particular discourse in the Bible concerning the rich entering the kingdom of heaven; Jesus looked at them and said, "With man this is impossible, but with God all things are possible." Matthew 19:26. Jesus was moved to compassion and intense care for all people; the poor, rich, and especially those lost and hurting. It is something that many ordinary people cannot attain, for many simply are not equipped to see with the heart and eyes of God.

At once I think of Marjorie, my neighbour and friend whose changing circumstances brought her into my path many years ago and how our friendship developed during one of the most challenging periods of our lives. Our friendship began with the death of her husband from cancer and her search for comfort and answers became what I can only describe as a spider's web; spherical, problematic and unremitting. Although she was in her early sixties, she was one of the smartest women I knew; she possessed many of life's answers for everyone else but could not apprehend and apply any to her own situation. She struggled to come to terms with her husband's death and for some reason she allowed me over a period of time to insert myself in the space that he had left vacant by her side, though guardedly. It was during this difficult period where she had lost the love of her life, that I had found mine! It was only a matter of weeks when I reluctantly shared with her the reason for the increased smile on my face that she took an overdose and tried to end her life. Marjorie recovered eventually but of course her life was never going to be the same again. She was no longer deemed as 'safe' to continue living alone and all the 'power' to direct her own life was given over to be state managed. Initially, she received visitors from every strata of her; politicians, entrepreneurs and all her well-heeled associates. Sadly, by the time she attempted suicide a second time, there was none of her former friends left, except me and her next of kin, an elderly lady whose life revolved mainly around her children and grandchildren. I continued going to see her wherever she was placed, especially after she was finally housed in a unit about an hour's drive away. I would make the drive four to five times annually.

I remember one day driving to see her and upon arrival she forbade the nurses to let me in and naturally, they took her wishes into account and asked me to leave but of course I am a patient person and so, I went to my car and sat there reading. Eventually after around half an hour they came and asked if I still wanted to see her because she had changed her mind. We greeted each other with our usual smiles, made our way into the visitor's lounge and not a word was mentioned of the earlier situation. It's over twenty five years since we became friends and although she has failed to say thank you for all the simple things, she nevertheless, accompanied me to court a number of years ago which, due to her eloquent assertion and wisdom, the case was settled in my favour. The most important reason I have remained reasonably close to her is simple; I love her and like me, she has struggled throughout her life as an orphan being shunted from one home to the next and being seriously abused by those in who she had placed her trust. My fate was sealed the day Marjorie's house was cleared to be sold by her family and they gave me a diary belonging to her. As I began reading through its pages my name was inserted on every page; what I had done or said to her that day or that week. Of course this is leaning towards a cultural bias which is unfamiliar to me for in my culture when something is important it is said every time regardless of immediate consequences but of course in British culture, feelings are often concealed in many instances to disguise vulnerabilities.

There are so many things that hinges on what we prioritise within our lives. Scripture is very clear on the acquisition of wealth and its effect upon our lives and Jesus was only too aware that even those who have less of an attachment to wealth could easily lose their way. It was for this very reason that he was so receptive to those who sought his help and although he was offended by many, scarcely did he offend anyone, except when a particular truth had to be harshly driven home to those who continue opposing him. I bear witness to a simple unspoken language common in all cultures; the language of grief. Only silence could suitably illustrate a more pitiful sight than a man or woman, beside themself with sorrow. In John 11:35, we read "Jesus wept," of course the full narrative must be read in context, for Christ was weeping when he saw Mary and Martha, their friends and family weeping for Lazarus who had died four days earlier in Jesus's absence.

This was where Christ the exemplified facilitator was excellent, for not only did he raise the hopes of those in turmoil, [he raised Lazarus from the dead] and he also offered them a future which surpassed all others. When we adopt the discipline of Christ we are enabled by the Holy Spirit, [God's inexhaustible agent], to move mountains of fear and doubts and permit ourselves to love those who despitefully use and abuse us and to bring lives back to value and identity. Undoubtedly, this is a large shift in expectations but remains a definite reality to those who are faithful to the truth of the gospel. This is one of the defining actions of ordinary men and women who willingly insert themselves in the spaces left vacant by false friends and genuine enemies. Should all our attempts at restoration and healing fail, we must swiftly discharge all our pride and affectations by kneeling in humility and contrition; since there is definite assurance of victory in every number greater than one. This assurance of victory stems from the idea of safety in numbers since one can watch while another sleeps. This type of victory far exceeds prizes or awards and monetary value simply cannot be attached to it. This attainment raises the hopes of a person from the dust and realigns them with their true humanity. Victory is simply standing throughout my life and daring to be brave enough during every threat, opposition or potential difficulty. What I perceive as 'victory' however, may be utter failure to a number of observers, since each person's theories are framed around a different set of values. Relativity also plays a significant role in many such instances, for what may be triumphant for me, may be complete humiliation for another.

I confidently assert that triumphs and disappointments transform ordinary lives into bold and durable characters. There is a constant force propelling me towards my destiny and thus, creating a greater need than ever before to find the solutions; not in the answers but in the questions themselves. This is not an unnatural phenomena but merely the ensuing tide of change which is not persuasive but brutal and rigid at every junction. I have simply never stood cowering in the face of adversity at any point of my life and even when situations was at their most vicious, I refused to accept defeat. In this defiance, I transmuted from a potentially flawed and dismantled person, to a courageous and unyielding one.

Life is a challenge…..So prepare to meet it

Life is God's Gift…….With a grateful heart accept it

Life is an adventure……..In faith dare it

Life can be a sorrow……In God, overcome it

Life can be a tragedy……..With courage, daily face it

Life can be a duty…..Without grumbling perform it

Life can be a game…. Know when to play it

Life is a mystery….. Wish never to truly unfold it

Life is a song….Let those who are worthy hear you sing it

Life is an opportunity…..So embrace it

Life is definitely a journey…By God's Grace complete it

Life is like a promise….Endeavour to fulfil it

Life begins with love…..To a special few please reveal it

Life is indeed a beauty….With every breath praise it

Life is God's precious spirit…So embrace it

Life can be a struggle….Of course you will fight it

Life, then death, the final mystery…..In Christ all will solve it

Life, God's gift to all….In Him all you days with thanks live it

I believe that in spite of some of the most exhausting circumstances, people are still capable of flourishing and growing. Furthermore, as attitudes begin to change there is a marked improvement in the lives of those individuals walking alongside us. Whenever I face positive criticism, I must endeavour to be better than before and rise to meet the challenges before me. Of course it is more favourable to receive praise - but what type of praise do men and women seek? It is better for the ego to hear that we are beautiful, smart and popular than to hear a barrage of truthful admonishments that would ultimately help to set us free. Pride however, [the precursor to every fall], hinders a number of individuals from being corrected due to their tangible and indiscernible fears.

The disabling and highly contagious condition that affects human beings is a common one; namely sin. Sin, though a small word has enormous consequences for the one whose life continues to be forcefully held in its prevailing grip. The manifestation of sin can be immediate or long-term and whilst many may disguise their attitude towards its nature and origin, the consequences are played out daily in the lives of people, regardless of cultures and creed. There are some people who endeavour to alleviate the suffering borne by others through their tireless and unselfish acts of service. There are others however, who continue to be influenced by sinful actions, which day by day continue to impair the lives of many innocent people around them. The glories savoured by a privileged minority, remains the silent struggles of a suffering and forgotten majority.

Serve or be served: A Life of Devotion

"If all men were to bring their miseries together in one place, most would be glad to take each his own home again rather than take a portion out of the common stock." Solon (638 -559 B.C). According to Solon, no one would willingly walk an inch in the shoes of another person, yet there are extenuating circumstances when such an encumbrance might be willingly shouldered. Service to others begins in humility and as exemplified in the life of Christ, one witnesses from the Bible's narrative how graciously and compassionately he cared for those uncared for by society of his day. During the last century, there have been individuals who were outstanding in the examples they set following the ministry of Christ. There were a number who simply left all behind within their own culture and inserted themselves alongside others in their suffering, rejection, poverty and shame. One such individual who immediately comes to mind was the unassuming and humble; Mother Teresa.

She was born Agnes Gonxa Bojaxhiu in Skopje, Macedonia, August twenty-six, nineteen ten. Mother Theresa developed a strong sense of calling from God at the age of twelve but it was not until she was eighteen that she left her parents' home and joined an Irish community of nuns who had missions in India. Of course her story became well publicised over the years, highlighting her gruelling and deeply moving work with the poor of Calcutta. I suspect Mother Theresa did not have to contemplate too many prayers with God and dialogues with superiors in order to put her faith and love into action. She appeared a feisty and resilient soul who asked few questions of herself but was in possession of many answers for the lives of others. It proves that very few real issues impacting the lives of people can in fact be resolved by means of lengthy mechanical debates, as those from political orientations. Since, many such dialogues seem to have the exact opposite effect on direction and outcomes. It's unthinkable that if a man holding a rifle was confronted by a hungry lion would first start a political debate or dialogue to establish what was making the lion angry, hungry or dangerous; he would simply aim his rifle and fire and then deal with the questions later. In the event of such nonsensical deferment, he would be dead and the lion would be free to kill another day. There are moments when questions and answers are not the imperative and a bold decision has to be made when much freedom is at stake. The calling of an individual to service has often been seen as a 'gift;' a person who possesses an ability which can be used to enhance the lives of others in many different situations. Although many actively pursue the gift they believe has eluded them for most of their lives, it is an enigma to me how they simply fail to recognise that everyone is already in possession of such gifts and all that is required is to seek God's direction. There are many people who seem unable to locate it but I simply refuse to ignore it.

I refuse to undermine the reasons why I came into being and refuse to have my life defined by others who themselves, have no definition for their own. From the very beginning there was an intended purpose to which my life was called and determined as I am, I seem unable to ignore or escape my destiny. I believe I am no longer under any unreasonable moral obligations, neither to myself, nor to other people. I can find no further questions to ask which will undoubtedly affirm my position - I was born, first to serve God, then to serve my fellow humans, in any and every righteous and holy capacity.

During the course of my life thus far, I have encountered many exhausted and overwhelmed individuals who have suffered emotional, physical and spiritual battles, making a number unfit for purpose. Many, like my friend Marjorie have related tales of unbelievable sadness, unbearable disappointments and challenges that left her defences shattered. These are the people I see as, needing a little push, a sharp pull or a ton of encouragement to get them back on the main 'highway' and out of their own secluded hideaway. Of course no human being should ever be robbed of their potential, their identity, dignity, or self-respect. I appreciate that what affirms a person's humanity can become a tangled mess and it is for this reason that I am able to live a hopeful and victorious life in Christ, from where my standards are reinforced daily. Since, without his presence overshadowing me each step of my journey, I fear that I too, may become loss under the weight of exclusion and rejection.

The standards I have created within my life are simply to reinforce the autonomy that was robbed from me in the past. I find that order creates discipline and in this space there is clarity for others as well as for myself. It is with this attitude that I approach every challenge I encounter. To some people I may appear somewhat one-dimensional. This is fine and I have no particular quarrel with those who retain such a thought since I prefer to live with a fastidious and orderly mind-set. Subsequently, my approach to life which initially appears one dimensional, allows me to steer my life into places I judge as both edifying and productive. I am not in the least interested in control over anyone but I am determined to control myself and those things that impact my being positively or adversely.

By approaching every situation from the same angle of calm, I will always have a measure of control over almost every event in my life. Even though a number of issues may initially appear overwhelming, if I remain calm, I can assert some control over my reactions and minimise undue stress and anxiety. This enhances my ability to move through each phase with confidence and level-headedness. First, I pursue discipline for my mind; what I think, how I think, the nature and orientation of those thought waves and patterns and at what point I want them to be arrested. As soon I find I am becoming entangled in a frightful mess, I halt my mind. After all, I am in charge of what happens inside me and in the swiftest period, those unhealthy or toxic thoughts are realigned with wholesome and morally sound principles. The same principles apply to my body. If I fail to exercise, I become less energetic when attempting more strenuous and labouring tasks. It makes perfectly good sense to me that if I wish to enjoy maximum output, I need maximum input thus, when both mind and body are equally disciplined, my entire being is in perfect unison. From this point I am much better equipped to meet and often exceed my own standards in light of the incredibly high distinction I continue to set for myself and whether I meet chaos or peace, it's no longer a question of how big the problem but how calm I am when facing it.

There is a theological conjecture which suggests that in the beginning God created 'order' out of 'chaos;' the world was in complete darkness and empty. Whilst this may seem chaotic to some observers, it is perfectly acceptable to me since, if there is no light, then naturally there is darkness and if something is empty, this does not immediately suggest that emptiness equates to chaos. If we should expound this theory of 'chaos' a little more in-depth and presuppose that this 'chaos' arose from the entry of sin which, resulted in the 'first death,' Adam and Eve's expulsion from the garden of Eden since, they were no longer in face to face relationship with God. Of course this is unsubstantiated conjecture on my part but is nevertheless supported in Scripture. 2 Timothy 1:9 – "This grace was given us in Christ Jesus before the beginning of time." Suggesting that, since Christ had redeemed us before we were created, sin had already proliferated the 'chaos' in the absence of everything. The fact that this verse is suggesting that God had redeemed something in the absence of everything, is surely a submission that sin was pre-existent? If for the briefest moment I should deliberate that the plan of creation was fundamentally flawed on the principle of redemption in absence of redeemable beings; was this in fact a mere theoretical inference? Does God speculate or could it simply be that in his infinite wisdom had measures in place for every stage of human life on earth?

Naturally, creation had to become redeemable because, it was in this action where its viability and potential was fully established and realised. Sin is the necessary evil which transformed the universe, highlighting the vulnerability of human beings as needy and impressionable and whose identity can only be confirmed through God. Of course God could simply have created replicas of him but this would have been futile and counter-productive for his ultimate purposes since, only God could exist as a perfect being in a perfect world. Creation beings were created from perishable substance yet, with the initial provision to live forever; another revealing thought. If the perceived chaos which was a direct tributary of sin and was within creation, then it could be the very reason God inhabited mankind with his spirit and the fact all were given a free-will to discern good from the pervasive evil which is wholly unavoidable.

The nature of sin as earlier stated cannot be underestimated. The Bible teaches in great detail of the beginning of sin and what it produces in the hearts and lives of men and women; always resulting in 'death', the second death. Since, the very fragile composition of human beings created from clay which was not made to withstand the pressures of the evil that beset the lives of all. Admittedly, one may ask; how could God being perfectly good, create a world in which evil co-exists alongside good? This evil is so corrosive that it dismantles everyone in its path. Many theologians have argued this point through the centuries and still the answer remains unsubstantiated; yet, the one thing which is clear to me and that is, no human being fully understands the wisdom or the plans of God. Perhaps both principles of good and evil must exist in order that such opposing forces on such a vast spectrum are recognised one from the other – pure conjecture on my part, admittedly.

Nevertheless, one could also debate the course and direction that God ordered from the outset; could He simply not have changed the direction of his intended history? Of course this simply ignites an already scorching debate on the idea that someone who is rigid and steadfast cannot change; what would he change into? It could simply mean that, if God had changed the history of humanity, he ultimately would have had to change also, implausible since, God is already all he is, unalterable.   It is for this reason, I firmly believe that God's original intention was to create a world without sin yet, we read in the Bible that Christ was slain before the foundations of the world were laid? The allusion here is that if God had not died, mankind would not have been and if creation is to become creative, there has to be life and inhabitants, making it possible, sustainable and redeemable. The act of a dying God was the upholding of the law of creation, the sustaining sacrifice that would transcend human beings into relationships and eternity with God rather than being suspended in the outer reaches of the laws of God's perfection and purpose which suggests that the only change necessary, was for all human beings to be transformed into the intended image of

God their creator, as each one assumes their full identity in him. Of course this human identity is full of faults and for this reason, I can deliberate on the validity of the creation reality which, according to those observers who pursue the 'fault' element, need to be reminded that the planet is full of faults.

The fault component is best exemplified in humans who all possess the potential to develop genetic culpabilities. Another area of fault is the earth's tectonic plates that cause frequent earthquakes and devastations. Similarly the sub-Sahara deserts are too hot to be fully supportive of many life forms and the Arctic Circle is much too cold to do the same and yet, many different forms of life are supported and have become sturdy and adaptable creatures. What initially appears as a 'fault' is in fact, God's perfection. The wisdom of God has to be above every shade of doubt and I don't believe I am in the least qualified to undermine the merit and on-going history of God who in his wisdom fixed everything into a meaningful place. While I accept that my identity was broken in part without Christ, I can gladly assert that it is now fully restored in him. For this reason, I have chosen to live my life without being in constant tension with the values and laws of the universe and not to become overly concerned with every possible motive and cause. Instead, I will humbly figure out my place and purpose within it.

I endeavour to live my life step by step and always mindful of everything and everyone around me. It is partly for this reason I pay particular attention to those people I encounter whose struggles are silent and painful but always with a real hope of the unexpected. This unexpected element arrived to me by way of fasting, praying and focussing on God instead of on my own pitiful existence. I seldom get angry, a man or woman who prays often is often the last to become angry since, anger is infinitely unproductive and so I offer prayers at every available moment. I pray upon rising, I pray fervently before retiring. I pray before I eat; in my home, in the homes of my friends but especially in the homes of my 'enemies.' I pray at the wheel of my car, I pray as I begin my day. I pray when the rain falls, whether a shower or a squall, I pray when I am triumphant, I pray when I am defeated. I live a life that is fuelled, not so much by food or drink; but by prayer, fasting and supplication to a most holy and worthy God. I pray expectantly when my guests arrive, I pray diligently and thankfully when they leave. I pray with my children, I pray for my children, I pray for my friends but especially for my enemies. I pray when I am busy, it doesn't stop when I am still, in traffic, in the school, by the gate, in the hospital, in the supermarket car park, at the airport before I board my flight. I pray with a deep conviction when I am flying or sailing. I pray when I have been humiliated, I pray when I have been exonerated, I pray when I have no idea what I must do next and I pray when all the answers are just a word or action away.

It's not so much that I love to pray but it's that I live to pray. Many may be disbelieving but my life of prayer is between my God and me, I pray in both expectation and anticipation. So that when the day of trouble comes, I can stand, as echoed in Ephesians 6:14; "Stand firm then, with the belt of truth buckled around your waist, with the breastplate of righteousness in place." I like to be in the present in the physical and in the future in the spiritual, so not being ready for every possible eventuality is not an option and sending many prayers on ahead gain such interest, I can live a relative interest free life in the present. I believe this is an appropriate way of maintaining order and discipline within my ordinary life. I embrace my ordinary life, the one God has so graciously granted me. This position may be viewed as disadvantageous to a number of observers but for me, it is the place from where I gain entry into some of the most extraordinary places.

Inside these places I can walk nosily with my friends, silently with my adversaries, I can weep with my sisters, and laugh with my brothers – and the world knows nothing of my existence in this space of limitless possibilities. I know my work is accomplished, the moment I see the transformation of a 'pauper' becoming a 'prince' and a barren life becoming fruitful and the chaos and disorder that enslaved a number of people, finally evaporates.

There was a time in my life where I had a need to learn everything as fast as I could. Now, I simply do not care who thinks less of me because of my reluctance to be cooperative in their world analysis since, I have come to accept that all that really matters to me is, as long as what I know or profess to know, continue to enhance my dignity, affirm my principles and direct my footsteps, I care to know nothing further. If I need a doctor, I simply call or travel to see one and similarly with any other professional whose skill I may need from time to time. I don't need to know or learn everything, this is impossible! Now, I spend time learning less in order that I may know more! It was from this point of understanding that I found the ultimate way forward and where I have learned to be prepared for all of life's unexpected events.

Preparedness equals Readiness

Preparedness equals readiness - for when I am prepared for life's nauseating occurrences the position I take and defend allows for a much better outcome in many instances. It is partly for this reason that I respond and behave in a particular way and what is appropriate for me could be simply unacceptable for anyone else. There are a number of things which I find completely unacceptable and so make conscious attempts to steer my life away from them. I totally deplore lateness, dishonour and bad manners [in anyone], myself included; all are inexcusable. This may be completely reasonable with other people who are themselves struggling to overcome such annoying traits.

Human beings simply cannot judge what they do not know; admittedly a majority of judgements are usually made from a very 'sound' place, - within the self. Many harsh judgements against others are often based on one's own values or lack of them. In all my searching through life, my most enduring quest has been for the truth. I am highly aware that each person possesses aspects of 'truth' within them but of course, everything we learn has to originate from another source, thus legitimising each person's claim to absolute truth, when in essence, is a fundamentally flawed assertion. There have been a number of occasions in the past, where I was completely disappointed with myself, purely with my lack of courage to challenge a particular truth. Truth is such a strange concept since, what is truth for one person, is a mass of fabricated lies to another. Naturally, there are aspects of truth, which can be fully substantiated since, it may be perceptible and whatever is visible, is often more credible. One such truth is my willingness to assert my standards in all areas of my life and to allow them to underscore everything of value to me. One such notable standard is my preparedness in every instance. This is easy to understand since, if I know there are hurdles ahead, I will prepare in advance to meet them at each point with the right attitude and appropriate shoes. Similarly, if the weather is inclement, I leave my home appropriately attired.

I promised I would always be prepared for everything but in addition to this, that I would also be ready with the right answers within me; should the wrong questions arise from others. The attitude of preparedness I adopted in my life enables a seamless transition in many areas. Regardless of whether I am teaching at church, doing a poetry recital going to the gym, travelling on an aeroplane, being admitted into hospital, or simply attending a meeting or an event; I like to be prepared. I have often been compared to five of the ten virgins in Matthew 25:6-8. There were five wise virgins and five foolish ones and each one had trimmed their lamps and travelled some distance to await the bridegroom. The five wise virgins had taken extra oil for their lamps but the foolish ones had only taken what was in their lamps. Of course, the bridegroom was delayed in his coming and the foolish virgins ran out of oil. Sadly, by the time the bridegroom arrived their lamps were empty; they were in complete darkness and were excluded from the greatest party of all. If I have made all the necessary preparations and I am still excluded, then I can do nothing further, what is done is done. These are essential traits of the Christian life but also of a victorious life. Logically, by our physical design, we live in the present but our expectations are indivisibly linked to future hopes and allusions of what is still to come.

There are so few things to which I aspire but there are a number of complexities in the universe that holds me in a perpetual grip. I never seem to have to go in search of pleasure because pleasure seems to be present whenever my mind is content and I am reasonably satisfied with my internal world. One of the things that reinforce this sense of satisfaction is my regular visits to my gym each week. The drive in the morning rush hour can take up to one hour but I would not change that for anything. There is a very simple reason for this which is the spirit of community amongst the members who attend regularly. I find that I can insert myself amongst them and become noticeable yet invisible. Nothing in life promises the 'perfect' experience and although the general camaraderie is upbeat and friendly, there is always at least one person who brings an ominous cloud whenever they insert themselves alongside others.

I remember one morning overhearing a conversation as I was running on the treadmill with my eyes shut tight. Although I was glad I heard it, (since I acted upon the information the very first time I had a chance to do so), I was also saddened that people can be so hurtful in some of the comments they make concerning others. The two befuddled young women were chatting about their antics at the weekend but my attention was particularly drawn to the mention of a young man who often runs alongside me on the treadmill. They were discussing his lack of personal hygiene as though he was an unfeeling object and emphasised how stifling the atmosphere can be when he is around, admittedly this was a fact but it would be far more beneficial to talk compassionately with him than to gossip indifferently about him. I made a decision that the very next time I saw him I would address this difficult issue. Of course I hardly require any prompting since, I become deeply offended when others engage in such malicious behaviour concerning others. It was Oliver Goldsmith (1730-1774) who said; "We must touch his weakness with a delicate hand. There are some faults so nearly allied to excellence that we can scarce weed out the fault without eradicating the virtue."

This highlights the delicate balance between fault and virtue but of course many attributes are directly alongside each other and a person should exercise every care in dispensing advice or criticism. I had to give a lot of thought to the idea of approaching this young man. Since, I had to effectively, place myself in his shoes and determine how I would feel if I was approached by a stranger who informed me of an unpleasant aspect about my personal hygiene. I find it so difficult to take a complicit view when others are being slandered and although I seem to care a great deal less about what is said about me, I dislike gossip about others. I knew that I had to be bold enough to approach this inoffensive young man and the very next time I saw him I took him into a quite area of the gym and began a very difficult conversation. I believed I started thoughtfully and compassionately but it's so hard to judge personally what real compassion looks like. I simply hoped that he would not be insulted and would be wise enough to see the merits behind my motives.

The next time he walked into the gym he was wearing new clothes and looking immaculate. Yes I thought, great! He came over, smiled at me, got on the treadmill and has never looked back. That young man became a good ally, assisting me in the gym wherever possible. He introduced me sometime later to his wife and family and I have been reasonably supportive of his local business. This was a few years ago and I thank God that I was given a spirit of boldness and not timidity. Of course he could have reacted adversely to my comments but I believe wisdom was instituted at the inception and I made a rigorous assessment prior to approaching him. I had to swiftly discern whether he appeared a gracious man and once this was established, kindness and humility created an opening. I approached him and began my conversation with just one question; "are you a Christian?" The minute he said yes, I knew the way to trust would be better established since, as a Christian myself, I no longer saw him as a stranger but as a 'brother.' I have no doubt that it was not what I said that really made a difference to him; it was the way in which I had said it. Since in me they are merely words, but when my Father comes, they are words full of power and healing. If we approach people's vulnerabilities in a supportive manner, with respect and kindness, our integrity becomes transparent.

The delicate foundations from where people balance family, work commitments, hopes and expectations can be swept away in the blink of an eye. These are the things that are worth fighting for; the ones people are more than willing to die for. With matters of principle in particular, every possible skill should be employed to defend them through to their final conclusion. It was Ralph Waldo Emerson who said; "Nothing can bring you peace but yourself. Nothing can bring you peace but the triumph of principles." It is imperative that the critical areas within my life are not measured unfairly against those in the lives of others; otherwise I would be in a permanent state of wretchedness. There is a need for sensitivity with others as well as with myself, a gentle exploration around the darker fringes that supports my present realities. There is an urgent need to deconstruct any unsavoury characteristics that may obscure my true realities and this is made possible when I become willing to change my approach to others. Since there are no identical views, I must be prepared to show respect to another simply because it is human to possess a variety of views.

Whether or not another person may agree with me entirely, I am simply exercising my rights as individuals to nurture the things that underpin my beliefs and values. In my constant pursuit for excellence within my life I realise that I may have inadvertently offended others whose lives are chaotic, purposeless and without the type of foundations that gives value and meaning. I have become increasingly aware that not every person will desire change; for some, there is nothing wrong with the way they have chosen to live and this is acceptable since, it is their choice and not what I would choose. Of course when a person like Katrina appeared from nowhere into my life, I should have known that her only desire was to attempt to alter my world beyond recognition.

Two Ducklings and One Quack

I remember a number of years ago driving through a beautiful village, when two very young ducklings wandered into the road, just missing the wheels of my car. All the cars were swerving around them but I knew they would end up dead by the side of the hedgerow and so, pulled over, gave chase and caught them both. "Now that I have caught them, what do I do with them?" I thought. I noticed one other car had pulled up alongside me and a young woman came over and said, "Hello, you caught them, I have a large pond in my garden and I will take them if you like." This was incredibly unexpected and I was so pleased that they would be safe in her pond. This meeting of chance would leave me years down the line wishing I had driven by like all the others drivers, not caring whether they had made it to the other side of the road or perished. I was on business about six weeks later in an adjoining village and bumped into the same woman, this time with her two young sons. As I walked past her she called out to me and we stopped chatting for a while and appraising me on the progress of the ducklings. We finally managed an introduction and exchanged contact details; and the day Katrina came into my life remains one of my most regrettable actions.

While I do not wish to relive every minor detail of the events concerning this woman I simply wish to highlight the fact that what can sometime begin as a coincidence can often morph into the most remarkable nightmare. Of course it was my belief that anyone who appeared so thoughtful by stopping their car and rescuing two vulnerable lives must be an inherently 'good' person. Some of the greatest lessons I learned in the ten years of my 'friendship' with this rather strange and self-centred woman was by far the most critical and life defining. I learnt that not all human beings possess inherent goodness and that not all wish for change and transformation; many are reasonably satisfied on their highways to nowhere. Katrina's life was chaos and mine was orderly. Her life was indolent and mine, embryonic, her existence was steeped in the occult and pagan rituals and beliefs. I suspected she held strange beliefs but she kept this aspect well hidden at the inception of our encounter. In contrast, I am welcoming, open and transparent with my faith and my beliefs are fully centred upon God. Of course I did not know she favoured dancing around Stonehenge and Machu Picchu during the full moon naked with groups of chanting strangers but my preferred garment is being adorned in praise and worship to God each day from sunrise to sunset. My prayers of thanksgiving and joy are fully demonstrated with the body of believers at my Christian church each Sunday morning.

Katrina and I were very different people but fate had malevolently brought us together. By the time I finally managed to rid myself of this scheming charlatan, my life was absolute chaos and her own became 'orderly' but only for a brief spell. In Leviticus 19:18 we are reminded, "Do not seek revenge or bear a grudge against anyone among your people, but love your neighbour as yourself. I am the LORD." Of course I loved Katrina; I saw a woman desperately in search of something to empower her life and position but sadly, this type of power is always short-lived. I cannot fail to appreciate the many occasions where she was kind and considerate, albeit with a sinister and underlying motive. In the past I was too ready to be open to anyone and everyone which propelled me into countless disadvantageous positions.

The day Katrina departed from my life was the day clarity and light re-entered; a dark and oppressive period had passed; thank God. I bear no lasting grudges against her since I might have offended her inadvertently by my strong Christian values, or maybe the visible lack of them, who knows! Naturally, the lessons in this situation have reinforced the things that I value most; my faith, identity, my family and my culture. I believe that if anyone wishes to get to know me, it is no longer my responsibility to remain, 'open all hours' but it's theirs to discover the signs marked, 'open' and 'closed.' In my culture there has been a marked shift in attitudes and behaviour in recent years. In the past however, our lives were reasonably open, so were the doors and windows of our hearts and homes. This is fine when you live in a community where everyone is a friend or a family member; there are never any surprises waiting. The change in culture for me having been uprooted from a very small country to a large and impersonal one meant a marked shift in attitudes and expectations. I simply had to learn that within my new British culture the majority of people operated a closed heart and door policy for safety as well as security; there were simply no hidden signs marked with 'push' or 'pull.' I am prepared to continue the process of learning and adaptation all my life since; I firmly believe that the process of learning continues from the cradle to the grave. It's elementary, because life is not a static non-entity but a continuum of growth through the processes of pain and sometimes humiliation.

Vincent, the young man at my gym received my encouragement graciously even though it must have been a difficult thing to hear. There are instances where I simply have to allow my heart to overrule my dictatorial head and approach my friends, neighbours and strangers courageously in an attempt to assist them to become the very best they can be. Of course I failed miserably with Katrina but I knew from the outset that this was a one way street and no amount of kindness and remonstrations would propel her along a multi-lane highway. In this instance, I simply had to concede defeat but at the same time recognised this period as one of the most triumphant in my life. It showed me resolutely the type of people I simply did not wish to encumber my life. There have been so many different occasions where I have quietly debated the rights and wrong of particular situations. The proverbial, "If only," which is natural in retrospect and serves only to remind us for the next time we are facing an enormous dilemma to work through systematically and applying both reason and logic.

My head is almost as compliant as my heart and though some observers may be alarmed at the thought of a 'soft head,' it suits me since; I prefer softness at the top and centre of my being because the outer casing has become an unyielding paradox in recent years. I understand the demands of my head, though I seldom give way to them. The gentle tendencies of my heart on the other hand is a different matter altogether; they are accepting and forgiving of many things and the only quarrels that ever takes place in my life, are those within my head.

I am constantly thinking; where is God? How big is he? How many species of fishes are actually in the oceans? What are its depths and intensity? Are there more than few 'good' men and women in the world and if yes, where are they? How does a Tulip bulb enter the ground so ugly in winter and burst out in the spring, fully dressed in radiance and splendour? How does the slugs and snails across town smell the French Marigolds in my hanging basket and in no time they are eaten to oblivion when their pace is a backwards crawl? I cannot go for more than a few meagre seconds without a major debate erupting inside my brain. I spend so much time going over and over events until I reach the most appropriate conclusions – my conclusions.

I don't believe that my attitude to reason and logic will be adversely impacted in the future, since my head remains a faithful servant, although it has proved an exceptionally poor master at times. The events which have shaped my life were not down to mere luck or chance but they were in fact, the exact routes that had been pre-destined for me to travel. Whether I meet my enemies or allies, I simply keep my allies reasonably close and am grateful that, I can draw more than a mere line between my enemies and me. I can draw upon wisdom, as I gain insight and am finally able to allow a healthy fear to occasionally come near, without dreading it will permanently disable me.

Head and Heart: Servant and Master

My head [brain], tells me when I am afraid because my heart starts to race within my chest and my breathing becomes both intense and rapid. My brain also informs me when there is a pain in some unpronounceable part of my anatomy; the brain remains the most mysterious of all the body's major organs. My head, a powerful organiser and skilful contender has been a faithful servant but in matters of conscience, my heart is always the master. The sub-conscious mind remains a hidden dimension, secreted away from all open judgements and scrutiny and where much processing and counter-quarrels take place. It is the large upper 'room' of pre-conceived ideologies and unfounded fears and without careful guidance from the less analytical heart, there is a real danger that over emphasis on one's own perceived reality could lead to such dismantling, that a previously whole person could soon resemble a fraction of their prior self.

What often begins in the brain as harmless thought waves can become so toxic that even the heart becomes endangered from complete paralysis. The questions that enslave a person in their mind could easily set them free within the heart if a bold approach was adopted to determine their exact nature. Whenever a person learns to be true to self, being true to others transpires into a seamless process. No one would be inspired by a word I uttered, if I gave instructions to others which I neither followed nor heeded. Similarly to the aforementioned thought, when my whole body is operating in unison, head and heart together, this lessens the possibility that my domineering head will perpetually outwit my compliant heart. One has to lead while the other follows - the brain is the cold, [Siberia] and the resolute commander. The heart on the other hand, is the warmth, [the Caribbean], of the human person. It is from this complex chamber, where my entire body is maintained and repaired by way of minor highways [veins] and major trunk roads [arteries], which are marked in their distinctiveness and specific functioning.

The rhythm of my heart, continuous from birth to death and around two and a half billion beats directs every operation necessary in an average lifetime. So, if so much thought and precision has gone into the creation of human beings, where each person is equipped with microscopic genetic data, a brain designed to guide and direct them into every judicious analyses and a heart that should respond to hurt, suffering and joy - why is it that so few people can confidently ask the right questions of themselves and others? For those who find it difficult to ask pertinent questions of self, will also find it particularly challenging to ask appropriate questions of others. Whenever a person's mind is open to self-evaluation, it is opened to all but if it remains closed to self, it stays closed to all. Whenever we become empowered to ask the right questions we are simply reaffirming our autonomy as individuals and inclusivity of the human community.

I advocate very clear boundaries within my life; this is an on-going sentience of what is permissible or not to be tolerated. Boundaries not only define the edges of safety but they also reduce the peripheries of darkness by constantly underscoring those necessary principles that are furthermost in my consciousness at the inception of every decision. There are some aspects that remain such an integral part of my sense of being that a mere glance or minor involvement would simply not suffice. As much as I would have occasionally liked to off-load a number of my difficulties onto seemingly 'stronger' associates and family members around me, it simply would become a wholly counter-productive enterprise. My un-refuted realities which are authentic become the essence and spirit of my unique humanity. I could never realistically wish for my troubles to be shouldered by another human being since, it is from such battlefields that new strategies and skills are developed. I would never wish for a crowd to share my favourite meal, nor would I grab a group of people at random to share my bath or my bed; God forbid! So, it makes a great deal of sense to shoulder everything that life brings into my path, willingly and single-handedly. I simply do not wish for a crowd to share the things which are the most enthralling; touching and tasting; these are undeniably my exclusive privileges and belongs to no other.

I particular like the analogy in Psalm 34:1; "Oh taste and see that the Lord is good." It's interesting in this passage that the reader is not being asked to get another to 'taste' for them; they are invited directly to experience the completeness and wholeness of taste for themself. Of course a person cannot physically 'eat' God but the writer is suggesting some aspect of God be tried out in comparison to what is currently held as 'good' and immediately one begins to imagine the enchantment of all five senses, taste in particular. As one becomes deeply absorbed within the dynamics at work inside the mouth and brain; taste can be a completely overwhelming indulgence and one that is absolutely unique to every person. However, if it were to be imagined that, I had never tasted sugar or anything sweet in my life, it would be impossible for me to describe what 'sweet' was really like to another person. Similarly, this could be applied to a number of other sense orientated objectives. If I had never heard a symphony, nor seen the constellations as they assemble in the sky at night, I would have no valid points of reference from where I could build or develop a particular discourse. It is only when I am able to identify and experience everything in its fullest capacity that I am permitted to make informed decisions that ultimately underpin and validate my understanding. When a person is invited to undertake a specific function, there is an expectation that they will undoubtedly be better informed at the end than they were at the inception; as hitherto defined. The explicit finding should be one which pinpoints ways in which we can be more honest, receptive and open to the challenges within our own lives and in the lives of those we aim to serve and assist.

Although realism is to be preferred to idealism since, every person's circumstances in life will differ enormously. Those ascendancies, to which one may be clinging woefully, may be out-dated and detrimental in terms of their present reality. As terrifying as this may feel, it will undoubtedly help to re-establish the trust of a person who is desperately seeking to regain confidence and faith in people once more. So staying with them as they pass through immeasurable turmoil is often the only way for them to gain new confidence as they begin to feel cared for and valued in the process of reconsideration and adjustment. The success of this process must take into account particular ways of thinking; since the result of a person's thoughts often ends with an action. Whenever a person's thoughts are inharmonious and delinquent there is always the chance of a complex and disastrous forward journey.

If I was to be judged by the thoughts secreted within my mind – if they were made open to public scrutiny, it is possible that many would condemn me as polluted, desirous or divergent? Sadly, our world in its present post-modern state advocate all such thinking and while I am not exempt from such decadent 'highways' in my private world of thoughts and analyses, I firmly advocate that; whatever a person thinks, is in fact the essence of his or her true humanity. Thoughts, though shapeless and formless and within the unreachable compartments of the mind, when empowered to life, are the beginning of a series of toxic and damaging future actions.

So a Man Thinks: So He is

A person who is persistently told that he or she is rubbish will invariably attempt to place themself in a 'bin' every time they pass one by. Similarly, a violent man who habitually beats his companion, then repulsed later by his actions, declare his undying love for her and promise faithfully never to beat her again; until the next time. It is unlikely, that a woman in this situation will ever progress to 'healthy' relationships since; there is nothing to assert what a healthy relationship should look like. She may continue to be drawn to the paths of aggressive men with a damaging belief that 'love' forms a part of such castigatory alliances. Habitual methods of thinking are incredibly difficult to overcome, as such thoughts can become so entrenched within a person's sub-conscious, that it could effectively take a number of years to be erased, if at all.

In recent years I have witnessed so many books written around the power of positive thinking yet, I cannot help wondering why there is still so much hurting in the world. If one could simply think themselves out of suffering and poverty and it was so, there would be so few people that were poor; there would be no further need for aid agencies and charities which would result in loss of employment and positions for many. Of course those affected would simply 'think' up new positions in their mind and it would be so; what a preposterous notion! In Proverbs 23:7 we see that; "As he thinketh in his heart, so he is." Authorised [King James] Version. This passage tells me of a person whose character is defined by their thoughts, eventually becoming visible outworked actions. There have been a number of occasions when I have held thoughts about people and situations that have momentarily paralysed me with fear.

I know that a number of people just like me, struggle to overcome profligate and unkind modes of thinking, as this can negatively impact our attitude and behaviour towards others. There is a distinct call for wisdom, for if we are to be safe and confident individuals in our own company, we are to limit the time we spend in such toxic energy waste and become better managers of our own thinking. Of course thoughts can be positive energy that helps us to shape and transform our world but we must have a desire to find these alternative pathways. We don't necessarily have to be great advocates of good but we must advocate goodness in our own lives which in turn, will impact the lives of others significantly.

If I were to attempt to understand the principles of 'great' thinking – centuries past and up to the present day, I may in fact be able to appreciate the intention behind the creation of humans on earth and their intended purpose. In all of the plausible concepts pertaining to life on earth and the origins of man - it is often the 'rouges' [the great thinkers] who stirs revolutions of every kind. There have been numerous individuals who have had far-reaching impact due to their single-minded determination to break through all the barriers of resistance before them.

Scientists in particular, are spending painstaking hours over many years analysing microscopic details in clinical laboratories to determine the exact composition of mankind. In recent years the focus has shifted to DNA and genetics since this is the blueprint of every human being. The imperative here is that greater knowledge is acquired in order to advance medicines ahead of their requirement in the treatment of future disorders; again I hear those rhetorical echoes of Christ being slain before the foundations of the world were established, [Christ wiping out the disease of sin to halt its impact on human beings] and science going to places in anticipation of a possible need; similar but very different results. Of course scientists have the human blueprint so they will know exactly how to meet the challenges that human genetics present to them; or will they? A rouge gene like sin will undoubtedly create a number of problems for an individual throughout their life.

In my observations of human thoughts and effectively its divergent nature, the most persistent theme from all of this is the fact that science merely shifts expectations and delay the inevitable – Christ on the other hand, meets and fulfils them all; ahead of, during and beyond time. Nevertheless, science and research still has much to celebrate. The flip side of this is thought highlights some of the most enduring testimonies of human beings whose incredible genius and opposing thinking established lasting legacies in medicine, music, theology, philosophy, engineering and politics to name a few, those same 'anomalies' became the standard to which many would aspire for centuries. The radical nature of their thinking was the very thing which set them apart and while many observers wished to silence them at the time, the futility of their quest could never diminish a light that was meant to shine brightly to illuminate a path for those who would follow after them. The key where many connections would be established and upheld was the very source of derision and hostility at the inception.

Nevertheless, it was from a number of such notable cradles where inspiration arose, simply because a person's ability to apply reason and logic to unreasonable and illogical situations were highly contentious and years advanced of their contemporaries. Imagine for a brief moment that I am thinking I would like to 'kill' a particular person over a dispute; I may not necessarily go after that person and execute them at my earliest convenience, for not only is this morally unacceptable it is also repugnant and brutal. Naturally, this would suggest that there are both morally right and immorally wrong ways of thinking which allows a person to soar or to descend into a pit which holds onto anything that dares to enter into its depth.

I have a tendency to link my theoretical discourses with aspects of reality which I believe helps to highlight a particular point more succinctly. In this instance, as painful as it is, I must bring to 'life,' Sonia, my childhood friend from our village, Newcombe Valley. Newcombe Valley is loved passionately by a number of people, myself included but scorned intensely by others. My father used to always say to us; "Curse where you are going but never where you have come from." Of course I could never hate the place I was born – all the love I have ever known was born and has died there. Furthermore, my enduring affection for my place of birth begins and ends with family, not only is my umbilical cord buried there, one day in the future, I wish for my body to be interred there; a reunification with my umbilicus.

So naturally, everything I understand of family; good, indifferent, beautiful and ugly is there. Another aspect is the intensity of the landscape – when the rains are abundant it is likened to paradise; flourishing and captivating. When the rains withdraw, it is transformed into a barren savannah, where the red dirt becomes overwhelming, clinging onto every aspect of life and making everything enflamed and beaten in its path. It is impossible to travel anywhere on the island without everyone knowing we are 'Savannah people.' The red dirt always betrayed us – on our clothes, in our hair, on the wheels of our vehicles and even inside our pockets! We were simply fighting a losing battle and eventually, a number of people began to recognised the richness of our soil and its source of bauxite and aluminium ore and so, instead of being ashamed of the red dirt that spoiled our clothes and our homes, we began to celebrate its strength, especially in view of the fact that our parish was the most prolific agricultural region on the entire island. The soil we had so grown to scorn was in fact, the same one that fed the entire island and beyond. Of course as children, we found it hard to stay clean but a number of families were rigorous in their attempts to keep children reasonably tidy throughout the day. Sonia was not from one of those families. In fact, she was from a different family altogether; a special family. She was born with what we now term as 'learning difficulties' and although attempts were made to get her to stay in school, she simply did not have the capacity to learn in a mainstream school alongside a number of brutes who habitually ill-treated and ridiculed her without mercy.

As I child I used to hear stories that I never fully understood but as I became a woman, the reality of Sonia's suffering was so brutal that I often wish I was a child once more. It emerged that my gentle, precious and vulnerable friend, with her albino skin, her blonde hair and astonishingly blue eyes was repeatedly raped by almost every man in whose clutches she became ensnared. The most unpalatable truth in all her suffering was that a number of men who violated her occupied prominent positions as teachers, nurses, magistrates and bank clerks – when they covered themselves with their exclusive cotton suits they could easily be mistaken for angels. It was one of those 'angels' who made her pregnant in her late teens and sadly, she was left to bring a son into a world that despised her and would ultimately despise him. No one ever imagined that she could care for this baby adequately but she surprised us all and was an incredibly attentive mother.

The most remarkable thing in this story is the fact that everyone treated that boy from the moment he could speak as they had treated Sonia, telling him he was 'stupid' and every derogatory term possible. Sadly, he grew up imitating what he was called and naturally suffers a great deal in much the same way as his mother did. He has learning difficulties and continued bed wetting into his early teens and there are a number of other issues. The way in which a fractured way of thinking can impinge upon those most vulnerable cannot be overlooked and I am astonished how callous human beings can be to those less favoured by society. I would seriously have to question my humanity if I found myself behaving inappropriately towards another fully able human being much less one whose challenges put her at a disadvantageous position in almost every situation. A few years ago I returned for a brief holiday home and for some reason Sonia and her son always walk miles in the hot sun to meet my car from the airport. There were two other people in my car that I had picked up along the road; in my culture this is normal, we always give strangers or anyone needing a lift a ride if we have the space. As I stopped to welcome them and give them a ride up the hill home, my other passengers began protesting vehemently that they would not continue to ride in my car if they got in. I turned round and calmly asked them to get out of my car and allow my friends to sit beside me; my car, my rules!

I remain grateful for one thing throughout my life and that is, although I have witnessed some of the most appalling behaviour by human beings I was determined to be different. I could have easily decided to seek revenge or something equally debilitating but I knew that this was never going to be the path for me and furthermore, I remain thankful that those few good role models who I encountered in the early part of my life have been the ones who have defined my principles and values every step of my journey. Of course I cannot protect them when I am not there but when I am – no one is permitted to harm them. I was deeply saddened to learn in my absence a number of years ago, that a boy had thrown a stone at this vulnerable woman and had left her blind in one eye. Of course, no one has ever been made accountable. I am grateful they permit me to insert myself in the space left vacant by their sides. During this same visit home, I remember being invited to a musical event one evening and was reluctant because my companion had not travelled with me on this occasion. In his absence, I made the decision to invite this young boy to be my chaperone and was glad that I had done so because he was determined to shine and I was humbled by his light.

In contrast to my friend Sonia who continues to suffer in poverty and want another woman in the same village with similar mental health issues was also made pregnant by an unknown male. The remarkable difference was, her son was taken away at birth and brought up within a loving and supportive family. This young man became an outstanding member of the community in every sense, as provider, husband and father. The contrasting lives of one who was exposed to the toxicity of human thinking and behaviour and one who was completed protected from it. My interpretation of this senseless behaviour by so-called 'normal' men and women remains the same. I often feel that for many people who live disagreeable existences under the pretentious banner of humanity, simply projects everything which is displeasing about themselves onto others. Many unsuspecting souls are carrying not only their own burdens but the conflicts of some most unlikely adversaries. Many of these people hate everything they see of themself in a mirror and so, find ways of reflecting it back onto others. There are a large majority of people who struggle to find value in aspects of themselves and are not actively pursuing others in a hope to apportion blame or anger; they simply wish to seek resolutions in order that they may find ways to establish the priority of their identity in every sense.

If what I thought routinely about myself and others was to be revealed openly and transparently to all, the world would obviously be a much more acceptable place. It is by virtue of the hidden nature of our irrational fears and thinking, from where so much toxic activity originates which produces irreparable damage to others but especially to a person's own sense of self and identity. These hidden thoughts are left to fester, gathering shape and form and enable us to create and dismantle whoever we chose. From my rudimentary understanding, human thoughts are methodical analysis of both coherent and incoherent random impulses passing through the brain. They come when we are sleeping as dreams in portrait, landscape and seascape and can leave us upon waking with such a tantalising sensation of 'having been there,' coupled with an overwhelming feel of a nonsensical reality which must be immediately apprehended. Thoughts are generated when we are fearful and can often morph into a toxic paralysis. The idea of being in 'love' is a typical illustration of an over-exaggerated series of complex thoughts. Of course, this hideous series of disinformation can open us up to intense psychological torture and abuse. This dramatically reduces our ability to function normally since, the idea of love has now become a paralysing agent and if simply left to run its natural disastrous course, will simply overtake us. Thoughts are an intricate blend of past, and present events which occasionally incorporates future actions not yet discernible; a psychological processing and un-processing of information and deceptions.

The mind is by far, the greatest of the unsolved mysteries of the human 'universe,' no reference to the universe that is; 'way out there' but the universe, which is tucked deep inside the human sub-consciousness. I can illustrate this idea a little more in-depth, in Psalm 42:7; *"deep calls to deep."* This Psalm speaks of roaring waterfalls and breakers sweeping one away in its might. Of course this is metaphoric language which is often used in biblical interpretation to present an unimaginable scene to the hearer or reader, yet the idea of something unfathomable and more profound than the cavernous aspect of my approximate humanity but is nevertheless reachable by mutual cooperation, is nothing short of remarkable. This complexity is hinged onto an outer dimension which is more than just a mere allusion yet, is physically unsearchable. Of course the mentions go way beyond the perceptible and begins touching upon the imperceptible magnitudes of the spiritual realms. Understandably, humans are both spiritual and physical beings; since, we could not be brought from nothing to 'something', by any other means. If this duality aspect was not present in humans, the world would largely consist of people who were devoid of what is perceived as 'normal' responses. They would therefore, be indifferent to pain, suffering and everything which allows human beings to merge at a common place and where the most constructive and brilliant aspects of their humanity become hinged to conscience, morality and social responsibility.

Thoughts are a powerful source of energy that links seemingly unconnected impulses to enterprising actions, making them corporeal. Yet, not all thoughts are destined to be tangible, for if one should image that they are a prince or a princess in the grand spectacular of a palace, with regalia, crown, man and maidservants, horse and carriages; who can stop such a foolhardy notion? Fantasy or reality, who can discern the inner man or woman and if their present reality is harmful to their general well-being, then, if a world of illusions and imaginings is a 'safe-house', then no one should extricate them from that safe haven. Whatever enhances the way an individual look and feel, either about themselves or what the wider perception is from groups and peers should not be discouraged unless it is harmful to that person or others. After all, how many individuals walk around with their chests puffed out high and lofty announcing their insalubrious intentions toward other human beings? The processing and un-processing of thoughts can be misaligned and could be likened to two high speed trains, which must never meet at any point where two tracks become one; this would naturally be catastrophic. In a similar way there is a definite need for a person to be mindful of their thoughts, the ones that are beneficial and good not only increase a person's ability to function within their own private world but bring significant improvements to all who share the company of a human being who possess morally good and pure thoughts.

Thoughts perfectly aligned to morally good and pure intentions are in fact rare since; the nature of human beings is in constant conflict to what is morally good and pure. Whenever this phenomenon occurs however, the human person is whole and is fully at one with self, with the world and with his or her creator. Of course you are asking, how is this possible? Immediately answering your own question by declaring, 'what a load of balderdash'; balderdash it may seem to a few but it makes perfectly good sense to me in every way. Since, it is only in the human mind, that unholy psyche, where one human being after another can create his or her own heaven of hell, success or failure, sadness or joy. The magnitude by which this can be generated cannot be physically judged but can reverberate both internally and externally for some time to come. When such thoughts are manifested, they can be observed as behaviour to self and towards others and often resulting in catastrophic decisions being taken.

I remember watching a documentary many years ago about the life of Sibelius, the Finnish composer who has contributed some amazing and breath-taking pieces of classical music to the world during his life. One of the most remarkable things in that appraisal of his life was the study of an on-going piece of music he had laboured over for twenty-five years to completion. When he decided it was ready for exposure, he descended in despair at its lack of depth and orchestra worthiness, so he threw the whole work onto a fire and watched in agony as it burned to rubble. This was his own private agony and in his own mind he had rehearsed that piece over a twenty-five year period. One cannot help wondering what he was hearing, since no other person had ever heard that piece performed by an orchestra, no one will never know the foundations on which his anxieties were based. It is a clear indication of the private turmoil people can encounter within the narrow scope of their tiny vacuum, with the potential to create a province, a masterpiece, a heaven or a hell.

One of the most distinguishing features between people and other beasts is the innate human ability to think logically, to make objective and subjective choices, to define others respectfully and be defined as and how one choose and to be totally responsible where they permit their internal thoughts to impel them. If I reflect briefly, over a number of events during the last few centuries, I find enduring testimonies of men and women, paupers and princes alike, pagans and Christians who possessed beliefs, gifts, talents and skills that would take them from relatively ordinary positions, to extraordinary heights. This transition, fuelled by their ambition to race, to conquer, to rule, to convince, to out-run, and to out-perform all of their contemporaries and competitors. Yet, those same fragile souls whose insecurities far outweighed their fear of climbing an icy glacier, or dying a gruesome death as a martyr and precipitating as though a divine call had led them to the brink of death on a great polar expedition. It may be possible that a number had been lead on missions to convert unbelieving pagans during every painfully obscure vacuum in history. For those who were able to fill those gaps, for some, it was the closest thing to heaven, while for others, it was bordering onto the first glimpses of hell.

A large degree of human thought processes are wrapped up in issues surrounding fear and insecurities. Fear is seldom recorded in the histories and anthologies of many gruelling endeavours yet, fear is indeed a major component that propels most of humanity's basic needs. The fear of failure, shame, disappointment and lack of recognition are the motivations driving a majority of people forward. After all, who wants to end their journey of life in a pauper's grave or even worst, no grave at all? It has been said; "One man's meat is another man's poison" and while one individual may be dreaming of plans on an astronomical scale, another may be simply worrying about where he or she will find enough food to provide the next meal for their family. Undoubtedly, the greatest adventures do not exclusively belong to the 'greatest men,' quite the contrary, they simply either got there first or they had the world at their feet to begin with. A number of individuals are able to align their adventures perfectly into history; if they cannot create their own landmarks, they simply assume the place of another.

So, if poor men and women can only dream and are buried in unmarked graves or no graves as earlier stated - is it only 'great' men and women who achieve great things? While a large part of my focus remain wholly upon much of my perception of the world and its peoples, I must also bear in mind the cultural biases from where ideas of greatest arise and whether or not there are distinctions between relative overvalued greatness. To redefine the term, greatness in a post- modern world, where greatness of mind, body and thought is to have an enviable bank balance, a top executive post in a bank or similar establishment, or to have six pairs of designer heels, five pairs of designer handbags and a body that looks remarkably like it has been ravaged by famine in the most pitiful and self-inflicted way; 'greatness,' or perceptions of exaggerated greatness?

In the ancient world much of what we now take for granted; rules, Christian values, and traditions were firmly rooted in a number of principles, albeit, a number were Christian but the majority pagan. Although our forebears did not escape changes through the passage of time, conquest and rulers; the overbearing ideologies of change were aligned with the purpose of unquestionable good for all concerned in democratic societies past. Of course, I realise that it takes a great deal more than ideology for the effective functioning of a nation since, all at its heart must be determined to fulfil their own individual obligations; both to self and to state. I am not convinced however, that modern societies embrace autonomous individuals at its heart since, many such people often refuse to align themselves with state and corporations that eradicate individuality and promote multiplicity. The problem that this thought continue to pose for me is – if I cannot find myself in this social engineering and manipulation, how will I find others who remain largely invisible in the vast sea of twofold minds? For this reason, I must maintain my unyielding position. I am better being identified by others, at least when they find me, I already know who I am and if they are lost, perhaps I can help to realign them back on track to the only route that every human should traverse; the route to fulfilment and potential greatness.

Route to Potential Greatness

Sometime ago I attended a celebration evening during International Women's Day, which was both an informative and uplifting experience. We were asked to identify a woman past or present, who had inspired us towards change, greatness of thought or action, or just one who had simply struck a chord with us, where we could identify aspects of our own persona and who had helped us to redefine the real tangible qualities and principles of greatness. Initially, I was uncertain of how my thoughts would develop around this but as I began to strip away the layers of what I did not like, what I was then left with was decidedly uncomplicated. I have never been an advocate of 'hero worship.' I simply cannot see the point of showing veneration to anyone who does not possess the power to change the meaningful and morally right aspects within their own lives, much less my own.

When I consider the essential qualities of who and what I am and who I wish to become, I always fail to see a fragile human being, with the potential to hurt and to fall, just like myself, becoming my all-consuming aspiration. While I value every human being as an individual with skills, talents and gifts to share, I cannot look up to one in wholehearted admiration, except a surgeon whose job it is to save every life, hanging in the balance before him. It was no surprise when I chose Ruth from the Bible and then had to quickly reiterate to the group why I had decided to make her my choice of inspirational woman. Ruth was extraordinary; she had married the son of Naomi and had become a widow at a most untimely hour and under a dreadful set of circumstances. The unfolding story of Ruth was both distressing and harrowing for any listener centuries in the future. Ruth possessed an unwavering spirit, a deep sense of loyalty, goodness and faithfulness. She also had a fervent disposition to adapt and change to future circumstances.

I saw a woman who was briefly clothed in fine silk and linen, metaphorically, only to be stripped 'naked' in full view of all her community, the shame and distress which this might have caused to another less level-headed and resolute soul could have been unimaginable. She was determined to follow her dream which, for many, would now be looking more like a spectacular nightmare. Ruth was defiant, she was not prepared to abandon the woman whose sons and husband had been taken from her and instead, chose to fill the space left vacant by the men at Naomi's side. This was undoubtedly, the most visible way of affirming her love and commitment. They intuitively recognised that their power of destiny was combined with each other and so began a long walk of faith beside each other, in their own shoes, as well as each other's since, there is always the assurance of victory in every number greater than one.

For Ruth and Naomi, there was never a question of what might be given or what had already been taken but was simply a story of love so pure and uncompromised. The two women, clearly empty and bereft emotionally, set off on a journey into an unknown future. As it turned out, the story of Ruth was one of the most uplifting and rousing piece of writing in the Bible. Ruth chose to define her own destiny by making an informed decision regarding the path her life should take. She was not prepared to have her destiny defined by another, not even the woman she most loved. This aspect in particular, is the basis of my deep love and admiration for her. In view of the enormity of the unfolding circumstances before her, she allowed the process of change to take its course without altering the things she most valued. In this depiction, we are better able to appreciate how the character of an individual is shaped through suffering.

I simply do not believe greatness is only affiliated with personal achievements since; there are a number of other factors pivotal in overcoming each challenge against us. Furthermore, so many would have opted to retreat and seek resolutions through a number of less testing means but for Ruth, the imperative was to complete the journey she had begun. Her courage was unquestionable. She was not only shaping a trail behind her but establishing a lasting highway ahead. In the true spirit of human desires to overcome tragedies and misfortune, to redefine purpose and destiny, to conquer, to dominate or to possess, we must be acutely aware of who or what underpins the essence of our tenacity which is central to our victories. Whether we seek to ascend mountains or simply, to stand and gaze fearlessly into the future, each challenge moves us a step closer to victory, from the moment we relinquish our anxieties and fears. Whether at the top of our world or the centre of the human psyche, we are able to defeat everything set against us by our enduring belief in the continuance of our limited faith, made inexhaustible by the God in whom we trust.

In our constant pursuit for human perfection, I don't believe we will ever tire of matching our skills, our pursuits for conquest and determination to push the boundaries farther and farther. What we then have is, a number of people who learn to appreciate their struggles, by facing every situation boldly and seeking resolutely, a way through or around every obstacle which is faced. When the destination begins to appear within reach, each person instinctively becomes a master and not a slave to past doubts. Naturally, the right attitude of purpose through accomplishment must be a presiding factor since; a number who were almost within reach of victory failed because of losing sight of what brought them to the boundaries of triumph. For those however, who affirmed their victory with a crucifix, faith, hopes or expectations, they realise at long last that they are in fact, intrepid conquerors but were simply waiting the moment to reaffirm their values, as they triumph in humility, at the top of their conquered 'mountain.'

"No place like home."   Newcombe Valley

Chapter Two

Mind over Mountain

When Sir Edmund Hillary conquered Mount Everest with Tenzin Norgay in 1953, it was reported that he had taken with him a symbolic token to highlight his achievement and that little but significant token has remained buried at the top of the mountain in a secret place; a small crucifix. (John Dickson–Humilitas: Lost Key to Life, Love and Leadership). At this point, I need to reflect on the aforesaid journey of conquest and examine briefly what exactly propelled Hillary, one of the most celebrated explorers of our time, beyond the borders of fear and embedded him, definitively within the pages of modern history. For although Sir Edmund Hillary's position of faith was never made explicit, he appeared compelled to take that cross to the top of Mount Everest with him; and I cannot help wondering whether he saw the cross as a symbol of triumph or indeed in its original historical context, [Graeco Roman world], or as one of defeat and humiliation? For if it was defeat and humiliation, this story would never had made it into the pages of history and so, if we are to believe that this action went beyond a symbolic one and that there was a need on his part to assert his triumph; publicly for the lasting gaze of the masses and privately, between him and a significant being.

If men and women from age to age are to continue to surpass difficulties and overcome conflicts, to ascend the peaks of mountains and to make highways in the valleys, to build enormous ships and sail through stormy seas, then there must be something profound in the idea of destiny being linked to personal achievements; since many begin to believe in the unbelievable and others start reaching for the unreachable. Human nature is at its most invincible when in pursuit of own glory and excellence and this quest become so compelling that it will persist until every mountain has been fiercely challenged and fully conquered.

I remember a number of years ago watching a presentation by one of the world's leading naturalist presenters - David Attenborough. In this production, the documentary showed a solitary Black Panther who had stumbled into the territory of a dozen or so aggressive baboons. The baboons were naturally defensive and puffed their chests high and with every ounce of brute strength tried to deter the Black Panther from passing by their terrain. The Black Panther naturally advanced against the threatening mob and was not in the least intimidated. The most astonishing development was not so much what happened next, we already know that, the Black Panther shamed the unruly pack due to his lack of fear and passed by unperturbed; it was the presenter's words that that held my attention; "It's not the size of the animal, it's the spirit of the beast." This show of strength when one is facing a mighty adversary is not to be underestimated, for there is a deep empowering that begins in the awareness of people and animals which allows each to step beyond safe boundaries into vastly unknown ones.

The story of David and Goliath in the Bible is a typical example of faith over size - David did not go against Goliath empowered with a mere sling and stone. "David said to the Philistine, "You come against me with sword and spear and javelin, but I come against you in the name of the Lord Almighty, the God of the armies of Israel, whom you have defied. This day the Lord will deliver you into my hands, and I will strike you down and cut off your head. This very day I will give the carcasses of the Philistine army to the birds and wild animals, and the whole world will know that there is a God in Israel. All those gathered here will know that it is not by sword or spear that the Lord saves; for the battle is the Lord's, and he will give all of you into our hands." 1 Samuel 17:45. This young shepherd boy's faith empowered him into the path of both adversary and destiny. It's a reality that; "Faith can move mountains," David removed the colossus before him which, paved the way towards his inescapable destiny to become king of Israel.

Faith, according to Voltaire (1694-1178), "Consists in believing when it is beyond the power of reason to believe." It is not enough that a thing be possible for it to be believed." The unbelievable daring of one whose faith propels them from known orientations to vastly unknown spheres, allowing seemingly ordinary men, [in David's case, an unremarkable shepherd boy] and women to perform extraordinary and unbelievable adventures. David surrendered his vulnerabilities unto God and in so doing, bypassed all his uncertainties. Although David's stature was incomparable with the giant standing against him, he focussed completely on the power of God above, ultimately, dwarfing and defeating the man Goliath standing before him. This is faith at its most audacious where a person is confident of victory before they have embarked on the task ahead. This is the irrefutable assurance of victory in any number greater than one. There are some individuals who refuse to yield to God and in particular those who possess analytical minds - for them, faith remain impossible.

Those advocates of science, who develop theories in advance, are impotent when faced with the intangibility of faith; scientists, theoreticians, physicist and all those who believe in the rationale behind everything cannot work in the blinding darkness of faith. After all, faith is about what the eyes cannot perceive [science much too tangible and objective], the subjectivity of faith is much too imperceptible, yet propels the observer to look beyond the meagre spectre of known equivalences. Science works within remits of perceptibility, substance and uniformities, where with faith, there are no constraints, except the doubts and fears, which one may hold in tension. It is unquantifiable and without boundaries and operating outside of the empirical spheres of human beings. Whatever it is that thrusts humans beyond the points of fear and endurance remains one of the greatest mysteries.

However much the lenses have changed over the centuries through which one observes particular patterns of behaviour, for some individuals who have seemingly surpassed the pre-set limits, there appears a common denominator; man against a giant and a mountain against a man. The fact that neither was concerned with the size of the task to be defeated before them but kept focussing upon what was underpinning their sense of identity. This identify seemed to have been confirmed when the enormity of the task was successfully accomplished; suggesting that each person has to know exactly who they are before they know precisely what they are capable of achieving.

Sir Edmund Hillary's conquest of Mount Everest may have happened over half a century ago, whilst David's story of rise to King of Israel was a few millenniums earlier, but the motif common to both men was their faith, naturally on very different levels. I am not for a moment suggesting that Hillary would not have made it to the top of Mount Everest without that little crucifix in his pocket; faith is not about a mere crucifix in one's pocket, it's an all-encompassing life choice which interlace into every avenue and path of a person's life, creating new highways and main roads leading in and out of every conflict encountered along the way. I for one hold a view which demonstrates the flexibility of faith; if I could not find a way to climb a particular mountain, I would simply go around it instead!

At the age of fifteen I was faced with such a devastating challenge that I simply wished for a mountain to fall on top of me and end my anguish. I remember two male officers from Greater Manchester Police who came to assist me with this very challenging issue. I simply did not have the words or the attitude of mind to direct them to help me in the right way; they terrified me almost as much as the experience had and to say they were lacking in compassion and care, was a serious understatement. I remember as I sat with the two officers I thought of something that was invaluable to my position and believed that this would assist the process in my favour. Those officers completely disregarded my pleas for help and had not gone to the place I had asked them to go which would have provided the proof that was lacking. Consequently, the case fell apart and I was left distressed and helpless. I feel that, due to the painful nature of this incident, it was better to omit the details since I would not be gaining any anything from outlining it in any greater detail. My decision to include it is merely to illustrate a salient point, which is merely to emphasise the need for patience when we seek resolutions in our lives. As the time progressed I felt that had I been from a middle-class family or was more eloquent, my story would have been more credible but I just felt they did not think I was worthy of their time or effort. Sometimes conceding defeat is like winning and we must recognise that just because a mountain is before us, it is not necessarily demanding that we begin to climb to the top. Sometimes it's enough that we are resourceful enough to find a way around it instead. I was able to find a way around, because twenty-six years later I watched the chief of Greater Manchester Police wept on my behalf for the abysmal way a young and vulnerable girl was treated. My father always used to say; "Day longa dan rope," [the day is longer than a rope], which simply means that, every wrong will eventually be made right; it just takes time and patience.

Naturally, this experience highlighted my need for patience and although it was often lacking in my youth, it has now become one of the bedrocks within my life. The mountains I simply failed to conquer on one occasion returned as valleys as I progressed through life and valleys are so much easier to negotiate. My view of the world has changed dramatically over the last twenty-five years but sadly, my feelings of my place within it remains unchanged; always on the fringes of every possibility, merely observing and waiting. With such apparent vicissitudes, it is hard for me to ascertain what symbols and motifs are valued, held or envisioned by those who must advance against armies, scale walls to freedom, or those who simply forage daily to find enough food and clean water to keep their families alive for another day. In the reality of people's suffering; what are the definitive strengths which enable each human being to reach the top of their particular mountain, however invincible it may appear? The idea of securing freedom reverberates in the world daily and although this assumed freedom for some may be bondage for others, the quest to apprehend liberty accelerates at many levels.

The past decade in particular has seen terror campaigns on a monumental scale around us; there have been conflicts and continuing wars, ravaging lives, homes, countries and nations. The news is dominated by the unbearable realities of refugees, victims of famine, genocide, earthquakes and many other natural disasters; one must ask the biggest question of all; where is God in humanity's suffering? My answer is not complex, nor is it far-reaching; it's as simple as outlined in every page of the Bible. God is where he has always been; close by observing and awaiting the invitation by those who wish him to participate in their lives and to do what he is best at doing; change, transformation and victory. The cross, a symbol of victory or defeat; victory for those whose faith and trust in God is unwavering and defeat for those whose faith stays buried at the top of 'that' mountain they hope they will never have to climb.

Some years ago I heard a story about a very young boy in a rural Welsh community who had wandered from his home and was found by the police miles away. The child was unable to recognise any signs which delayed the process of reuniting him with his parents and in desperation to the point of giving up, the police officers decided to return to the station and used their typical protocol. As they began the drive back with the boy in the car he suddenly recognised where he was and shouted; "Please take me to the cross, from there I can find my way home." This was a large crossroad which was known locally as the 'cross'. And sure enough, they took him there and he assessed the direction and in no time was reunited with his anxious parents. There are many things that inform our sense of identity in the world and when they are given the priority they deserve within our lives, there is less chance of uncertainties regarding destination and purpose. The idea of a cross that holds so many within its power has not diminished with time and the brutality and disputes which it symbolised in its original context still demands attention and continue to command respect from a number of faithful sources.

To understand the dispute of the cross in our modern world many centuries removed from the time of Christ, we will explore retrospectively the Graeco Roman world, where in historical terms; the antiquity of the cross was in fact a sign of both degradation and brutality. These symbols however, underwent a major transformation with the dying and resurrection of the Lord Jesus, whose presence and anguish upon the cross, could only but transform it from defeat and humiliation, to genius and absolute greatness.

In Latin, "humility" is known (*humilitas*; tapeinos in Greek), was not a virtue in Greaco Roman ethics. The word meaning to "crushed" or "debased", and associated with failure and shame. (John Dickson). So, not surprising that a motif of shame and disgrace, has now become a theme, encompassing a joyous redemptive action executed in God's righteousness and has become an enduring testimony for all times, yet there are of course those who do not see Christ as triumphant on the cross. Having died the death of a criminal, his divinity became questionable, for the immortal God, simply cannot die, thus, disillusioned the promised hopes of Israel and initially, creating many ambiguous questions and few transparent answers. At the time of Christ's crucifixion, I don't believe there were scores of sympathisers asking him to stand in his place, in his shoes or inserting themselves in the space visibly empty at his side which was previously filled by his faithful, but timorous disciples. While this is true in every case from New Testament narrative, it must be conveyed that Simon, the man from Cyrene, Matthew 27:31-22; was forced by the guards to help Jesus carry the cross; a reminder of the assurance of victory in any number greater than one.

For as long as I can remember, I have witnessed a number of people who take great delight in the suffering of others, even to the extent of contributing to that suffering. Many individuals are living wholly pretentious lives under clouds of misconceptions regarding their treatment of others. So many believe they will glide elegantly and painlessly into an appointed mansion in heaven and continue with every aspect of their earthly lifestyles but only this time, forfeiting all the mansion tax! People seem to arrive at different junctions in their lives and for some whose suffering apprehend them when least expected, I generally have an image of many such souls demanding the one answer that money simply cannot purchase; "Why me?" Suffering is universal but a price was paid by one, for all human beings. It simply could never have been a transaction undertaken through money or precious stones, since they are deemed unworthy but this suffering in all people was purchased by the blood of a righteous Lord. I believe every human being possess the answers to everything that shapes and confirm their lives but many choose to ignore them since, the moment something is acknowledged, it demands a rigorous amendment from that individual. Sadly, there are a number of people who, instead of tackling unhealthy issues within their own lives, proceed along a malevolent path in order to dismantle the lives of others.

I believe human nature is both constructive and destructive which makes it impossible for any person to live an average lifetime without offending a single soul. There are some people however, who appear to spend much of their life in the 'offending business,' not those individuals who are repeat criminals, traversing back and forth through the legal system but those incapable of a deep self-exploration to eradicate their own narrow fields of view and so, enhance their interference skills when assessing the lives of others. My father always used to say; "Duppy know who fi fright'n," meaning, people will take advantage of those most susceptible in society," once again highlighting the most inexcusable sides of human nature. The life choices made by a number of people, will invariably take many of them into the wrong paths which can be unscrupulous, amoral and dark. Although a majority are retrievable, they can nevertheless, leave deeply entrenched scars to all who are gripped in such immoral highways. "It is better to limp along the right path than to walk strongly in the wrong direction." (Thomas Aquinas). Of course, I echo the sentiment of Aquinas since; I would sooner be along an unpopular path alone, than with a noisy heard with no idea where I was headed but was simply going along to remain part of an exclusive fraternity. The problem rests heavily upon the nub of values and beliefs. If a person has no idea of right and wrong, they will not be aware when they are overtaken by indecorous values and fraudulent principles. It is so easy to fall, so easy to practice untruths and to ignore the underlying ethics wherein one's life has been shaped. I am so aware how seamless the transition is from a noble path to an unsavoury one and how easy it is to learn crudities in preference to sound principles.

The protracted nature of suffering and its impact upon the lives of individuals, is evident on many levels, for the dreaded highways leading to such wretchedness are neither signposted to get on nor to exit. I have spent many years seeking ways through, around or off these multi-lanes of despair and had to keep reminding myself that, the greatest lessons in life are to be learned in the places that has caused me the most anguish. Whenever I was encouraged to climb those foreboding mountains and scale walls to freedom, it was often in the very action that I was empowered and better equipped to determine my own conclusions. There are however, those who are swift to judge, to condemn, vilify, ostracised and to apportion blame since, they are mere observers of various situations from the margins of the lives of others, they simply cannot understanding the lengths to which a number of individuals will go in order to remove themselves beyond unhelpful criticisms. Nevertheless, it is a common human trait to hurt others and then pass the blame onto them. Since, it's easier to condemn another person, while absolving one's self of guilt and blame, all at the same.

I have never understood this reverse psychology; for if someone steals money from another person and goes to court to prove or disprove his or her innocence, if the case was conclusive by a unanimous guilty verdict, the judge would simply not release the offender because he defended his position convincingly and go as far as suggesting that the victim was the one responsible for his action. Since, they did not secrete the money away and temptation got the better of him. Yet, on the same principle, many people hurt others and justify their actions everyday by blaming the victim. This is especially true in rape cases where the rapist will often try and pass blame to the victim; suggesting she dressed too provocatively, or she spurred him on. What does a statement like this really mean? Our societies are a convoluted mess where almost every view has become distorted and tarnished that the boundaries of right and wrong are now precariously hinged upon fabrics of both truth and lies. So much so in fact, that both has merged into one and has become indistinguishable.

It would appear that matters of principles seldom triumph over money and power. In the end everything is based upon who has the finest barrister, the most money and the most collaborative witness statements. For such people, freedom takes priority over integrity and all other values from where justice, truth and morality are drawn, become out-dated and irrelevant. This is the world in which we live, we can simply choose to love it or hate it but we simply cannot ignore it. Although I find myself despondent at times, I remain confident that a life of integrity is more than possible, perhaps not for all but definitely for an open-minded majority.

A Life of Integrity

How many times have you found yourself asking a person to undertake a task on your behalf that you would never do for them? For example, a foremost politician asking his wife to accept a speeding fine, completely against her better judgement and admits guilt and blame to the police, when in fact he was the culprit. The honesty that many individuals seek from others is often desperately diminished within themselves. I am particular fond of dismantling the schemes of others since, anyone who blatantly ask another to commit a gross offence on their behalf, is also capable of committing a transgression against that person and also a number of others. One question that I have found particularly helpful in recent years is simply asking; "Perhaps someone else may forgive me but can I forgive myself?" With that thought pivotal in mind at the inception of every potential wrong-doing, it makes it that much harder to contemplate immoral thoughts, resulting in erroneous actions and not only do I have a burning conscience, I include Christ at the centre of all my actions and thinking. Of course, no one is a saint, all are woefully inadequate when it comes to matters of principles but my best strategy is to limit the frequency of which I need to seek the forgiveness of another and so, have made it my on-going aim to only ask of others, what I would willingly do for them.

I remember the men and women for whom I cared during my thirteen years in charge at Woodend residential care home in Disley and in every sense cared for them as I would like to receive in return. I remember attending so many funerals that I simply lost count. There was one old lady in particular who was really hostile and would look for the weaknesses in every carer and attacked without mercy. Naturally, with me it was my brown face and she was relentless day after day. I continued to deliver the highest standard of care to her and all the residents whom I loved dearly and I was by no means discouraged by her vile abuse. I remember standing in the crematorium chapel on the day of her funeral; just the vicar, the undertakers and myself in attendance. She had no next of kin and in the silence of that moment, I knew my brown face mattered to her, but finally for the right reasons. There was never a question of doubt for me regarding attending her funeral after all, I am human and have been equally guilty of many transgressions but I simply did not wish to add one more to the list by disregarding a human life who simply had no valuable reference points from where to base her judgements of others, I did and so, acted accordingly.

Of course a number of individuals, like the aforementioned elderly lady are unable to move through a process of change and conversion and sadly a number would sooner die than to attempt to believe in the unbelievable. Admittedly, this covers a wide range of individuals in every society but for some reason, I have been particularly drawn to those with scientific backgrounds. Logically, I must reiterate once more my leaning towards those individuals with scientific backgrounds since; they are the very ones with whom Christ was so concerned during his ministry. He knew exactly how difficult it would be for them to make the transition from incredulity in the intangible to conviction in the unbelievable. Who knows, perhaps there are a number of scientist willing to disarm their pride and become humble and open to potentials beyond their seeing, hearing, tasting, and touching. For me, science emphasises calculable values at its core, where Christ encompass incalculable magnitudes at its foundation, to which no one can make convincing judgements, save the ones to whom such knowledge has been revealed. I do not believe everything in the universe is worth seeing, tasting, hearing or touching. The difference for me is that my life is centred on Christ – but of course this life brings none of those outstanding personal achievements. In science however, every scientist is a potential prize winner? It's a fact that people award prizes to each other because God is not interested in knighthoods and prestigious awards but cares deeply and passionately for the hearts of those who love and worship him, those to whom he has revealed himself.

The most remarkable members within society are often overlooked in preference for those who can generate interminable amounts of wealth for their sponsors. A surgeon is a typical example of one such person whose aim and purpose is to save every life which is before him and who, although generously rewarded in financial terms, is not always seen as a height of absolute aspiration, compared to footballers, soldiers, musicians and actors. A soldier for example, is routinely awarded with honours and medals for bravery when they execute orders in which they are highly specialised and trained; they kill men, women and children to win the affection and esteem of their fellow countrymen, yet surgeons whose skills are the highest of all men but whose dedication and excellence is taken for granted in many ways.

While the position of a surgeon is less dangerous; since he functions in a safe and clean environment with every disposable convenience at hand; the soldier on the other hand, is in hostile territory and must safe-guard his own back and that of his comrades.

The uncertainties of the world in which we now live multiply daily and the culture of individualism and greed is a by-product of post modernity. The decisions made by many people whose aspirations are to become soldiers, surgeons, teachers or pop stars, will not be made in obscurity but will be informed by what they seen in the media every day or whatever they value in terms of culture and religious orientations. Many such uncertainties are coupled with the sheer weight of expectations that we shoulder from birth to death; all of which are familiar with Christ our Lord, who for a brief moment came amongst us. If we become so enthralled in our own glory and achievements, then there is simply no room left to celebrate any other since; the egotistical human nature refuses to give acknowledgement to anything other than self. This self; a brute at times, will stand for a majority of life but the inevitable fall is only whispers away. Since God in his wisdom recognises the vulnerability of all people and allows all to fall to see whether in humility we will reach for him; for it is only those who reach out with hands of faith to God, will rise once more and continue to stand. In our refusing to stand for the beliefs and values which underpin our lives, voices remain suppressed by fear or weakness and remain largely unheard, yet those who propagate violence and intolerance, continue to drown all other sounds. Invariably, the world has become increasingly secular and intolerant of differences. Many Christians continue to face persecution for their beliefs – often in 'Christian' countries. Those leaders who continue to amend the law in order that everyone may be accommodated within the remits of 'inclusivity,' are by no means unaware of the actions they instigate in regards to the commands of God and although many fail to admit to errors of judgement, it is the fastest way possible to take a 'great' nation to its knees; since it is only when enormous challenges begin to overtake an entire nation, that God is sought and reinstated at the centre of their overwhelming struggles.

There is an enormous vacuum of 'good' role models who inspire lives to real change. A majority of young people today seem to be aspiring for careers which are excessive in every sense; wealth and lifestyle choices being the most sought after elements. Who realistically believes that they can be given 'everything' for doing virtually nothing?

When a gardener plants his flowers from seed he or she has to lovingly care for them for a specific period and even as they grow the routine becomes more demanding. After they have flowered at their best and dying at their worst, they still require work. This is the same for the farmer with his crops; from seed, then harvest, to the market and finally to the table, this is complete dedication and hard work. Yet many young lives wish to be propelled into the maelstrom of fame and opulence, without giving a thought to what is to be gained over what will potentially be lost.

Everything today appears to be fuelled by selfish ambitions and there are many people who simply never give a thought or consideration regarding the lives they could potentially crush in pursuit for own glory. Some are like juggernauts racing at speed, oblivious to everything in their pathway as they apprehend the first step on the ladder to climb above the lower echelons of society. Their blinding determination will ensure their success, but it's debatable whether their lack of humility, integrity and compassion will concede their defeat at a future date. This lack of humility, integrity and compassion is evident on every level and it is difficult to contrast the nature of Christ against the debilitating human nature that is sadly at its most enterprising when consuming everything which appears to threaten its existence. Society consists of two types of people: those who forgive freely and those who are unable to forgive anything. In the Book of Revelations God called them; the 'sheep' and the 'goats.' Forgiveness lengthens the days of men and women on earth and allows each person, through its power to forgive others. In Christ's death and resurrection all have been duly pardoned and given the freedom they yearned but did not deserve.

God demands that humans go further than ever before, beyond their own meagre conditioning and forgive one another just as he has forgiven us; many who are actively forgiving everyone of everything, should empower them with the meaning of real forgiveness. There are many people who have been forgiven of some things, others of everything but were never told by those who forgave them and consequently continued in the misery of the reverberation and impact of another's hurt and suffering. In just the same way, many people remain oblivious to the fact that God in Christ has forgiven them of everything and so, remain in bondage. There are so many who walk alongside us in the world who have no idea they have been absolved which, may indicate the reason why so few have the anticipated outcomes towards the end of their lives. With real forgiveness comes a new type of freedom previously denied and from where a person is able to navigate their own pathways rigorously, assured that the 'demons' that held them rigid is no longer able to keep them. The human spirit is free to a large extent, it possess the power to choose from a variety of options and in essence, there is a sense of unity; in suffering, in conflict, in rejection and in humiliations which are inescapable to many.

Some time ago in a nearby neighbourhood, an intolerant minority group decided to march in support of what seemed to be an unprovoked attack on two young men late one evening. The most interesting observations to be made by those living and doing business in the town was the impact the march had made on their normal days business and although they would have preferred if it had not gone ahead, those in charge chose to ignore their wishes and carried on regardless in a time of severe economic unrest. Interestingly enough, the parents of the boys in the attack, completely distanced themselves from the march and refused to play any part in it. This is redolent of mob mentality and served only to disrupt the lives of the very people they were supposed to be supporting. I particularly like to assess mob mentality, for in such gatherings there is a great deal to be determined from attitudes and behaviour. Are all those people standing together, standing in unity or are they just simply standing? The idea of Strength in groups is based on shared or comparable values, yet, there can be a number of underlying conflicts which become the catalyst, leading to the dismantling of all such alliances.

To contrast this thought, I would like to examine briefly the night Jesus was arrested; he was surrounded by his disciples who, up to this point believed themselves to be completely faithful and loyal to Christ. It must have been a dreadful blow for them when Jesus told them; "This very night you will all fall away on account of me, for it is written: "I will strike the shepherd and the sheep of the flock will be scattered." Matthew 26:31. Of course Peter denied all knowledge of him when questioned some time later by the authorities and his betrayal by Judas was both timely and seamless. As the situation worsened one of Jesus' companions drew his sword in his defence but Jesus said to him; "Put your sword back in its place, for all who draw the sword will die by the sword." Matthew 26:52. It is often in situations such as this, where a number of people are able to identify what is most valuable to them. The disciples exemplified goodness but not perfection, so when their mountains became too precarious, they simply retreated. Even with strong principles and integrity, they could not bear to suffer with him;

thus abandoning him to be humiliated and to suffer without their support. And similarly, those who stood by in the crowd as the Lord Jesus was mocked and degraded as he hung upon the cross to die the death of a criminal. Many simply believed that justice was accomplished. Sadly, all those who stood by, cheering and watching as Christ languished were in fact, the same ones whose freedom was granted by the act of his dying; in essence, his perceived hopelessness was to become the freedom and hope for all.

Arguably, the intelligent and compassionate approach by this group of intolerant individuals would have been to listen to the voices they were supporting but admittedly, it appeared the imperative for them was to have their own voices heard and views expressed, at whatever cost. In Romans 12:21, I am reminded; "Do not be overcome by evil but overcome evil with good" and in the same way, I must try and understand the mind-set of those who prefer to be retributive, than forgiving. Naturally, a majority of human endeavours are principally for own gain and the idea of unity in strength, can be a leaning to a 'pack mentality' which is contrary to strength. This relates to lack of courage and according to Confucius; "To see what is right and not to do it is a want of courage." It is far more beneficial to forgive through the most profitable means of dialogue and consideration, rather than marching in aggression. The transference of anger and guilt has been a cunning plan of mankind down the ages, since from the moment we place what we hate towards another object or subject, we relinquish all our association with it and become 'free' to absolve ourselves from any blame. In the instance of Christ, a good and holy being, crucified in premeditated ignorance and even as he was tormented to his last breath in the hope of an ultimate and divine, God inspired revelation, "Wake up people, do you want God to open the heavens a second time and come down at will to satisfy your unbelieving and callous hearts? 'The divine revelation you are seeking in your blindness, is hanging right there in front of you, open your hearts and close your eyes in order that you may gain just a glimpse of the king of heaven and earth amongst you." It was Saint Augustine (354-430), who said; "Seek not to understand that you may believe, but believe that you may understand."

The number of times I have gazed daringly into the narrow conduit between heaven and hell but without faith and belief did not recognise where I was standing. The days I feared would merged into the ugliest nights and in meagre faith holding fast to the certainty of another new morning breaking but without convincing faith, my hopes perished in the stagnant darkness. The times I was convinced I had met with an angel in the most inhospitable and remote of places but did not have the courage to trust my heart, for without real trust and faith, I could not find a way through. And the number of times I encountered a demon but hoped that they would be converted into a saint before my eyes. Saints are transformed sinners on the road to victory, those who have acknowledged their errors and are being enabled by the mighty hand that has transformed and healed them inside out. This same hand is patient, it is kind and it approaches with openness, it is never overwhelmed by the unexpected; since all things remains under his control. He is the one in whom confidence and trust is inspired and in turn inspires the same in others. He is the only one who stands underneath every hazardous precipice waiting to catch everyone who unintentionally falls.

I Promise to Catch 'You'

I recently underwent a medical procedure where I had to be anaesthetised for the fifty minute process. I was met beforehand by my consultant and was given a full appraisal of the procedure, in far too much detail but was really grateful that he had taken the time to explain everything so thoroughly. I seldom feel afraid of anything but this occasion was the exception, for my typical lack of anxiety to many major concerns is definitely one of my faults. Fear in general can be a healthy emotion, setting limits and boundaries for our protection as we navigate through life. I started to feel a little concern as he was leaving my room, realising that I would not see him again until I was escorted down to the theatre for the operation. As he was leaving he saw the apprehension on my face and he patted my shoulder and said "Don't look so worried, you will be fine." A few hours later I was taken down to theatre and was escorted to a preparation ante-room where, I was met by a lively team of nurses and an incredibly upbeat anaesthetist but I could not see my consultant. Nevertheless, I did not wish to sound too familiar by asking where he was.

I was asked to lie down and just as I was about to be given the anaesthetic to induce sleep, my consultant came in from the theatre. There was a great sense of peace and relief within me as he walked over and said a few affirmative words and shared a joke with everyone. I was anxious for one particular reason which was simply that, I needed to be certain he was the one doing the procedure since, he was the one in whom I had placed my trust for that moment. This placing of trust in another human being has been one of the biggest burdens of my life and there have been times where I would sooner perish than to allow anyone to care or administer help to me. There have been so many seemingly outstanding and well-meaning individuals who impelled me to believe they could in fact, make every dark place light and I was further convinced they could consolidate the oceans into a single measured drop.

This occurred over and over again for there was a deep longing in me to see a human being from any class or race being the 'good' he or she was created to be, sadly each time I awoke from my 'day-dreaming' and realised I was once more in the middle of another remarkable nightmare. I have met so many brutal and manipulative individuals in my life that it takes me a long time to figure out the 'angels' from the 'demons.' I am now however, acutely aware of the subtle differences between the talkers and the doers, the angels and the demons; the angels [the doers] promote my well-being and they always prioritise my dignity and most importantly, they always return to see how I am progressing and healing. They are never afraid of my peculiarities, for they also require the same things I need; love, encouragement, honesty and respect. The demons [the talkers], propagate their own agenda, remain distant and unmoved and are terrified their true identity will be uncovered. I remember holding my oxygen mask as I began falling asleep and desperate not to capitulate to the strangers around me, until my consultant said convincingly; "Don't worry, I promise I will catch it." There are journeys where we are accompanied for a long way, others we may be joined for only part of the way, this one was both to some extent and I realised that mutuality of trust and faith are essential merits I hold passionately; for without trust, nothing can be built to stand and without faith, there are no claims of that which is unseen.

If I am to understand what the Bible teaches, I see that according to Hebrews 11:1, I know, [Faith in Action] "Now faith is confidence in what we hope for and assurance about what we do not see." This is a real promise of those things unseen but with a palpable allusion of what is still to come. In strident contrast to the things of humans and the things of God, there is no doubt; the things of God far outperform the seemingly good and virtuous acts and intentions of mankind. God's enviable position is that, wherever we his children go, he can accompany us for the entire duration and even better than this, he has gone to some dreadful and frightening places so that we never have to traverse those dark seats of despair, alone and in anguish. The reality of God is his divinity and his humility, making it unimaginable that he would readily allow a person who deserved severe hardship and difficulties to go into places where only shame, fear and humiliation will result. A frightening thought it may be but it is never the intention of God to freely punish those whose trust impinges upon his unfailing love. If love is about sacrifice and he made a holy atoning gift of God [himself], back to God for the healing of humanity's sins then, the precipice beneath us was no longer permitted to engulf us. The potential to fall and hurt had to remain to highlight the dangers to those who are blind to the fact that, in order for God to save them, they had to permit him to convict, then restore them and finally set them free.

This is a remarkable God who is beyond the understanding of scholars, teachers, preachers and many believers. God is the one whose love and presence is both indispensable and invisible; he stays with us not just for a while but remains throughout our pain, anxieties, in our sleeping and waking moments. He is also with us in our addictions by empowering us to rise through them and becoming the source of great testimonies of triumph and healing. God remains trustworthy and faithful in all things from birth through to the end of our lives.

I remember waking up in the recovery bay about an hour later and was in excruciating pain, I felt invaded, fragile, pathetic and vulnerable. It was the very first time in my life that I recognised and acknowledged this feeling of vulnerability, this created awkwardness and annoyance for me. I consoled myself of the fact that there will be times such as this, when I will encounter feelings of helplessness but I must be prepared to set aside all my affectations and immediately replace them with humility and unreservedly accept any help and support which is offered with grace and dignity. I was more than willing to show a temperate and courteous disposition since, no one could exchange places with me as this was my journey to complete the healing I needed. First, there had to be anxiety and pain, before any restoration could commence.

Although my sense of the universe may be somewhat rudimentary, I am nevertheless guided along by my deeply held views and concepts around Christ, human beings and their roles within the scope of the wider world. My cultural values which embrace at its heart the idea of strong family bonds are one of these immeasurable concepts through the years which have become my greatest expediters in the understanding of suffering; since if one suffers, we all suffer. This idea of suffering is always best illustrated when contrasted to the suffering of the Lord Jesus, who being an equal part of the Trinity, would suffer both in his humanity and his divinity.

It is conceivable that God in Christ would suffer as much as God 'apart' from Christ, yet present in and throughout his suffering. I understand the Journey of Christ in part, his exit from heaven and entry into the sinful and barren human wilderness of lack of genuine emotions, forgiveness, humility and compassion. His fateful journey from Bethlehem as a baby to Calvary, [born simply to be sacrificed], in my place and what I see is not someone standing there offering to 'catch' something belonging to me but one mightily pulling me, all of me back from the very brink of eternal death and decay. Just as my consultant had said earlier before my walk down to the theatre; "Don't look so worried, you will be fine," I hear rhetorical echoes of my Lord saying in John 14:1; "Let not your hearts be troubled, you believe in God, believe also in me." The major difference to these very contrasting stories is that my consultant was paid in full for the service he provided to me; Christ on the other hand, underwent the procedure for me and absolved all fees, which he himself had paid in full, both in retrospect and for all future indemnities.

There are simply no ambiguities concerning love, gratitude, or loyalty, for even though I have never met with Christ face to face, I love him beyond the rationality of my heart and perplexing as it may seem, my love for him grows day by day and it is unwavering and remains undiminished. Did I love my consultant? Christ entreats us in Matthew 22:39, to; "Love our neighbour as ourselves," for he, [Christ] loves us with an everlasting love and when we display a high regard for others and wish nothing in return, they will know we belong to him.

Although my consultant was an impeccable professional with a kind and personable disposition, I know that as soon as the job with me was done our journey was complete; the road reached its natural conclusion but not so with Jesus. The journey which started way before I was born, just gets better and better and it continues along a never ending pattern, running straight through to something the Bible calls 'eternity' and as David stated in Psalm 139:15-16; "My frame was not hidden from you when I was made in the secret place, when I was woven together in the depths of the earth. Your eyes saw my unformed body; all the days ordained for me was written in your book before one of them came to be." Imagine a God who knew me even before I was; imagine a God who allotted my days with thought and precision, imagine a God who knew every pain and struggle that I would encounter; but imagine him there in the midst of it all with me?

I arrived in the world through my family from where I learned to love, to be principled, strong and confident. This was the basis for a life which would interleave into the lives of others from every orientation and background in society. It is my desire to continue meeting a variety of people and it is my hope that at least a handful will be impacted positively by my association with them, however brief or indefinite our encounter. I would simply see no further point to my life if I could not find meaningful ways to insert myself amongst a variety of people. If my life is a gift, then this gift should be redeployed wherever permissible.

In my culture, whenever we were given a gift, we were taught to share it equally amongst every person within the family and so, I believe that since, it is God who has given me the gift of life, then I should spend the majority of it in thanks and celebration to him and the remainder in devotion and service to others. I neither wish to solve this mystery, nor understand why God would want to receive such a friable soul like me, who; invariably, through fear or a lack of faith may one day resist the opportunity to stand up against an angry mob on his behalf?

It is unbearable to image that so many stood by as the Lord Jesus had his life brutally crushed at Calvary but in the spirit of true humility in his dying moments, his divinity shone through by granting pardon to one of the thieves on the cross beside him. I wonder just how many of us have felt that one of those thieves was 'me' but which of those thieves were you or I? Christ is a God who 'catches' us when we fail and also when we fall and particularly when we breech the boundaries of trust with him and with others. The cross is symbolic of many different things but one which should be distinct is that it symbolises the end of one way and the beginning of something new. This newness is only to be achieved however, with unquestioning faith, unconditional love and perseverance through each bitter sacrifice. There were so many who touched the place where God in Christ had stood, so many who refused the offer he pledged to rescue and catch them from their lives of sin, for in 'catching' someone, that person must disarm and surrender all their fears and establish a level of trust with another that can be incredibly terrifying.

The unbelievable revelation that God, through Christ, stood for a brief moment amongst us, willing us to relinquish all our anxieties and to trust what his love is capable of doing in our lives. There are many today including me, who wish we could briefly turn back time and insert ourselves in the space left vacant at the Lord's side - to be face to face with humility, with love, power, grace, and mercy. It is a fact that, no one will come as close to God again until the defining eschatology. Sadly, there were only a pitiful few who stood alongside him, who found the courage to choose right over wrong and truth over lies. This action on their part steered their lives away from the edges of sin in the gracious acceptance of the new life God had given them through Jesus his Son; a complete epitome of the New Testament elucidations from beginning to end.

From New Testament interpretations, I understand the earth will be transformed from its present unsustainable position, to a redeemed and viable proposition. This transformation, similar to the conversion granted to believers in the death and resurrection of Christ, promises a newness and splendour, the likes never witnessed formerly. This is not conjecture but is fully supported in the Book of Revelations, where the signs alluding to such manifestations are both comprehensive and forthcoming. Not surprising since, the transparent bias towards a select few simply cannot be sustained indefinitely. There has been a manipulative and precise engineering over the centuries which have enhanced the success and safety for the most privileged in society and the failure and insecurity for the vast majority. Needless to say, people will continue to strive for excellence, regardless of the ultimate fate of the planet and just as in centuries past, the pursuit for excellence will not diminish. A vast array of knowledge has been granted to a select few but one has to ask that nagging question; "Will there be any imminent revelations and new discoveries to further advance our civilisation or has humankind simply exhausted all of their innate potential for good?

The course of human history has witnessed some of the most remarkable events and explorations and while many have been attributed to individuals, some have been attributed to groups, companies and fraternities. It is only at the point where the human spirit becomes confident to relinquish its constricted hold on everything, which is perceived as being in opposition that human beings will be able to excel into new discoveries as they widen their narrow fields of acceptance. This action will make way for those previously excluded on the outside, those deemed to fail, since; society is engineered for their failure and not their success. Yet, I am irrefutably reminded that, the assurance of victory is only guaranteed through the inclusion of all and not just a few, designated ones.

I make a number of my observations in relation to what I value and what my priorities are at the time such perceptions arise. My culture however, has a large bearing on all such acuities. Since, it is from within my defined cultural boundaries where a majority of my greatest lessons have been learnt, especially those lessons concerning the way people are motivated to function within society. Of course I believe that if a person is qualified to teach, then so be it, let them teach but this is by no means suggesting they are inadequate at every other discipline. Admittedly, some of the wisest people I have ever met have never been inside a school and some of the most uninspiring and dismal have been submerged in the most prestigious seats of learning and yet, they could not outperform such neophytes on the mysteries of life and the universe. It is only when those who walk on the 'outside' of life, [the fringes], are invited on the 'inside' and be part of the revolution of science, technology, engineering, physics, media and every field of potential excellence that new discoveries will be made.

I find that I can get particularly somnolent whenever I keep traversing the same ground over and over again and it is for this reason a number of exhaustive methodologies must be adopted to enhance results in a number of specialist fields of knowledge. Although the world is complex at one level, it is a most simplistic planet at another. It consists of every type of life form with humans at the centre of the pathway to knowledge. I refuse to accept there is only one authoritative pathway to discovery and enlightenment for mankind and yet, the centuries have seen only a small majority leading while all others have followed submissively and accept the denunciation of their ability to contribute towards the furtherance of understanding for all. Needless to say, if I need a dentist, I can find a hundred in a square mile and the same for any other expert or clinician I may need to consult routinely.

While I would prefer to have a wider scope to reflect the diversity of the planet, I know it's a reality a long time in the making. I am however grateful, that while everyone is busy being qualified to the extent of having so many pieces of paper to write letter after letter, I gain confidence that whenever I need someone to insert themself beside me, just to be with me, I simply kneel in contrition. In the same way, there are a number of individuals who willingly insert themselves alongside those who are suffering consistently yet, they have no recommendations and no blood ties but are entrusted as friends, sisters, mothers, fathers, defenders, neighbours, keepers and brothers; the qualifications that outclass that of any other.

My Neighbour's Keeper

I was born into a culture where much emphasis is placed upon sharing; sharing possessions, food, time and even a bed for the night. We were a closed knit community and the only notable thing was that, my neighbour's daughters across the road had blonde hair and blues eyes. As strange this may sound, it was down to their maternal great-grandmother who was of English descent and was not that unusual for our parish. My own maternal great-grandmother was also a legacy of a time in our past best confined to the pages of history books but we loved her character, her strength and the fiery nature which was attributed to her English heritage. She was alleged to be one of the most beautiful women in the whole community during her life but a shrewd and beguiling one who was my mother's guardian and carer in the absence of her own mother for the first seven years of her life.

I remember as a child how protected I was from everything. It was unheard of for one person to be seen walking along a road alone and since there was no electricity during that time, it was an absolute rule that the sun should never set whilst journeying home, otherwise the return walk along dusty red dirt lanes was completely unbearable. The darkness was just about sufferable but it was the horror stories we were told as children to keep us in the house at night that made us cling to each other as we negotiated our way along familiar daytime pathways which became hideously unmanageable, barefooted under the darkness of night.

I remember my neighbour's daughter's all five of them, beautiful and so 'perfect.' I remember wishing desperately to be miraculously granted flowing locks of hair like theirs; but what utter nonsense! I was born with little hair; the burden of my childhood and my early teenage years, it gave everyone the right to use every derogatory term possible when describing my tiny braids. I remember being told that during our appearance on earth that, the queue of little girls waiting for hair was so long that when it came to my turn, God ran out of hair since, I was the last girl in line. Of course I am always last in line, because I have made it my goal to push others ahead of me in many instances. I simply do not crave what a majority of people crave and as I have pushed others further and further along naturally, I have fallen in the shadows behind. This is my joy and my strength the one true definer of the person I was created to be. My joy is seeing someone accomplish something greater than I could ever dream of. In the meantime I watch, wait and observe, for when they are exhausted with the playing fields of life; I remain filled with inexorable energy. Admittedly, I always place myself at the front in every room where there is the potential to learn; in school, church and any other meeting place. Those who know me well always know exactly where to find me. If I cannot find a place at the front, I would rather leave than insert myself at the back and be at a disadvantaged position. Of course I had no choice on what was allotted to me at birth but would rather have changed other things than to have the overbearing vanity of whether my hair was long or short; life is much too critical to concern myself with such trivia, in view of what I now understand and value.

Painful as it was, I simply did not wish to spend my entire life seeking answers that could not be found for when one begin to compare their own position against that of their associates, friends or neighbours, they simply become entangled in a perpetual cycle of misery. It was at this point I instinctively knew that I would have to finds ways all my life in every potentially disabling and unfavourable position to make the very best of my 'worst' rather than to make the worst of my best; though I still seek diligently to determine what exactly is my 'best'.

I simply cannot imagine what constitutes worst and best assets adorning a human being since, no singular part stands alone in perfection but all are dependent on the other parts to be whole and complete. An arm by itself would be simply hideous. Visualise the most astonishing pair of eyes that was 'blind' to everything of wonder and beauty inspired in creation. Imagine not being able to appreciate the sunrise or to become lost in a sunset's incandescence glory across the evening sky; what loss and unreconciled sadness. It was partly for this reason that I became determined to be the best that I could be and to refuse emphatically to be defined by others. It was from here that I sought constantly to be defined by those standards I set for myself; especially those lived in full acknowledgement of my God who has so generously given my life to me.

Admittedly, there were moments when I did not like the person whose identity I framed and carried but have nevertheless, continued to walk convincingly and to find every way possible to make my life, my hair and everything I value to be as beautiful and as pleasing as it could possibly be. I am only too aware of how not to become obsessed with the possessions, status or personal features of others. I thank God that in view of what I learned as I grew older, I would never have swapped one tiny strand of hair on my head to be in the shoes of those young girls at any time. For it emerged years later how they had endured the most horrific physical, mental, psychological and sexual abuse imaginable.

Much of this abuse began to surface when Hanna the eldest daughter ran away from the family home at the age of thirteen to avert the despicable and abusive behaviour of her father towards her. This devastating action forced her to seek occasional refuge from neighbours and friends, with our house becoming a regular place for her to sleep at night. Hanna was at the grace of anyone who was kind enough to offer her a bed for the night and the mercy of the men who routinely raped her night after dreadful night but as a child with no support, she had no choice other than to return home and that was evidently much too painful for her to reconsider. I was much too young to recognise what was happening at the time but as I got older, I realised their father had continually confronted them with the repugnant idea of sexually intentions but each daughter would repelled his advances, only to flee the family home for their safety but often ending up in a more challenging situation. My eldest sister Carol, who was a year or so older than Hanna, often rescued her from the clutches of many abusive men and on one occasion waited alone for some of those responsible and set about whipping them into retreat. My sister though only five feet tall, earned a reputation for determination and audaciousness at a very young age and the stories about her bravery are still often talked about. She would never allow anyone she loved to be subjected to any form of brutality, as long as she found a way; she was there like a one woman army, proving, even in such distressing situations, there is a type of victory in every number greater than one.

Hanna has endured the most dreadful experiences imaginable and I cannot recall a time in her adult life when she was not in conflict with diseases, family, demons or men. The rest of her sisters also managed to escape but have had equally appalling times adjusting to normal lives, as wives, mothers and sisters. For one to try and imagine the horror of being put through such a gruelling and torturous experience and the lifelong impact that something like this has on a person, is bordering on impossible. Yet, Hanna is the humblest and most genuinely open person I have ever known with all her suffering. Of course I can immediately tell that the spark has long evaporated from her soul but there is nothing she would not give to another. She exemplifies the idea of victory in suffering; which is simply to forgive those who have harmed us, for in forgiving them we release ourselves to become rocks for others, while those who caused us pain are mere pebbles being tossed at will by their evil desires and actions. The imperative in pain and suffering is to search everyday deep inside to see if forgiveness can be found, just one more day so that a hurting heart can get beyond every ounce of its demoralizing agony.

I cannot reconcile the way people behave and admittedly, I had an intense dislike for my disagreeable and cantankerous neighbour but put that down to the fact that both my parents disliked him along with many other people and so, it did not seem so unusual. The one thing I found the most disturbing of all was when he died. All his children were there weeping as though for a noble king. This merely proves how misleading grief can be; how often the tears, that are falling are the ones meant to heal the past, close the door and heal into the future. Tears for the father they wanted but was not given, tears for their childhood being robbed, degraded and erased; "With the persuasive language of tears" Charles Churchill, (1731-1764). We can be deceived by falling of tears, for those tears cried are the years of confusion, being given the much needed freedom and release that was previously denied. "If the tide is rising high, the river must burst its banks, if the heart inside is breaking, the tears must flow with ease, until mind and soul is emptied of all that makes it grieve." When the dead are buried the only hope that remains is the one which inspires something within the hearts of men and women. This hope is the relinquishing of the old and an embracing of the new and as the past is perpetually sealed; we are merited an occasional glance backwards but must be determined to keep looking forward.

Looking Back to move forward

It is my belief that, anyone who does not understand his or her past will never be able to grasp the future since; the past has a way of repeating itself in a number of irritating ways. There are naturally those who wish to keep certain doors closed tightly from the past to the present and especially, if there is a slight chance that the past may catch up with the 'perfect' future. This is particularly true for those people who have committed criminal offences and struggle to overcome the stigma of past records and wrong-doing. They may have been sentenced lightly by the courts but have paid for their crime by way of a blot on their record which becomes problematic when re-assimilating back to work and into society. Of course we can gaze back from time to time but only if this helps to close doors firmly, or if we are assisted to solve issues in our present situation by asking a number of pertinent questions. "Life is not a problem to be solved but a reality to be experienced." Soren Kierkegaard (1813-1855). Kierkegaard, I believe, is suggesting that far too many people become preoccupied with seeking answers without first asking the right questions. In many instances, a number of individuals tend focus on everything negative and are unable to move a safe distance away from pessimistic influences. If we somehow allow ourselves to see beyond our meagre perceptions and look more daringly ahead, what may emerge is that our focus have in fact changed, and when this occurs our expectations will also shifts enormously. What initially appears as despondency in fact becomes a test of strength and fortitude.

Some time ago, I heard a story about a young man who pleaded with God to increase his strength. The man was directed by God to go and stand for an indefinite period in a barren wilderness in front of a mountain. Of course he became disillusioned after many months since no further instructions were forthcoming from God. In his impatience he began a daily routine of trying to scale the face of the mountain in a hope to increase his strength, when in fact he was simply depleting his meagre resources. Of course this is often the point where God steps in with terrifying wisdom. "What are you doing" God asked the man. "I am trying to become stronger, so I am climbing the mountain to increase my physical strength," the man said. "Did I ask you to do that" inquired God. "No" said the man. "Then why are you doing it" queried God – when you asked me to increase your strength, it was your character I was building not your arms."

There are so few of us who are able to be still, as it is often from this place that we are able to hear through the silence in a deafening world. The instruments of change that we possess are not 'way out' there but are embedded within each of us. So many of us become weary with our efforts to grow and change and are no nearer our goals than when we instituted them decades earlier. It is better to learn from painful situations, those that impel us to take an exhaustive view of what we value in our lives. Everything in life does not demand active participation; we simply do not possess the physical strength to engage with everything. I for one, welcome every opportunity where I can observe those who enjoy participating. On a number of occasions, I need others to set the standards for me to follow. I can illustrate this thought more succinctly by one of the merits of the British legal system. There are historical cases that set precedence and from these all future laws stand and are upheld. If people were able to formulate such primacy in their attitudes and relationships, using others as their measuring line, a good deal of heartache and grief could be spared since, outcomes are visible and pre-determined.

For those things in my life that I value and onto which a number of my future hopes are pinned, it was a catastrophe when one such qualifying joy shake the ground on which I stood. I remember a number of years ago reading a story of a doctor whose young daughter almost died from meningitis and when asked how he had missed the symptoms, his response was just like that of any other parent. "She was my child I just couldn't see it." Of course there have been times in my life where no amount of prior knowledge could avert me from making some of the poorest judgement calls. Those spiteful demons who listened to my secret fears and waited for an opportune moment to package and deliver them to me the day before I set off on the trip of a lifetime. I have never been a woman who throws her hands in the air and scream in despair when I am facing a crisis, I much prefer to find a quiet place, close the door and stand before God in silence then speak when he permits me to do so. I have learnt to be patient and prayerful in situations I cannot alter but if there is a single thing that I can change, I will effect that change forthwith. Of course I can be clumsy and infantile in the same way as a number of people I know but I suppose, to be these things is fine as long as they do not seriously impact my ability to function in my usual buoyant way.

I simply endeavour to map out my life with as much depth and clarity as I am able since, it's in this process where I am able to memorise past events and find resolutions to any amount of difficulties. Even though I may not have the same tenacious spirit as I did in previous situations, the impression on my map remains unchanged. Whenever I have reasons to doubt my strength, it is at this point that I remember the words of Paul the Apostle in 2 Corinthians 12:10; "That is why, for Christ's sake, I delight in suffering, I delight in weakness, in insults, in hardships, in persecutions, in difficulties. For when I am weak, then I am strong." In humble acknowledgement of my weaknesses, I sought God's grace in order to be transferred to a higher place; perhaps a mountaintop instead of a valley. Whenever I meet with God I naturally have expectations; be ready, patient, and yes or no. Without expectations I simply do not know how to be before him because he is God and not a human being - I have learned never to have expectations from people, only from God. There is always a gift, an answer or the healing I desire and his answers are always a timely revelation. I recall my mother, so passionate on the attributes of God and always advocating how God helps those who help themselves. She would often remind us not to go looking for, or to create unwarranted trouble within our lives; "Don't go looking for trouble, for trouble has a way of finding you, or that trouble nuh set like rain," this simply means that trouble does not give a forecast like the weather, and problems always come unexpectedly. In spite of this, I have gained much confidence in the fact that, although I am powerless to change the weather, there is influence within me to change any number of pessimistic outlooks I may temporarily hold.

The Bible supports us on this very matter of excavating paths leading to difficulties in our lives. In Matthew 6:34; "Therefore do not worry about tomorrow, for tomorrow will worry about itself. Each day has enough trouble of its own." As a woman, I am now better able to discern those necessary details surrounding my self-worth since I have tackled them confidently and have secured a deeper meaning and purpose to my life. While some may choose alternative pathways towards their idea of peace and perfection, others would resist all such pathways that do not carry symbols of the triumph of the cross; I for one, could never envisage a road that was not along the, 'Via Dolorosa', "The way of suffering"; for although the walk is lonely and bitter, the ascension is full of promise and extraordinary genius.

It is only in the pursuit of God's righteousness that I am empowered to graciously and loving accept the wonderful gift that Christ gave after his ascension, a life made worthy and exemplified in him. Anything else is desolately short of the expectations I have for myself and those that God has set for me. I believe all human beings were born to fulfil specific purposes, yet at times it seemed I was constantly in a maze, going round and round in a repetitive loop to which there was neither beginning nor end. A decision to eject myself from this thought pattern was necessary, so that the Holy Spirit could reinstate knowledge and insight to me in order for me to reassert my rightful place back into the story of God.

The credibility and authenticity of the story of God is unparalleled, for each time I read His word I find myself amongst its pages; wherever I see a disobedient and suffering people, longing for grace and pardon. Whenever I see an orphan, a widow, an alien or a person rejected or excluded on the basis of their difference; in their midst, I am there. There is nothing greater or better than when one comes to a profound understanding of where they fit into the purposes of God. When this happens, there is a sense of inclusion into something that surpasses all previous knowledge and understanding. Everywhere in God's word I find men and women being excluded but God went beyond including them and adopted them as 'sons' and 'daughters' and giving each person a new identity and ultimately raising them above every one of their fears and disappointments. I hear so many grumbles and complaints from so many sources concerning the hardships they have endured daily; rhetorical echoes of a diaspora people traversing the Sinai wilderness and who often failed to see the miracles immediately ahead of them.

Human nature is a complicated and unfathomable mass of needs, desires and wants and so few are able to reasonably separate them in appropriate priorities. If someone appears to be suffering an incurable illness, one would imagine that this was the overbearing priority. However, he or she may simply wish to be flown to the moon in a rocket and bid a sombre farewell to the world; when in fact he or she could have lived if they were wise and humble enough to assess their priorities differently and first sought the help and skill of a surgeon. Of course this is a tedious analogy but I used it simply to highlight the lengths a number of people go just to avoid facing the truth.

The on-going conflicts between peoples is the tragedy of humankind but even greater than this is the fractured views, the bigoted ways and the objectionable and unforgiving nature of so many. Although there are some who profess to have unconditional powers of love and forgiveness; while this may appear reasonably true to them, may paint a vastly different picture to others. Our view must be embedded in an untarnished optimism that cannot be discoloured by external factors steeped in pessimism. This optimism should have a shape and form and be given a name in order that it may be 'captured', possessed and accessible within the immediate reaches of human fortitude. Optimism should encompass the nature and behaviours of all since, so many people wish to hide themselves against the hostility of the world in something which gives them hope. When optimism is the preferred view to pessimism the things we crave move a step closer as we are better able to discern good from the pervasive immorality. As I muse over a catalogue of feelings, actions and behaviours, I realise of course, that I am no different from any other human being where needs are concerned but I believe what excludes me on a number of levels is my undeniably love of prayer and worship to God. Since, without him, I simply could not find the hope and compassion I have craved interminably. Praying is the most powerful way of communicating with God and it is, the most direct way to safeguard what he has already placed within me. I meet with him to honour him, to give thanks for my life in whatever situation I find myself. It is especially consoling when I am unwell; since it's during these times I am impelled to meet with the wisest physician by far. While I prefer to be healthy rather than sick, I am grateful that it is in my illnesses where God is most present. If I did not seek him with my heart I would never learn the rapturous and tantalising feeling when in a second, God would appears and shows me he was there all along. It's such a comfort to know that God never leaves when the so-called friends I trusted have all deserted me; yet, God remains faithful.

A number of years ago I arranged to take my children along with my sister and a friend to Florida. Within three weeks of departure my friend had to abandon the trip due to unforeseen circumstances. I was left to find a replacement and since my friend had ample insurance covering this eventually I promised faithfully that every penny would be repaid in full on our return. Admittedly, I was rather hasty in my attempts to find another person to take her place since, there would be a lot of driving and I knew it would be a tedious undertaking, being the only driver in the group. Suddenly I thought of my 'good' friend Gloria and even before I had ended the conversion with her she had asked me to ring the travel agent and put her name in the place of the other person. This was done with the explicit understanding that the money for the trip would be paid fully to the person who had opted out as soon as we returned to Manchester. Of course she refused to pay a penny and I was sued under an obscure law because I was the one who had made the promise of repayment. I had to go to court on two occasions to defend my integrity when it should have never been in question.

The amount of times in my life that I have suffered because of others people's lack of integrity and decency, I have simply lost count. She finally conceded and wrote me a cheque for half the cost – the holiday had cost over one thousand pounds; I was still quite angry with her. I went to court accompanied by my dear friend Marjorie whose fortitude and knowledge gained the respect of the judge which resulted in the claims against me being dismissed. I was free from any further pursuits from the claimant who accepted the cheque covering half the original price and forfeiting the remainder. Of course, in every matter of integrity, there is always assurance of victory in every number greater than one!

The amount of times I have been pushed on the outside by devious and wilful individuals is beyond counting. Yet, whenever I have been appraised by a number of trustworthy characters regarding the perceptions they hold of me, each time I was surprised by what I heard. I don't believe I am a great deal different to my special childhood friend Sonia since, we both look and behave differently and are excluded on the outside of almost everything. Sadly for Sonia, if there is a party, she is outside the house with her son. If there is a joke, she is it; always the derisory humour of others. If someone gives her a nice clean dress to wear, someone else takes it from her. Thankfully, I am most at peace with lonely, hurting and displaced people - the only answer I have is that, I am also one of them; "Birds of a feather." I believe the only difference between me and the people I love and care most about is the fact that I can engage fully at all levels in life and my confidence have soared through the years in spite of a number of malicious individuals. I have rarely encountered threatening mountains or walls in my life purely by chance; they have always been placed maliciously ahead of me by others. When walls separate us as 'foreigners' on the outside of every potential good and the mountains before us are threatening and when each road is unfamiliar and full of potential wrong turns, I am grateful that God has a way of turning up uninvited! In Joshua 6:2-11 we read of God's amazing power at work as Joshua in obedience marched around the wall of Jericho for six days and on the seventh day, in anticipation of victory the priests began to blow the trumpets.

The guarantee of victory was based upon the promise that God had given Joshua proving that, although we are limited, God is inexhaustible and that we should never attempt to restrict God because of a lack of faith or vision. I believe firmly that my on-going security is predicated on the command of a righteous and holy God and divine performance is based on right and meaningful perceptions which I believe are given to each of us directly by God. The beginning and the end of every matter is whether I hear correctly what is demanded or asked of me, or whether in impatience I go ahead in my own delusion and blinding darkness. Despite the clouds which may hang ominously above me, the sun continues to shine upon the earth from where my fertile hopes and schemes continues to grow and prosper. Although I was limited by the level of my understanding when I was younger, I have nevertheless become more cautious and selective as I have grown older in terms of the decisions I take, the company I keep, the organisations to which I choose to become affiliated and the ways in which I pursue matters of principles in my own life. Every action I undertake in life speaks volumes about the type of person I am and yet, so many continue to refuse to allow God to be the companion he promised he would be. I celebrate God because he has never taken but only added to me, he has never actively seek to harm but only to strengthened me and he has never despitefully used or abused me but has only encouraged me in every possible pathway of goodness and integrity. Many refuse to allow God to be the ultimate companion and friend, perhaps due to pride or the fear of becoming ostracised by family and friends. I can see no other way through life than the way of Christ, for in him my confidence and faith increases daily.

We increase our faith when we are placed in adverse circumstances and feel perilously near to giving in; "True faith and courage are like a kite- an opposing wind raises it higher," (John Petit-Senn). Surprisingly, faith is not an object which can be measured until, of course we are in dire circumstances and suddenly realise that there is actually something greater holding us than us holding ourselves. The things which are held in prominence in my life have not changed since I was a child; Christ, family values and a number of unwavering principles. It is from these values that my confidence has accelerated, making me reasonably fearless in many situations. "Experience tells you what to do; confidence allows you to do it." (Stan Smith), that we possess confidence is a truism but seldom are we able to harness its full potential due to fear, for no one wishes to be dubbed; 'a know it all' but I would sooner be called that than; 'a know nothing.'

In contrast to Sir Edmund Hillary's conquering of Everest, I have learnt to accept the limited nature of my human potential yet, my prospect to rise in Christ is immeasurable. Naturally, all my efforts in life are not to be viewed as 'conquests,' like Hillary's Everest undertaking since, I believe I am simply living. It is for this reason that I hold firmly to my Christian beliefs and allow them to inform me unfailingly, whether I ascend enormous 'mountains' or barely visible hills. While I may have preferred an alternative outcome to a number of situations, I must accept that outcomes are always based upon the things which are held in greater or lesser priority in my life. It is unclear to many commentators whether Sir Edmund Hillary was a religious man or one possessing any type of faith but one thing is reasonably clear to me and that is, he left that cross at the top of the mountain simply because it got him there. Not because it contributed to the sheer hard work but because it increased his resolve and the idea behind his pursuit for both perfection and completion; which are inner convictions borne only from ideas of the deity.

My deep convictions are the reasons I continue to meet and overcome a number of challenges in my life. Naturally there were moments I could have easily succumbed to despair as I found myself traversing back and forth over the same ground and could not find a way either round or through a particular difficulty. This is natural, for the human mind will always seek to find the swiftest resolutions without the painful encumbrances. My courage is most evident during such times and it is often when I am most strengthened to raise my expectations from myself and others. What begins to emerge in difficult and painful situations is the fact that there are a number of people in the world who are compassionate souls and who are prepared to go some distance with their friends, neighbours and even an occasional stranger. These people are almost invisible alongside us but are somehow the most daring. They appear to possess courage for themselves and compassion for others. They are somehow determined to find the perfect realignment and insert themselves alongside others as they push them; back on top of the 'world'.

Back on Top of the World

I have entered some dreadful places, well one or two in my life and was only too pleased to walk in at the front and continue straight through to the back door. I have gone to the cinema all excited at the thought of watching an entertaining film, only to be verbally assaulted by a barrage of profanities. In such instances, I remove myself from my seat faster than a thoroughbred racehorse and exit the building by means of the fire escape route. I simply cannot see how anything that damages my perception of others is of any moral benefit to me or them. I was twenty seven years old when I entered my first night club. Well, there was music and music is fine, there was also a vast number of people; old, young, strange and destitute and there was nothing to be gained there, except, the music was great and I loved to dance and so, I continued dancing in the same place for three years, then decided I had danced enough in one lifetime in a public place and walked out the door and never returned. I am so aware of the toxicity of a number of things in the world around me and it is for this reason I analyse everything so cautiously before I attempt to embark on anything new.

I was twenty-one years old when I married my first husband; I lived at home with my parents up until then and had no aspiration at that time to live with any person unless of course, I was married to him. I simply could not abide the thought. I may not have an overbearing desire to control others but I will endeavour to control every aspect of my life as I move in and out of good and bad paths moment by moment. Naturally, no amount of precautions safeguards everything since; I am a curious individual who will never allow an opportunity to pass from where I could learn something inspirational. Although I prefer to observe nine times out ten, there are moments when participation becomes the imperative but of course, with participation comes the inevitable conflicting values.

There is a comforting promise that; "The steps of a good man or woman are ordered by the Lord and even though he or she falls they will not be cast down for the Lord upholds them with his hands." A reassuring declaration which highlights the fact that, wherever a person inserts themself, God continues to care unreservedly for them.

Naturally, at each stage of my life I have glanced behind me and have been so grateful that all my footprints have been erased by his love. The only proof of having traversed a number of places is a vague recollection from time to time. This remarkable Father, who is both loving and forgiving, allows suffering to apprehend the lives of those whom he has called but at no time will he permit suffering to overwhelm them. It is always in the most dire and adverse of situations where I have been able to reassert my rightful place; in family, community and within groups and associations. It's a blessing that not all minds and attitudes are identical to my own since, people behave in two ways regarding what is least understood; a majority will completely disregard it and the inquisitive ones like me, will develop a keen interest in its orientation and purpose, then begin the task of unravelling what is misunderstood, until it becomes distinguishable. The majority, who disregarded it, are those individuals who are generally apathetic towards a number of other pertinent issues affecting others around them but are too wrapped up or overwhelmed with aspects of their own lives.

To illustrate this thought, I would like to explore the concept of 'suffering' briefly since; it forms a substantial part of my journey. So, what exactly is suffering and who suffers most? Although I believe I have suffered to some extent in my life, a majority of my difficulties was created by some of the most disagreeable characters imaginable. What transpired from those encounters has admittedly changed a number of my beliefs and concepts but overall, I believe in spite of them, I have become a stronger and more determined person. It is for this reason I hold an optimistic outlook regarding certain types of suffering, especially in view of the outcome of such difficulties.

I can quite easily imagine what makes a number of people afraid since, those same sarsens may be the exact ones that makes me anxious. Although I have no accurate reference points in regards to strategies developed by others when they are hurting, suffering remains the true definer of our humanity. The distinctiveness of each person, their values and bedrocks, will undoubtedly become affirmed during periods of anxiety and change. All human beings imagine all types of indiscernible fears, this is merely our way of affirming it is normal to be afraid and by doing so, we are strengthening our humanity with others. "That we cannot be human alone, we must be human together." Desmond Tutu – God has a Dream: A Vision for our Time. Bishop Tutu is asserting that our common human values are drawn from each other and that we simply could not exist without other human beings alongside us whether we scale walls or climb mountains. Our approach to everything as individuals is different, yet our common values are interleaved with each other. I believe I respond positively when I am encouraged, defensively when I am threatened, angrily when I am condemned and lovingly when I am cherished. It is within the human community that everything of value is upheld or crushed, celebrated or denigrated.

Admittedly, each person has a rudimentary sense of right and wrong but nevertheless, a great number find it so easy to cause hurt to others. Everyone is endowed with a free-will – the main characteristic separating humans from all other created beings. God as creator simply could have created beings with limited potential and possessing an inferior image, rendering them pitiable, insubstantial and marginally above despairing. But God was only too pleased to give all human beings every potential to succeed, to be excellent, to be humble and to have a mind and heart to exemplify him since, all are created in his image; this image is the unquestionable human identity that is found in God alone.

In Genesis 1:26; And God said, "Let us make mankind in our image, in our likeness, so that they may rule over the fish of the sea and the birds of the sky, over the livestock and all the wild animals and over all the creatures that move along the ground." There have been many furious scholarly debates over many centuries about what this 'image of God' looks like, whether it is indeed an actual look or is it the essential components which differentiate the human animal from the brute beasts, roaming the forests and desert wastelands to satisfy hunger. If we are the image of God then, this suggests to me that we should live godly lives as exemplified in Christ, since this image forms the essence of human identity and values. The image of Christ during his life on earth would give no rise for concern; he was perhaps 'ordinary' in appearance not wishing to be conspicuous.

He was however, visible in matters of principles. His judicious and unwavering tongue set the Graeco Roman world ablaze when it came to the delivery of his message of repentance and forgiveness. His integrity was unquestionable since he cared for others more than for himself. His humility was undefined because, at no time in the history of humankind has another being displayed such virtues as Christ. I am not for one moment deluding myself that there are not a number of people who feign humility to dispossess others of their assets and dignity. There are numerous individuals who are stealthy and cunning when it comes to inserting themselves in the vacant space alongside others; Christ however, was most definitely not one such individual.

A number of years ago I was on a study programme where I befriended by a young woman from Swaziland. I took her under my wings and opened my heart and home to her after noticing how she was excluded by all the others students in the classroom, library and café. I could not help noticing her sadness and made the effort to offer her friendship and support. It was my belief that, although culturally we possessed some microscopic differences, overall we had a number of shared principles and values. Of course I was wrong and she gradually began to morph into a greedy and materialist woman whose expectations soon outstripped my wardrobe! The noticeable change in her began when the very people who had in fact treated her with such indiffencence, began to pull her back towards them.

Human nature at its worst is the most disturbing thing I have witnessed in my life and although death can be an abysmal thought, it does not frighten me half as much as the evil concealed within the hearts of men and women. Those individuals knew they would not be able to feign humility and win my support since; I am only interested in those people who are genuine and are always on the fringes of society. Those habitually overlooked because of their 'difference.' Her difference sanctioned rejection rather than acceptance and advocated judgements rather than meaningful valuations. I am interested in an unusual form of genuineness though sadly, have seldom found it.

I believe that for every cause there is a visible effect and as long as I can, I will continue rejecting the ruthless sides of human nature. I have finally given up my attempts to work out the darker sides of human beings and I am confident that I am not the only person to whom such callous individuals are attracted. In the past I used to spend hours reprimanding myself for my foolish actions and trusting nature. Nowadays, I simply allow God to choose my friends and in every instance my expectations has been exceeded and my hope restored. I have as many genuine friends as I have eyes; it's easy to invest in them because they receive my undivided attention. I have been particularly grateful for Winifred, whose love and encouragement continues to surprise me. She returned after several months after I had closed my door in her face. Remarkably; she is the only person who thought I was worthy of a second glance. I have grown to love her because we pray, laugh and eat together and her words of truth continue to impel me towards my destiny. There are so many men and women who appear completely ordinary in the world but are empowered to go between the suffering, the rulers and those within the compromised echelons of power and remain fearless throughout it all. These souls seem to have the innate ability to attract people to them like the unmistakable firefly. In my continuous observations of the past – I seemed to have attracted a number of angry, disillusioned middle-class women and self-contained, accomplished European men.

Of course in order to make sense of this I lean towards a cultural bias from my early years where I was brought up to be open. There was simply nothing to be guarded against since; I was always with 'family.' Of course this view was dismantled in part by a number of ruthless individuals when I was 'discarded' momentarily as a child but I continue my quest to unearth goodness in the hearts of people. I remain confident the world consists of many good people but they were not to be found in the places I had been looking. It was in this exhaustive period that I chance upon Harry – and it was during a trip to Raleigh Durham, that I was propelled into one of the most life-affirming happenstances.

Raleigh Durham

Some years ago I took a trip to North Carolina to visit a Paediatrician friend who was as delightful as he was mysterious. Delightful because he was amusing and a little reckless, mysterious because he was called by many names: doctor, egotistical, father, brilliant, successful and self-contained. People who achieve so much always seem to lose a majority of life's defining virtues as they become morbidly attached to their success and possessions. My friend was a keen yachtsman and had a substantial yacht moored at Lake Falls. As the days passed I began to evaluate the disadvantageous position I had placed myself in and this thought lingered heavily throughout my two weeks stay. For some reason European men seem to possess rather an enquiring nature towards me and while I try to overlook this, I seem unable to avert their inquisitiveness.

These men, often successful in their chosen fields, are often self-contained and complex individuals who find it difficult to be open with those around them but seldom with me. Harry was no exception but was such an anomaly; he was moody and unsettling yet genius was present within him. The way he cooked a meal and prepared the home grown vegetables and the way he would administered care and attention to the children and parents who sought his help was exceptional. They all held him in the highest esteem - but if he knew it, he never found a way to be inspired by it. The strain of being miles away in a strange place all began to take its toll. One evening we went out for dinner to a little restaurant which was a welcome change. This nightmarish situation was months in the making and sometimes it's so much easier to turn over and continue 'dreaming' than to wake up and scream. I walked out onto a veranda to get some air into my toxic lungs from the cigars and the gloomy atmosphere.

As I began contemplating, I heard footsteps behind me and not daring to look around me, I heard a voice as deep as those southern breakers said a very warm "good evening." I looked round and for a brief moment thought that James Earl Jones the actor was staring at me; of course it wasn't him but he could have been a stunt double for him. He spoke with me as though he had known me for years and I must have made the right judgement call trusting this endearing stranger. For once I was with an 'angel' and not the habitual demon. He informed that he had followed me outside to check that I was not being threatened because of my Caribbean origin since in this part of North Carolina many people can be extremely hostile to people like us. I was pleased to be cared for in this way but saddened at the same time at the unreceptive nature of a number of people. It was one of the few times in my life that a man had followed me but not to make inappropriate suggestions. He had been with a group of around ten people dining and when he saw me leaving my table and headed for the terrace, decided to come over and talk with me. All the people he was dining with were pilots and crew from Delta Airlines and in no time we were joined by all the others. By this time I had forgotten about Harry but I knew him well enough and figured out he was probably finding courage and strength in the red wine but I always prefer to seek it from kind-hearted people whenever I run into them. I was completely taken by surprise how this group of strangers cared for me and at every point I kept waiting for them to ask for something in return. They asked for nothing and for a long time into the future would continue to give me more than I could have wished for.

As the evening drew to a close they exchanged contact details with me and there was one stewardess in particular who asserted the position of 'mother hen' and took me under her 'wings' from that moment until the day that I could fly again. Just before the evening drew to a close they informed me of their regular stops in London and that the next time they were there they would definitely call and check in on me. I am so used to meeting insincere people that I thought sarcastically; "Who do they think they are kidding?" The evening with them ended and with Harry, there was no happy ending in view of the ambivalent beginning. About a month after I had arrived back in Manchester I received a phone call from Selfridges Hotel in London and was surprised to hear four of the Delta Airline crew on the other end of the line. They invited me each time they stopped over in London to join them for lunch but my work commitments made this impossible - this 'checking in' happened routinely over a two year period. The day that they heard me laughing again, really laughing, was the day they knew that their job was done.

I found myself at a really uncomfortable and painful place, all of my own volition and had to concede that this situation was much larger than me, so big in fact that I could barely stand. Immediately ahead of me was a defiant 'mountain' demanding to be climbed. I had neither the will nor the desire to do so since, there would be nothing to be gained from putting myself through this endurance. Instead, I retreated to the safety of what I trusted and valued most and although this action took a lot less courage, it was nevertheless, a painful position to choose. For in choosing, I immediately reconciled what I had gained over what had been lost. Those men and women, who stood alongside me, were able to focus on my potential and not what had been lost. This was the beginning of a new course for me since, it was one of the only times in my life that I had encountered genuine compassion from strangers. I never forget kindness and compassion because it has been the rarest occurrences in my life. I have found the worst things when I have been looking and the best ones when I least expected.

Sadly for Harry, the drink he liked so much consumed him and ended his life two years later at the age of forty four, proving to me once more that sometimes to concede defeat is actually the best form of winning. I simply cannot reconcile those in society who appears to be given the most, becoming so paralysed when faced with invented phantoms and doubts. The fact success propels them to such heights means they go way beyond the reach of their 'true' friends and whenever a need arise for someone to insert themself alongside them; they cannot disarm their pride and seek help from the most appropriate sources.

The crew from Delta Airlines however, are used to soaring high everyday above the world but the difference is clear - their feet never leave the ground. They understand suffering and pain and wherever they saw it, acknowledged it and intervened when permitted. They went beyond their remit by choosing to stand alongside me and inserting themselves in the space left vacant by Harry. I remember the Delta Airlines commercial back in the nineteen eighties, "Delta Airlines, on top of the world." When they departed from my life I was able to fly once more and without thinking in any great depth, I recognised instinctively, I had in fact, arrived, "Back on top of the world." I remain in deep acknowledgement of the fact that, there is always assurance of victory in every number greater than one.

Sorry: I wasn't thinking

How many times have you accosted a person and demanded an explanation for an ill-advised action? The response is nearly always the same; "Sorry, I wasn't thinking." As frustrating as this is, one has to accept that many people simply do not think in advance of their actions.

Although a lack of thoughtfulness could present serious consequences in our lives and the lives of those around us, we must also recognise the times when we ourselves have been thoughtless. Thinking is not merely in relation to a set of well-aligned assumptions, for if all were able to compartmentalise our thoughts the solutions that followed would be consistent and far more productive. For those refusing to venture beyond the meagre pre-set boundaries, will invariably limit the range of life experiences especially those with the potential to change attitudes and encourage strength and resolve. It is during such times of severe hardships and difficulties that character formation is intensified and from this reinforced position that a number of people, like me, are enabled to conquer a number of hidden fears. Effectively, I am advocating a different mode of thinking and analyses.

Whenever I become engaged in a different form of thinking I immediately discover a number of new revelations. The human mind; a battlefield at its worst and a harmonious orchestra at its best, possesses the potential to be malicious, successful, good and even humble yet, many seem unable to find the appropriate routes that propel them in these directions. The greatest battles known to humans are those 'played' out every day in the vast 'battlefields' of the mind - against visible, invisible, credible, implausible, tangible and fictitious opponents. Thoughts naturally, are out of reach and sight of both thinkers and observers. A person's appearance may suggest they are completely whole and unaffected, when in fact they are broken and can neither be influenced nor apprehended. Is the inimitability of the human person based entirely upon culture? I do not necessarily advocate a wholly and consistent belief that a person must readily assume their culture in order to work out their own unique identity. Identity can often be defined in separate partitions of: family, religion, or place in society; which sadly includes wealth and status. These values that are accepted in many modern societies simply cannot delineate or endorse a person's individuality since; such things are incapable of hermetically sealing anyone's core distinctiveness. Although identity is inextricably linked to culture and also the position a person holds within the broader spectrum of society, one must also appreciate the dynamics of community and beliefs and when off-set against world-views, can become potentially toxic factors, which are changeable and susceptible to many ephemeral menaces.

I would find it far too disparaging to insert myself amongst my own culture and believe that to be my only place. As menacing as assimilation can be, I would sooner find ways to break down barriers which prevented people from other cultures to come alongside me in every situation. Since, the way I view myself is not hinged to culture alone. Much of what I think forms a large part of how I behave but it is how I think that should affirm my place alongside others. I often wish I did not think as much as I do but I cannot stop the endless debates that are created within me. As a child, those caring for me were often perplexed how little I spoke but I simply had too much to think about: the beautiful humming birds, the stars in the night sky, the roar of the thunder, the moon so perfect and welcoming to lessens the darkness. I could not help thinking who was wise and prodigious enough to make the sky sparkle at night. I spent much of my young years gazing up towards heaven and often missing what was right ahead of me. If ever there was a child who had her head perpetually in the 'clouds,' it was I; for I was simply born to look upwards.

Human relationships are balanced upon some of the most fragile foundations and the slightest shifts or tremors are potentially catastrophic. There are many who are afraid to go deeper than the surface and the irrationality with which such fears flourish are disconcerting. I am convinced that we would become paralysed if we were granted additional foresight, where each person was permitted to look years ahead into the future – the world would become a very sparse planet indeed. There would be so few people who could actually live what they had envisioned.   Admittedly, I consider myself as privileged, knowing that I have been granted the spirit of foresight and discernment. I don't need a person to speak to me nor do I need to hold their hands, or toss stones to invoke the power of some unknown source, I simply allow the Holy Spirit to inform me of every necessary detail concerning the hopes, disappointments and fears of anyone who choose to insert themself alongside me.

While it is never my intention to invade the thoughts of those beside me, there have been times where the noisy clatter inside their minds is much too difficult to ignore. Of course I don't need permission to 'ransack' the minds of anyone but I remain cautious of what I may uncover. A number of years ago a very young woman was imploring me to 'read' her mind and reassure her of a future full of sunshine and flowers – my reluctance was palpable since there was no future for her, only the grave at short space in the distance. There is never going to be a gift as this without such onerous burdens. Each time I look to the future the past is there and whenever I look to the past I can only see the present and I cannot change a single thing. It is for this reason that I often close my eyes in a hope to stop believing in the unbelievable. The more I believe the greater my clarity and the greater my clarity the more intense my faith. I continue to seek God through these revelations but faithfully beseech him to empower me to adjust the future, where permissible. In view of my conviction of what is unseen: does seeing affirm belief?

Does Seeing Affirm belief?

Every human being possesses a number of gifts and regardless of their appearances; each person is a spiritual being in custody of particular qualities to warrant their purpose and plan. I accept that God is a spirit and that all humans were created in his 'image,' which is an extended dimension of their physical state of being. So, it makes perfectly good sense to me that it is our spiritual aspect which allows us to move freely beyond physical confines. African and Caribbean culture has been heavily impacted by the idea of the spiritual realm – both positively and negatively. As a child, I remember being told such dreadful stories of spirits and ghouls which would make me afraid for months. Of course this was merely tactics by my mother to keep us all in the house after sunset but we did not recognise this as being so at the time. It is difficult to imagine that spirits can be 'visible' and that they can be guiding lights to those still living. I remain open to a number of possibilities but refuse to accept anything other than those which are rigorously defended and supported in Scripture. My view of death is the end of one pitiful fantasy and of life after, as the beginning of humanity's true reality. Of course I cannot substantiate my own thoughts; nevertheless, a majority are rigorously defended in Scripture. The Bible is also clear in regards to those individuals who profess the ability to direct the lives of others with what we understand as; 'psychic ability.' This is a salient issue and the Bible is not silent on the matter of those who 'tell fortunes' for money. People who are hurting will seek almost every possible way to end or alleviate their suffering.

I remember some years ago shortly after my father had died, I was walking through a shopping arcade when I was approached by an elderly lady who said, "I can see a man around you stroking your face, has someone close to you passed away recently?" Of course I was surprised by her statement and although I love mysteries, I much prefer those that are of a 'holy' nature. I talked briefly with her and she said some very accurate and telling things which admittedly, I cannot deny, even though I did not care for her method. Eventually I left her, dubious of her claim as a 'psychic healer' since I am confident that the idea of psychic and healing together is exclusively pagan. This is a centre I visit frequently and it became apparent after a few weeks that she was no longer there. Several months later I was walking through the town and bumped into her while she was being pushed by her husband in a wheelchair. Naturally, I enquired how she had come to be in the chair – I always ask questions. I believe a number of people prefer this straightforward approach than the usual façade. A few months earlier she had been involved in a road accident as she crossed the road and was left badly injured. I believe a number of observers know the direction I am heading and for me the question I must ask is; "If we possess insight for so many others, why not for ourselves?"

For those of us who refuse to believe unless we see, the edges of darkness remain much closer than we think. When we believe in the invisible, [love and hope in particular], it is from here that we are better able to affirm the actions we take in every aspect of our lives. Every day I witness pain, suffering, deception and evil in the world. Is this my reality or that of another? Simply because I see something with my eyes does not make it any more real since, it is what I am seeing and not my reality. For me, the only true reality I have ever known and understood is the one which is embedded deep within and can neither be seen nor apprehended by another. This is my avowed reality and whether I choose what I see or what is chosen for me remains unquantifiable since, realities cannot be measured in perceptions only in what is apprehended. I refuse to think that in order to believe I must see the object or subject to which that belief is pertaining. In any case, just because I observe something, does not necessarily make that object or subject of my observation my exclusive reality. It is far more beneficial to me what I value in my life since, what I value will invariably form the basis of my fundamental sense of being. Regardless of how I am shaped, whether by toxic or harmonious influences, what I hold as indispensable should not impact another person in the least. It is only when I begin a process of actions and counter-actions that I become capable of dismantling the lives of others and more importantly, my own.

So, if I choose to climb a mountain just to prove I can; how would that be beneficial to me? I much prefer to climb those that are necessary in order that my character become strengthened. I am aware that each challenge brings it dangers as well as its rewards and it is for the latter reason I believe Sir Edmund Hillary chose to remove himself from safety and faced the terrifying quest of Mount Everest. In my ascents and descents throughout life, I have lost substances of my intrinsic sense of being but there was also much to be gained in many instances. It is difficult to imagine that anyone is ever certain what awaits them on the far side of someplace unknown but I am certain that Hillary knew exactly what awaited him at the top of that mountain. It was for this reason, unlike a number who failed in their attempts, he pressed on in blind faith to the top of the world. Who knows whether he held doubts over the existence of God or not but I suspect he held many doubts about his own life, his achievements and purpose and his commitment in his pursuit for excellence.

I have never questioned the validity or the veracity of God, yet day after day, I pose questions from every conceivable angle regarding my own fragile life. I have never asked God for miracles just to prove or disprove his presence, for every time I examine my heart and hear it beating, I know the only proof of a miracle I need is right within me. And each time I look to the heavens and the sun, moon and all the constellations display in wonder, I see the beginning and the end of the one who has set them high above me in the firmaments in order that I may look up in delight, to honour and praise him.

I do not wish to climb mountains for vain glory, prestige, honour nor wealth but only as a means of fulfilling my destiny. Throughout my life I have climbed through the barriers of pain, heartache, rejection, prejudices and violation of trusts; not to prove I am strong but because I had no alternative. When so much energy is spent in preservation and subsistence, there is simply none left to face challenges which bring renown. I do not wish to become great in the eyes of my fellow men and women; though I have had to overcome great and mighty adversities. Greatness happens to a number of people, or is initiated by those fortunate enough to know others who possess sufficient kindness and acceptance which allows them to soar high above their own pride and fears.

I have many memories from my childhood that are largely untarnished by evil and the very first memory I have of God was around five years old when yes, my mother again, asking me to bring something for her when I really wanted to continue my game of 'marbles.' This was the best game in the world and I was much too busy beating the boys at their own game but she kept imploring me to come, when she suddenly declared; "Only those children who are obedient to their mothers will get to be with Jesus in heaven." I recognise once more, though not at the time but in view of maturity that, my mother was setting the conditions of my self-worth which would become the proverbial 'albatross' around my neck for much of my adult life. It was all about how good I was in terms of what I did for others and I am confident she was naïve in her admonishments but many children assume what they are taught and if not corrected, will invariably cause them much heartache throughout their lives. I abandoned my marbles and winnings and ran faster than an athlete hurtling through bolts of lightning and in no time, I was there.

I remain thankful I grew up in an age of relative innocent and was so protected it was unhealthy as I became an adult. I did not even know the real difference between boys and girls; I simply saw people with long hair in beautiful hand-made dresses and miserable bowed legged ones always bemoaning their lot in khaki shorts and orange T-Shirts. I understood the things that were of value to me as a child and I learned to cherish them. My mother, the strongest and most determined woman I have ever known and my courageous and disciplined sister Carol, who was more like a second mother to us all; my recalcitrant brothers in particular. But I remain grateful that my brothers, though often unruly and disobedient, excelled in the long unbearable evenings as we took advantage of the darkness and would sit together patiently on the cool marble floor as they taught me to read around a small table assisted by our faithful kerosene oil lamp.

Naturally, the oil in our lamp would need replenishing from time to time, just as in the exact way that the human body needs to be replenished with sustenance in order that it may continue to function effectively since; everything in creation is of limited capacity. There is however, an unlimited and inexhaustible power which remains undiminished and this same power allows each believer to draw from the source of its flow. It is from this action that we become empowered to face every physical, spiritual and emotional challenge and where we are permitted to stand instead of the inevitable fall. This is supported in Ephesians 6:13; "Therefore put on the full armour of God, so that when the day of evil comes, you may be able to stand your ground, and after you have done everything, to stand. Stand firm then, with the belt of truth buckled around your waist, with the breastplate of righteousness in place, and with your feet fitted with the readiness that comes from the gospel of peace." Christ came to the world to reveal God to humankind and that revelation is a Contiuum. In the midst of this revelation, I neither resist nor do I question the unquestionable for I know that it is God who keeps my 'lamp' burning as stated by the David in Psalm 18:28; "You, Lord, keep my lamp burning; my God turns my darkness into light." Invariably, whatever good and noble pathways I seek, God will be along those same highways and he will become my light in every dark and threatening space. This journey with God is different, it does not feel like a journey because as physical beings, our walk alongside God only happens in the spiritual dimension where he inhabits and we are graciously permitted to do so because of his Holy Spirit.

I remain pragmatic and allow the world to progress and at the same time not to become wholly dependent upon its instructions concerning moral guidance. If anyone should stumble as they negotiate through particular difficulties, it is important to acknowledge that this is acceptable from time to time since none are perfect and all human aspirations are lower than the angels; "We are men and not angels, we walk on earth not in heaven." There are so many individuals who wish they could be good but are unable to find the appropriate point of entry. There is an expression in my culture; "If you cannot do good things, refrain from doing evil ones." It is by far the strongest people who prefer to stand alone for the right than to be with a stampeding herd pursuing the wrong, for whenever a person follow those whose intentions are largely against the populous, they invariably become ostracised and so, are no different to the ones who chose to stand alone. I refuse emphatically to set my standards high above the clouds because, I would be beyond the reach of anyone whose help I may need from time to time. I remain grounded in my locus and firmly within my principles. I have never wished to become another person, assuming his or her identity and living his or her life. My father used to say; "Yu nuh kno how parson get 'im gown," which simply means, we must not be envious of the achievements of another person, for only they know what they have sacrificed in order to achieve their status or possessions.

Similarly, no one would wish for my life since, they have no idea what it comprises of, or what I value most and what are my defining virtues and humiliations. I have conquered mountains and have walked in valleys through blinding tears but none of these compare with the boldest thing that I believe I have ever done. The boldest thing that I have ever done in my life was not the day I decided to put an end to the teasing and torment by the girls at my high school in Manchester.

When I arrived from Jamaica my English was broken, along with many of my dreams; Manchester was wet, cold and appeared very harsh and ugly to me. I thought all the trees were dead but it was December and winter was a totally unknown concept to me. I thought going to school would alleviate some of the loneliness and uncertainty and opened up new pathways but every day I was teased relentlessly, because many of the girls saw me as 'strange,' compounding my sadness in a foreign and hostile environment. One day I was accosted by a girl and thrown down a flight of stairs much to the amusement of all those watching, this was a just another assault of an ever increasing list. I realised that this girl who had assaulted me was the most feeble in the year group and if I failed to defend myself, it would be 'open season' for everyone else; I knew if I did not fight today, a different person would come back and fight me every day that I was in school. I picked myself up and just when they thought I was about to walk away in shame, I grabbed her by her long black hair and effectively pulled her down the stairs from the position where she had thrown me; this was the only occasion where long hair was better on someone else than me, for once, I had the advantage.

That was a bold but foolhardy action which I hated but was compelled to do. Needless to say, from that moment I went through school with no further beatings and enjoyed the opportunities to learn from my wonderful teachers, leading to success in my CSE examinations at the end. Yet this was not the bravest thing that I have ever done. Neither was it the night I stopped alone on a deserted highway and offered help to a young man broken down at the side of the road. It wasn't the time I was seven years old and stooped down in the long grass to rest with my one year old nephew Andrew and gashed my leg open on a bed of broken bottles; seeing the blood gushing out and the white of the knee bone protruding, I calmly got him to climb onto my back and limped home to the horror of my mother and older sister and brothers. It was a horrific injury which they cleaned, packed with cooking salt and I was sent me to bed; the hospital was much too far away and stitches; what were they? I thought they were what my mother sewed into dresses as a seamstress!

It certainly wasn't the time I had to take my ten year old niece Sherine back to her family after the death of my mother. Sherine arrived to what she believed was my father's funeral but at the age of five, found herself clinging hopelessly to her mother Vivene as she was told she would not be going home with her again. My mother simply could not live alone after my father's death and she made a decision to 'adopt'

Sherine who was her youngest grandchild. This compounded the rawness of having just buried my father at the back of our home where the burial plot continued increasing while our numbers on the ground was rapidly depleting.

The healing for both Sherine and my mother began when we all left and returned to our various homes abroad. Sherine was the apple of her eyes and naturally her ears in everything; the phone, the doctor, the teachers, the bank manager, the pastor and all those with whom she did her business routinely. This was Sherine's life for almost six years until the death of my mother in February two Thousand and Nine. I remember the days following my mother's funeral and how numb everyone was feeling and as the time passed swiftly no one dared address the reality of this little girl being thrust back into a life of want and poverty.

My mother's death was unbearable in so many ways, for although she possessed a beautiful home, acres of land and many other assets, these things were no use to a ten year old child in deep crisis. The mountain ahead of us was too high, too wide and incredibly dark. I remember arriving for my mother's funeral after thirteen hours from

Manchester and went straight to the funeral home to look at her. Everyone told me to expect the worst but in my heart I had hoped for the best and that was exactly what I was given. I saw a peace in mama's face which was absent during her life and as I touched her hands stroking them in my usual way, they were still my mother's precious hands. I knew from the scars where she was accidentally burned many years earlier and it was when I touched her face that I knew she had entered a special rest.

Carol and I arranged every aspect of our mother's funeral from start to finish. We chose her coffin and dressed her in white silk from the Middle East. We chose the flowers, I wrote the eulogy and we chose the head stone on which I had a poem inscribed. We lead the mourners in the church and celebrated her life then carried her coffin to the car. I have not found it necessary to cry for the woman I have most loved and admired, yet almost every day I deliberate over my own fragile existence. I could never understand how my mother loved life so much with all her difficulties and challenges. Mama suffered from high blood pressure, diabetes, and survived breast cancer nineteen years after a mastectomy. She was deaf for forty years, partially sighted and finally died from bowel cancer; her life was over and to me, God's will had been fully accomplished. In all her life, none of her children ever saw her as disabled or less capable; she did everything and was excellent in all her undertakings.

Sherine and I collected her possessions, almost too many for the boot of a large estate car, considering when she arrived five years earlier with just one small rucksack. The entire day was a bleak one even though the midday sun shone at its most brilliant above us, the way ahead was a dark and foreboding one. We phoned ahead of our arrival and were met by a sea of children; even children who had started having children! By this time my heart was somewhere in my shoes and I could not coax it back into my chest however much I tried. Saying goodbye is fine when there is a supportive and trustworthy network but saying farewell to a vulnerable young girl who had no idea who would be ultimately caring for her was simply horrendous. This remains one of the bravest things that I have ever done but is still some distance behind the boldest action I have ever undertaken. Was it the day I was marched up a darkened stairway with a shot gun to my back and a hand grenade held to my head? I lived and was ecstatic! Since that time I have counted each step on every stairway I climb; every escalator, every hotel every house, every castle. I have memorised the number of every one in every place I have ever been. Every time I do this, I am grateful to be alive!

I can confirm that the boldest thing that I have ever done, was the day I asked God to forgive my sins, both secret and exposed transgressions. I asked him to insert himself permanently at my side, in the space that was manifestly vacant. I told him that it was perpetually occupied by those who used it to get close enough to maligned, covet and discourage me; of course he knew this, because he is God. It was at this point that I finally began to understand that, from the moment he filled the vacant space by my side, no one would be permitted to occupy it while he was there. This was the moment I learned of love, real uncompromised love and genuine forgiveness for myself and for those who had caused the greatest pain in my life. Real love and forgiveness is only made possible by the compassion of God who understands the fragile nature of each human life. I must humbly acknowledge that one of the paradoxes of God is that he seldom approves of those people I chose as friends, companions and lovers and regardless of who has caused pain in my life, I must forgive them in order that his forgiveness for me is complete and that the space beside me remain full and overflowing with his presence.

Remarkably, in the fulfilment of God's purposes within my life I must learn to be many things; joyful alone, lonely when I am pleased and to bear solitude and suffering with humility and dignity. I am encouraged by the fact that while I belong to God, I simply do not need the approval of anyone and throughout my life; God's love will continue to interrupt my journey in order that it flows in the direction of his choosing. Some may view this as foolhardy as opposed to bold but for me, it has been the only real definer in my life. In the past, my trust was based on perception and I would often be robbed of my joy. Now, I trust completely in what I cannot see, for when God opened my eyes to new possibilities, my mind and heart also opened to his powerful life changing revelations. This exposé positively impacts my dignity, humility and integrity and become priority to God who is willing me to flourish like never before. I enthusiastically assert that what I see in the world is only a fraction of my true reality.

For a majority of my life I have been imperceptible to many people but have been grateful to remain a whisper upon the breath of God. In the presence of God he affirms my humanity and each day his whisper becomes purer. While a number of people may find my assertions without logic, they are nevertheless the openings through doors leading to forgiveness and love. The idea of real forgiveness is way beyond the understanding of many people since, so few believe they have anything to be forgiven of, or indeed to forgive. I do not believe for one moment that I would have been able to forgive another human being had it not been for the divine power of God at work within my life. When he chose me, it wasn't simply that I may gain entry to eternal life but that I should grow in wisdom and live the merits and virtues of Christ. I am so grateful that God selected me and in turn has allowed me to choose him. In God I have found all the answers to my existence and these answers have transformed a once bleak view to an optimistic and hopeful life.

Of course I have searched for love all my life but not the 'love' men pursue when they desire the sensuality of a female but the love that supersedes this most basic obligation. Whenever I meet with God there is grace and tenderness, he is my king and I am arrayed in my pauper's gown, just momentarily, until I am touched by the splendour of his crown. The inexhaustible nature of love, its unrestrained orientations, though sadly lacking in those people from my past, remains life's defining privilege. Who could fail to be inspired by the way in which God defends his people? And in return I am strengthened to defend him against everything which makes a mockery of his sovereignty.

The fact that God is invisible does not make him any less real than my own reality, for in my struggles he simply asked me to disarm my fears, close my eyes and open my heart. If I imagine God to be 'small' enough to enter my heart and allow me to be transformed from one state to another, it is plausible that I am master of many things – visible and invisible. I believe that whatever the size of the mountains before me, that I am in fact, the one who possess the aptitude to reduce their sizes but should I imagine them to overwhelm me, I have already conceded defeat. When I imagine myself to be proud and supersize, it is at this time that my adversaries also inflate themselves against me. This thought may be in contrast to the convictions of Sir Edmund Hillary but I can imagine how he may have approached his chosen mountain; with equal amount of fear and respect. I am confident that whenever I proclaim my beliefs, I am in fact defining my own perfection; since it is from all such principles that my hopes arise.

The power of God at work in my life is the one thing that has brought me hope and whether I stand or fall, be triumphant or face defeat I know that the pursuit of excellence is a continuum. Sometimes the measure of a man or woman is not the prizes they are awarded for their endeavours but the fortitude they display when they have had their awards withdrawn. Some people find it so seamless to breech the rights and dignity of others. They simply refuse to acknowledge that everyone is guilty of malice and wrongdoing. There are some people whose record of offence should shame them into contrition but they continue regardless. I am aware of many human complexities and the intense nature of malice, hate and prejudices. I simply cannot abide those people who are always first at the scene of every public execution, those eager to accuse and throw insults and stones. If I must witness the degradation of another human being let me hold my head as low as my heart since that person may be in that position only a day ahead of me. So, whoever is without sin, step forward and throw the first stone?

"Family - Nothing Compares"

CHAPTER THREE

Pocket Full of Stones

The *Pericope Adulterae* is the traditional name for the famous passage in John 8:1-11, where Jesus rescued the woman who had been caught in the act of adultery. There is of course the customary confrontation between Jesus and the beguiling Scribes and overtly righteous Pharisees, presiding over whether the woman should be stoned to death, as was the tradition of the day. For the sorrowful and deeply contrite woman, this was a timely intervention by Jesus, who in His wisdom dispersed the crowds by shaming them, thus saving the woman's life. Towards the end of the passage in Chapter 10-11; Jesus straightened up and asked her. "Woman, where are they? Has no one condemned you?" "No one sir," she said. "Then neither do I condemn you,"- Jesus declared. "Go now and leave your life of sin." In this the final admonishment to the woman, Christ, being fully aware of the type of woman standing before him was neither prepared to reinforce his judgement of her, nor was he about to condemn her and so, by allowing her the opportunity to make a promise of a dramatic U-turn, she not only saved her life in that moment but for the future eschatological glory Christ promised.

There are so many instances when it would be simpler not to judge a particular situation, or indeed the action of another person, since human beings possess critical attitudes of others but seldom of themselves. Our own memory lapses seem to serve us well, as we become anaesthetised in regard to our own faults and weaknesses, it's worth remembering the words in Scripture, where Christ was speaking about the issue of 'faults,' not the ones we imagine to be in other people but the ones actually present within ourselves. It would seem there are far too many individuals who are so grossly preoccupied with the lives and concerns of others that they appear to know other people much better than themselves! I would be deeply ashamed if I knew so little of myself and so much of others, when in fact, what I declare to know of others is based upon imaginings and speculation.

A number of years ago I was invited onto a committee along with eleven other people, to give feedback regarding the performance of a number of local businesses. There was a lively mix of people from various backgrounds, although all were from middle-class upbringings, except me since, I consider myself classless as a Christian. I believe I have no need for class because it is mankind's standards, as opposed to God's standards. When Christ called me to himself, he called me from the trappings and allure of the world in order that I would advocate his truth, as I became fully immersed in his holy anointing and words. There was one lady in particular, Lara, who was more lively and friendly than the others and we eventually became quite friendly outside the group, meeting for the occasional lunch or coffee.

As a rule, I do not lunch with middle-class women, especially those who talk incessantly about their acquisitions and lifestyles; for me, this is boredom bordering onto misery. If I am really honest, I don't like lunch or coffee with women - full stop! I am much too comfortable in the company of my male companion and I have found that the opportunity to engage intellectually with a man is greater by far. While I possess a deep level of admiration for a handful of men, especially those driven by integrity and excellence in their chosen fields, I have admittedly, never found it easy to place trust in men such as these. Sadly, I would sooner fasten a giant fish hook through my tongue, after attaching it to the Sydney Harbour Bridge then hurling myself off than to trust any woman other than my sisters. Needless to say, this is merely my own opinion drawn from years of observations with both sexes. Lara was interested in all the visible details of my life. She seemed genuine and so, I did not feel I had to be overly guarded with certain aspects and so, was foolishly open regarding some of the lifestyle choices I made. It was a number of months before I realised this woman was less of a friend than a Russell's viper and was in fact, cataloguing every aspect of my life in order to use this information at a later date against me.

What transpired twelve months later was a bitter woman who had made a callous judgement against me and my family regarding the way we had chosen to live our lives. She was angry that I found a way to pray when she was hurting, since she had lost her faith completely. She was annoyed that I could choose freely and prioritise my life with fixed principles. She was also angry that, somehow I had broken through the stereotypical mould of what the 'world' expects of me and how I spoke and behaved. Okay, so, I did not live in a high rise apartment in an 'undesirable' neighbourhood, neither did I have five children by five different men. Instead of traversing back and forth through the jobseekers route and the benefits agency, I was travelling around the world with my companion and enjoying every adventure as though still a child.

I was both saddened and astonished the day she sent me a barrage of abusive test messages, suggesting she found my life style unacceptable; she simply could not reconcile the way I had chosen to live. Now, I was slightly confused at this point since, I am one of the most transparent people I know and while I do not, as a rule share personal issues with people outside my immediate family, I have never found it necessary to deceive or behave with double-standards towards anyone, not even obnoxious individuals like her. Initially, I was surprised at her action but upon reflection, it all made perfectly good sense. Lara, an Oxford graduate, living in a three million pound mansion in a stockbroker belt, with all the trappings of success which she believes is a privilege for her and not for others - this was the real conflict! There is one subtle difference between me and a vast number of people I knew and have deliberately left behind since, unlike them, all the material possessions which surrounds me, are by no means the ones which defines my life. My life is defined in every sense by my love and understanding of Jesus Christ as Lord and it is for this reason that I set my own standards and live effortlessly within them. I simply do not care for wealth, status or possession. Of course, it is better by far to live well than to be in want. The other minor difference between us is the fact that, I am only too aware of a life of want and deprivation but Lara's idea of being disadvantaged was to have her top of the range sports car scratched going through the car wash. She simply judged me as being unworthy of the life and situation God had granted me, not because I am good, but because God is good. She does not want anyone to measure up to her level, especially someone like 'me.'

Although I have failed on many occasions to understand resentment and jealousy, I have learnt to treat it with indifference. The story of the unforgiving human race is steeped in so much angst and negativity. There is always someone ready to dismantle another, simply because their face does not fit the stereotypical images. Joseph, for example, was thrown into a pit by his own brothers, only to be rescued by a contrite Reuben who later sold him as a slave to Egypt. Families are no different; some of the most difficult relationships begin and end in families. My father used to say; "Seven brothers, seven different minds." It's incredible sometimes how a person who is essentially bad can produce something so pure and so good, yet it happens. To think that Lucifer [the devil], was in fact the angel of music before he was hurled out of his position; it cannot bear thinking that; someone so repugnant was in charge of the heaven's orchestras! Sadly, Lara was a completely self-absorbed woman, who could not see the endless possibilities within others because they were absent within her.

The amazing paradox in the story of Joseph being sold as a slave in Egypt was the fact that his brothers had to beg his forgiveness years later when their own situation had changed from prosperity to dire want and poverty. The objects of our repulsion at various points in our lives have a way of returning at an unsuspecting hour and force us to accept our own failings. Not surprising, even the devil, has to bow in humility at the mention of name of Jesus. This is the mystery and wonder of the creator, from where I continue to prosper and grow, not because I am good but because I seek goodness for others, way above my own selfish motivations and desires.

I have often been reluctant to talk openly about myself since; there is not a great deal to capture the imagination of those who are merely curious or idle gossips. The world is full of people who share a great deal in common but so few are able to understand the depth and complexities present within other people's lives. I would like to illustrate this thought very briefly. A number of years ago I was invited on a shopping trip with an acquaintance, who I am delighted to say never became a friend. The day in town was reasonably fruitful and friendly but I could see the increased frustration on her face each time she pressed me for opinions of other women to whom she was connected. At the end of the afternoon she dropped me home and her parting words were simply; "I am not taking you out again you are so boring, you have nothing to say about anyone." As far I was concerned that was perfection.

I am only too aware that, whoever gossips to you will also be a gossip of you. Jesus said; "Take the beam out of your own eyes so that you can see clearly to tell your brother to take the mote out of his eyes." Matthew7:3. It never fails to astonish me just how deep the Lord Jesus would go into the hearts and minds of ordinary men and women. Just imagine having a friend like him constantly by your side, reminding you of all life's salient issues. We can see in Ephesians 4:15; "Instead, speaking the truth in love, we will grow to become in every respect the mature body of him who is the head, that is, Christ." Unlike Christ, there are so few people who possess good arbitration or negotiation skills, in fact very few people are thoughtful in their dispensation of advice or criticism. They are often pre-occupied with the lives of other people and ready without the least provocation to throw insults, stones and meteorites at whoever they manage to apprehend. I am a pragmatic person in many ways and is much more task oriented than people. I immediately know who approves of my presence and who finds being around me unsettling. I don't have enough energy or time to worry about what pleases or irritate others and my riposte remains the same; if you don't like me or being in my company, then don't be. We all have a choice. Of course in public spaces I have to walk through crowds of people laughing, enjoying life and just being themselves – this is fine but in my home, my scared shelter, I will defend my right to choose who is permitted to enter.

I am sure there are a number of people who understands what a home truly is but I will briefly say what it is for me. The most important thing about my home is that it provides the obvious safety and security that I have always sought. It is within its walls where love is granted the freedom to grow away from the glare and scrutiny of everyone. It is where I discuss tête-à-têtes about treasured goals, hopes and aspirations.

It is the only place where I am free from pretentions and can step inside the realness of self. My home is the place of light that defines the truth of every meaningful reality, whether day or night. My home is also where, if I choose, can deliberate in uninterrupted silence and the world is none the wiser. For me, it is not the cost of the soft furnishings or the price of the bricks or stones but the softness in his heart, the gentleness in his touch, the vivacity in his eyes whenever I call his name and the reassurance of his smile. It is from home that all my plans are supported, my dignity upheld and where all my dreams are encouraged to grow. Whether we are encouraged to be strong in our homes or just be ourselves, we are authorised to stand in the midst of every mighty adversary. The biggest challenge to all of us is not whether we will receive the attention of the world and maintain it but whether in fact, one single member of our own household will believe a single word we utter. My home is not a place of conflict neither is it a place where antagonists are welcome but is exclusively reserve for family, friends and appreciative guest.

I have often been surprised by the unwarranted actions of many people, and one such incident has proved to be a titanic turning point in my life. It was Christmas Eve a number of years ago, and I was certainly not expecting to be verbally assaulted and condemned in my own home by yet another, angry middle-class woman who sadly, possessed a diminished view of herself as well as others; me in particular. Her anger merely highlighted her growing insecurities which were present long before I became the focus of 'blame.' In her eyes I may be guilty of a number things but I am not guilty of those things which became fractured in my absence during the early stages of her life. In recent years I have barely given a second glance to the stones others have thrown at me, I have simply grown tired with the anger and misaligned feelings of others. In my life I have learned to look critically at myself and pursue the answers I seek. If they are not forthcoming then, it simply means there are no answers to those issues and so, I must find ways to create at least one further meaningful question.

I continue to live a victorious life and I am constantly reminding myself that; "I not outstanding because I have a pair of legs but I am standing out because of my outstanding faith in God." My life, gifted to me by God is a continuous celebration, as I allow Christ to inform every aspect concerning direction, meaning and determination, which is by no means a matter of chance. I am grateful for the kindnesses that has been shown to me, often by strangers and saddened by the hostility I have encountered from 'friends,' family and neighbours. I have often met the direst set of challenges from within my own family since, those within striking distance knows exactly where my weaknesses are and how best to breech them, for in my naïve and trusting attitude towards others, I unfortunately allow them closer to me than ever.

Do I stand above reproach? God forbid! For even I have been guilty and found seriously lacking. I abhor retribution even though my life is not exemplified in goodness. I simply wish to be treated as I have treated others and will continue to praise the courage of those who instructed me with kindness whenever I have faltered. I continue to thank God that he saw something in me when the world only saw a source to off-set their derision and disparagement. This place of hardships is a fertile ground and although no one would wish to build from such foundations in these conflicting places, the majority of my learning and strength has come as a result of many such trials. I stand firm and embrace every good principle from where my life is guided. I see from Scripture and my life experiences that the general tendency of human nature is to dislike 'bad' people but the reality is they hate 'good' ones more, much more; the Lord Jesus supports this thought! Christ simply refused to deny the truth and kindness to others which was denied him and at no time did he compromise the goodness and truth present within him and neither must I. In my life I seek only honesty and integrity; first from myself and then from others. I would simply not wish to ask something from another person which I could neither do, nor had any intention to fulfil myself.

I have few pretentions, neither am I proud; vanity displeases God and with pride, one always falls. I know for when I fell, it was hurtful and demeaning but the decisions leading to that situation was mine entirely. Similarly, I think back a while ago where a Malaysian student, accidentally caught up in the riots of two thousand and eleven and just when he believed that he was being rescued by two seemingly 'Good Samaritans,' he was in fact being robbed of both his possessions and his dignity. This was an unfortunate event for him but we must be bold concerning the unpleasant events we create within our own lives. At some point in every person's life they will either fail or fall but this is inevitable, for it is in our falling or failing where God catches us and makes us his very own.

I have endured suffering and overcome adversity but remain grateful that it has been in these situations that my character was formed. It was during such times when God granted me the knowledge I needed to re-evaluate the depth of my hidden strengths. I know I have escaped a lot of demons of the past and although I have fallen on a number of occasions, I got up each time because I know I was born to keep standing. There are those who seem to prefer a horizontal position to a vertical one and invariably become ensnared in the irretrievable traps of dependency. The misplaced generation who rely heavily upon sympathy and medication - to wake up, to sleep, eat, to stop eating, to dream, to stop dreaming, to laugh to cry, to stay still and to keep moving. A generation lost in renunciation to the support mechanism directly in place to curtail their cognition and development as fully actualised human beings. Even so, humans are well equipped with every sense to possess and dispossess nations, rulers, friends and neighbours. They are complicated and intricate in every sense.

I have seen one person cried because they had to eat an inferior meal one night and another cried because a child many thousands of miles away had nothing to eat for days. I have seen some hopeful and expectant because they could smile through each bitter tear and those who danced simply, to be set free.

Dancing is like Love: the more Intimate, the more Satisfying

Human emotions can be surprisingly misunderstood, for what moves one person to tears may have another in fits of laughter. "For those people that think, the world is a comedy and to those that feel, it's a tragedy." Horace Walpole (1717-1797). Regardless of whether a person is always processing everything demonstrably or subjectively, everyone possesses the potential that will either empower them to move beyond their prejudices or permanently disable them in their fears. From here, a number of people are able to relinquish out-dated views and become more compassionate and supportive to others. I have a firm belief in the power of actions. It is in such outward displays that I am permitted to expose my vulnerabilities, which are by no means a shows of weaknesses but is unequivocally, a major display of strength. In this display of strength that has been more obvious to others than to me over a number of years, it would appear that those observing me have been acutely aware of a variety of gifts I possessed. Many of these perceived 'gifts' are directly attributed to my culture since, it is a pre-requisite for women to be multi-dimensional in almost everything but it is my love of dancing that was most perceptible. Dancing for me cannot be justifiably enunciated with mere words yet, if I could give it a sense of reality it would be defined thus; dancing is like love, the more intimate, the more satisfying. When I dance and begin to move, the freedom inspired in me is visible with every single step. It is like newly aroused passion, lingering past the prelude of dawn. Dancing is my footsteps before they hit the ground. It is the contagion to which I seek no remedy. Dancing is my secret joy and my susceptible delight. Of course for me dancing is an art form since, it was within the walls of my home that I was able to perfect my attempts to dance like never before and once perfected, I was confident to dance in view of others. It was my love of dance that gave me the opportunity to spend an evening with a vulnerable but incredibly high spirited young woman.

It was almost my birthday and to celebrate, there was an arrangement made a few weeks earlier to spend an evening dancing with a number of my closest friends. Of course this pattern would be repeated in the future where another person would choose to spend an evening with me, only on that occasion, it was actually my birthday. On the evening of our outing no one turned up, I simply could not believe that this was happening and as I was about to slump into deep anxiety there was a knock at my door. There she stood laughing in the pouring rain with her clothes and long auburn hair soaking wet. It was Marina.

Although she was only nineteen years old she possessed wisdom that would shame many people twice her age. She had worked with me for almost four years and was a little wild and very reckless. She was a young woman who had shouldered a number of deeply troubling issues and had left home at the age of fifteen and was living nearby with a very supportive family. We headed into town and had an enjoyable evening of non-stop dancing from the time we arrived until we left in the early hours and for once another person had clearly out- danced me! As we arrived back to my house she asked me faithfully to give her a wakeup call on the morning of her next shift at work then headed home.

This would be the last time I would see her alive. Admittedly, no amount of foresight is ever believed until it has come to pass, and by this time, much too late for any measured action to be implemented. As promised, I called her only to hear what I feared to some extent but was hopeful, as always of a different outcome. "Sheryl, Marina is dead and we are waiting for the police." She was dead and that would never be reversed. Dancing with me that evening was her farewell, to the life I believe she could no longer live. I fail to understand why she chose to end her life at such a young age or indeed, whether like the coroner's speculations suggested, she did in fact intend to end her life or that it was just a tragic 'accident.' The real answers went with her but at least I did uncover something a little sad some time later on, that she had in fact sabotage our evening so that none of the others were present.

This became a significant turning point in my life as I was acutely aware that my gift of discernment and foresight was more accurate than I had initially thought, and that such a gift deserved respect and was to be used more effectively in the lives of others, not just within my own. Much of the suffering I have witnessed around me from a young age has always been attributed to a lack of love. It is a fact that whatever else may be missing from a person's life, if love is present they are better equipped to meet and overcome many challenges. It is for this reason I am so aware that if I do not have love, I simply cannot find my way and everything becomes a corpus of blinding darkness. Since love is the only platform of absolute truth. It is from where all other truths must be defined and it is the beginning of life and the impelling force that equips each person with adequate strength to trust in the kindness of strangers. Love is the light that penetrates every dark place. It reminds me of my childish fingers stroking the soft brown skin of my grandma, soft velvet and ageless in its perfectness. It is the hopefulness through adversity and the one known source of goodness and calm. I know what love is but not because I have an inexorable amount hidden in the depths of my heart but because God is love and the one who remains my wisest and humblest teacher.

I remembered my father saying; "The humblest calf always gets the most milk." This means that humility always reaps rewards in life. Farmers always take good care of their cattle since, they depend on them for their sustenance as much as they rely on them for his livelihood; there is an unacknowledged mutuality of trust and interdependency. There is much knowledge in nature, if we but take the time to stop and learn. As a child, I too would love to watch the calves with their mothers and those who were too boisterous or aggressive would find it difficult to make a connection and take milk from her. The little one however, who approached the mother with fear and timidity, was always the one she allowed to take the most milk from her. In much the same way, humility and love are aspirations of the same thing; one must actively be involved with the other, not forcing, not demanding but with mutual respect and understanding. As an adult there were times when I felt the least loved of my mother's seven children, [perhaps this feeling was just another undefined level of unfounded insecurity] but in spite of this, I learned to become infinitely loving and forgiving. I loved my mother more than life. Was she perfect? No! Not in the least but it was for this reason I loved her beyond my understanding. I did not need my father's love or his approval since he was just someone always at a distance except on the one occasion when his care for me overcame those many years of absence.

I arrived in Newcombe Valley after a long and exhausting journey from Manchester a number of years ago and was really pleased to see both my parents looking healthy and joyful as they welcomed my family and me. As a very young child I was often plagued with a number of minor annoying illnesses which resulted in me being taught to self-administer natural remedies to aid a speedy recovery. There were two in particular that made my life miserable when they attacked me; tonsillitis being the most prolific offender. The other condition was painful and annoying but I routinely self-administered ancient remedies which always seem to halt the symptoms. I remain uncertain why my tonsillitis was left untreated for so many years but this is routine in my culture, since, if something is not killing you; you leave it alone! As I got older my tonsillitis became more aggressive and I simply kept traversing backwards and forwards to my long suffering doctor in Stockport.

The night of my arrival to see my parents, I went to bed at a reasonable time only to be awakened a few hours later by the most acute pain in my throat. "Oh no, not an attack of tonsillitis here in the middle of nowhere," I thought. On top of all this there was the usual power cut and my disturbance woke the entire house. I remember my father approaching me with a candle, to illuminate the darkness surrounding me and as he looked down my throat, was aghast by the size of those white ghouls, advancing across my airways. He calmly lit another candle and told me not to worry and to be patient as he would be right back. In no time he came bearing a gift, which was to become the greatest gift that he has given me in my entire life. I was directed to gargle, then drink and get back to bed and for the first time I obeyed him, doing exactly as I was told.

I slept remarkably well and awoke in the morning to calm in my body and throat, the likes to which I have not experienced for some time. The white spots on my tonsils had vanished, so had the swelling and all the symptoms. That was ten years ago and since that night I have never had tonsillitis again. When I consider how it had preyed upon me between two to four times annually for over thirty years, I am so grateful that I was finally free of this wretched condition. I never asked my father what was mixed in that potion but I have a good idea. I thank God that gifts have always come to me when the need was at its most acute and because I was obedient and trusted my father in that moment, I was made free.

One of my key observations   regarding the peculiarities and behaviours of my father in his later years has actually revealed to me that I am in fact more like him in some ways than I am my mother. My father was a loner who chose gardening and animals in his leisure time over people; these are two of my passions and although I love people ardently I enjoy regular space and distance between me and them. He was highly critical of others and the life choices they made; although I try not to be critical of others I remain excruciatingly critical of myself. My father never drank alcohol in his life, unlike me who was as equally poor a consumer of alcohol as I am a swimmer. I simply hate the taste and smell and the inevitability of loss of control and dignity and so after a few attempts in my younger years of trying to apprehend the 'wow factor,' found it decidedly insufferable and tedious. I find getting intoxicated on life is more thrilling by far since, from this position of clarity I can observe and recall every small detail and continue to make sense of everything way past the morning. For me, this exceeds the misery brought on by recurrent inebriation. Where my father had struggled to read and write, I decided I would be the change in the family and began reading as soon as I could and every night would sit with appreciation around the oil lamp while being taught by my two older brothers. He was a man whose idea of perfection far exceeded his intentions to put those thoughts into meaningful practice. I am hopeful in my pursuit for perfection, not because I believe I possess the required virtues to achieve it but simply because the one possessing me is unquestionably perfect. He cared sporadically for others on one hand but was selfishly determined on the other.

What can I say here? I care deeply and passionately about a variety of things and refuse to allow others to define my destiny, thus may appear selfish, when in fact I am simply being autonomous. He was simply like every other human being with the potential for both good and evil, just like me. Did I love my father? The pain of love, the anguish it brings when it cannot be perfectly defined. I simply do not know the answer to this question but the one thing that has propelled my life forward is the fact that everything I was not given by people, I was able to secure in God - the perfect father I wanted became an on-going reality.

I do not understand how imperfect beings can set such high standards of perfection. I have no idea what perfection looks like since I have never seen God, the only perfect being because, perfection is not an enduring human virtue. The idea of perfection began in my family at a very early age. Of course, I would try and understand what constitute this ideal but knowing full well that I had often struggled to feel as valued as others, perfection would continue to bypass me due to a growing number of insecurities. There were times when I was compared unfavourably to others in my family and although I don't believe it was from a malicious orientation, it nevertheless exacerbated a number of fears as I matured. The fact that I was the fifth of seven children seemed to me the perfect alignment, since in Hebrew culture, five is an auspicious number, meaning grace.

I cannot simplify the meaning of grace and would never attempt to do so and the fact that I was born on a 'Tuesday,' reminds me of that old rhyme; "Tuesday's child is full of grace," so, with so much grace around me, I can never abandon my pursuit for both grace and perfection. My father was far from perfect and admittedly, I was deeply hurt by his refusal to walk down the aisle with me on my wedding day; instead, I had to ask David Williams, an Englishman to insert himself at my side in the space left vacant by my father. I could have asked one of my own countrymen but that would have been more painful so, my only option was to choose someone who was nothing like my father. My father's refusal to be at my wedding was the simple fact that my husband-to-be was a white Englishman. He simply could not accept this inter-racial union. For many years after my marriage, I was excluded from the affections of a number of my family and had to work extremely hard to gain re-entry. I cannot condemn another human being simply because they failed to provide the answers I sought, only myself for not living the questions. Naturally, I would be a step closer to freedom if I could simply declare a resounding yes - I loved my father. But I cannot at this moment, I will say however that, I loved his wisdom for others; he just had little for himself. This is always a tragedy in every human life.

My mother on the other hand had sufficient wisdom for the entire village! Her determination, her resolve, her character and her formidable personality made bypassing her wishes a matter of life or death. When mama said, 'no,' all discussions ended. One vexed word from her transported me into a deep paralysis of helplessness. My mother's eyes were naturally her ears and when she did not wish to answer, she simply closed them. I had issues concerning mama's strength but when it worked for us, no one stood against us but when it was against us only God could defend us! Yet despite all this, I admired her values and principles. If my mother had shown signs of weaknesses during her life she would have been crushed in a world she could not hear.

I am grateful that at every stage of my life I was always happiest next to her - as a child on her knees, as a teenager lying draped across her arms and as a woman, kneeling by her feet with my head on her lap while she played with my ears. It was on such an occasions when she was stroking my petite ears that she always found so perplexing, because even though the rest of my body was growing, my ears refused to budge a single inch and it was at this point where she looked at me and said, "Musmus, as a baby you entangled my feet, Sophie, as a woman you entangled my heart and now you are entangling my feet again musmus and these tiny ears, they are telling me of a challenging and extremely difficult life ahead for you."

My mother was always forthright in her prophetic revelations of future hardships concerning her children. Of course there were times, I did not wish to hear of continued struggles but the fact that she was nearly always right compelled me to pay attention every time. I loved her and decided never to disobey her. Our relationship, though far from perfect was one based entirely on trust. My mother would often remind me of my vulnerabilities - what better place to be reminded. These moments are my enduring memories of unadulterated happiness. Whenever her strong arms embraced me, I knew heaven was closer than ever and although hell was often within my mother's mouth, in moments like these, heaven was within both.

If ever I was hurting, I would simply travel see my mother wherever she was in the world. As soon as I knelt down by her side and placed my head upon her knees, my healing began. I have been healed in almost every instance throughout my life each time I have fallen in humility upon my knees. There are all types of 'calves' born to many different mothers and just as my mama used to say to me; "Dawg mawga but im hed big," when translated means, the dog is meagre but his head is big - which simply means, you may be small in stature [with miniscule ears] but you are a smart child.

There are so many people who are aggressive and demanding and who believe that everything should be granted them regardless of effort, [like the angry middle-class woman who stormed into my home that

Christmas Eve for the sole purpose of abusing me], I don't believe for one moment that love is an inherent human right and gifted free of cost to all but in every way must be proved over and over again. Furthermore, I do not necessarily believe that it is always within our families that we are most loved. How many of us would realistically choose the people who are permanently attached to us as: step-children, sister-and brother-in-laws, cousins, nieces, aunts, uncles, nephews, or even brothers or sisters? Perhaps I have been fortunate at one level, because I have been given brothers and sisters that I love as much as myself. There are a number of people who do not share my blessing and for them; family is an unbearable reality. I take a naturally optimistic view of everything in my life and see the merits of harmony as well as disputes. A majority of the lessons I have learnt in life began in my family and even though I could at times throttle one of my own siblings, or some other obscure relation, I would never allow another person to do the same to them. While they may not always approve of my words and actions they have the assurance that in our struggles to become autonomous beings, my regard for them remains largely unaffected.

If anyone is reluctant to walk alongside me because my views have changed dramatically, does not necessarily mean I will force my own beliefs unto them since, this would be totally unacceptable. I have never witnessed a rich man refusing to walk alongside a poor one merely because of their different values but we simply must learn to become more accepting and tolerant of those beside us. He may have objections regarding the merits of walking in his companion's shoes since, the exercise may be totally unproductive but choosing to walk alongside another person can bring both enlightenment and wisdom. In every instance where someone has chosen to come alongside me, I remain grateful. For in their decision to allow themselves to be vulnerable, they are also permitting me to a better person than before. These are a formidable type of people who are full of resolutions for their own lives and kind-heartedness for the lives of others. They possess love which is sincere, as it is neither founded upon needs or desires but is instituted by a natural regard for each human life.

Bishop Samuel is one such individual. He is a unique man and has been the only one I have known that, whenever he opens his mouth, 'fire' comes out. Yes and before you ask, of course I love him! He reminds me of a mythical dragon, setting everything ablaze around itself, and without observing, consumes itself with the intensity of its own heat. While it may be completely acceptable to have a 'dragon' walk alongside me, I must first appraise the merits of allowing him to do so since, I have no desire to be enveloped by a forceful conflagration at any future date. Bishop Samuel may appear quite unassuming but is a man on fire for truth. In recent years he has become one of my most influential teachers and while I could unpack a number of his vices as opposed to his virtues, this would save no purpose whatsoever; since I deal with the reality before me and God deals with the vices before him.

Although like me, he is not perfect by any means, I have nevertheless been encouraged by his ministry of power and healing. I cannot fail to acknowledge his compassion when others displayed hostility and derision towards me. He continued to encourage me towards the fulfilment of my destiny and it was from his meticulous sermons that I was able to make my own appraisals on the matter that continues to impact me and will continue to do so into the foreseeable future: the question of 'pure love.'

I have to reiterate the fact that I am a very pragmatic person, one who understands a number of complex debates and issues but those that initially appear the simplest have become the most problematic to disentangle. In my culture there is no shame in poverty nor is there any in failure – only in failure to try. There is however failure in falling. It is for this reason that I struggle to accept the rather absurd notion of, 'falling in love,' what is this supposed to mean in any culture? By virtue of the fact that one has to fall into something is a clear indication that they have immediately rendered themself useless! If I should fall into a pit I would need rescuing and what if the one rescuing me is less fit for purpose than me? This same rule applies to almost every eventuality when one is walking in total blindness. Every time I have fallen I have acquired a number of injuries – although not always physical but of course ones pride is always first to be wounded and it is for this reason that I prefer to stand vertical and resilient in love. When I am able to stand in love at the inception, I will remain standing throughout it all, through the traumas, heartaches, disappointments and the betrayals often leading to the inevitable separations.

I know that love is painful, both from observation and participation. I have observed the anguish of those who believe themselves affected by its power and those rendered powerless by its affects. Although I can display love by my actions towards others, love has nevertheless, remained the most mysterious component of the universal triangle: God, love and humankind. In this triangle, God and love takes the prominent positions yet, people's ideas surrounding love has been largely developed from their continued associations with each other. I have often doubted the authenticity of a particular thing that had its origin in a pure source only to become contaminated by many other impure origins. This undoubtedly leads me to question its legitimacy and purpose. Imagine that love had lost its essence, its loveliness – what other virtues could be assigned as the platform of truth in the world?

I believe it is love that provides the platform for excellence and perfection, even though not immediately explicit. I know that nearly all human life begins with an attempt at 'love,' though some observers may debate this thought. I simply do not believe that everything that looks like love is in fact love. A human being forms the final part of the mysterious triangle but due to a lack of knowledge regarding the position God asserts in our midst, Christ was chosen to fill the increasing vacuum created by us. I accept that not everyone will be able to understand or accept my beliefs since they may appear rather implausible. This is no different for me when trying to understand some of the values to which others may cling. I am simply not here to throw stones or to dismantle those values but only to reaffirm those things that are of value to me. The world can be a hostile and threatening place on a daily basis and it would be foolish for me to add to that despair. I believe myself to be a different person than the one I was a few years ago and it is my intention to become a better person each day as my life presses towards its conclusion. I am only too aware of the few dark places I was foolish enough to enter in my life and if I am aware of my past transgressions, Christ is aware of my need to seek his forgiveness but of course this must begin on the winding road of obedience.

Christ is never silent on culpability and while I may have attempted to exonerate myself from fault and blame, it is an acknowledged thought that all human beings are guilty of every type of transgression. Of course there has never been another who exemplified obedience and humility quite like the Lord Jesus and through his divine nature men and women from all creeds would become free from internal bondage to sin and oppression. Christ was able to dispossess the possessed, forgiving sin wherever he found it and setting free those with faults and addictions. Of course no one wants a 'know it all' to upstage them and it was for this reason that the pious high priests and teachers of the law became so eager to convict him and it was ultimately their mendacious smears against Jesus which led to his crucifixion and death as a common criminal, hanging outside the city walls in the midst of two thieves. I refuse to be further surprised by the extent human beings will allow themselves to be deprived, for when we sink below the surface of truth we become destitute of all life giving endorsements. Yet, we see clearly from the crucifixion reality of an innocent man – an unbelievably good man who was brutally executed simply for speaking truth over institutional lies.

He was mocked and ridiculed, since he had raised others from the grave but when his moment of shame descended, he was judged as pitiful since, he could not remove himself from the cross. The enduring hope in this universal triangle of God, love and humankind, was the fact that it was not hopelessness but love that kept Christ on the cross and this universal triangle has now become a personal circle; the Lord Jesus our personal saviour, bringing the purity and meaning back to love.

I do not care for the 'execution' of another human being, only their exaltation. If I cannot feed my enemies, neither will I never sit or walk alongside my friends. If I should choose to fill my pocket with stones it would be in the hope that if I should lose my way 'out,' they may be left as a trail in order to find my way back. I continue to ask pertinent questions of myself in order that I may be able to ask them on behalf of others. There so many people who have forgiven me and in so doing have empowered me to forgive others. The 'pocket' full of stones which accompanied many of the witnesses who came to mock and gloat as Christ's life ebbed away on the cross must have never once asked a single question concerning matters of principle or conscience. The 'crowd' mentality pushed them beyond the peripheries of hate and malice. In Isaiah 53:4-6, are the most profound words of truth and wisdom:-

"Surely he took up our pain and bore our suffering,

Yet we considered him punished by God, stricken by him and afflicted.

But he was pierced for our transgressions; he was pierced for our iniquities;

The punishment that brought us peace was on him,

And by his wounds we are healed.

We all, like sheep have gone astray,

Each of us has turned to our own way;

And the LORD has laid on him

The iniquity of us all."

Isaiah 53:4-6

Immediately my thoughts are focussed on the current discussion, [asking the right questions]. These are expressed by Isaiah in verse eight of the same chapter; "By oppression and judgement he was taken away.

Yet who of his generation protested? There are so many 'good' men and women willing to watch innocent lives crushed and denigrated every day but do nothing, a disheartening reality in every sense. In every period of history there have been miscarriages of justice, where a great number of people have suffered under brutal and oppressive regimes but those largely unaffected continued their lives irrespective.

There are so many who are protected from stones being hurled at them but are often the first to step forward and hurl them back at others. I am uncertain whether apathy or cowardice is the disabling factors in many instances but what has become abundantly clear to me in my observations over a number of painstaking years is one major revelation and is the fact that many people prefer lies than fighting for truth. Since truth has a way of unhinging the realities of many people, causing unsubstantiated fears and irrational behaviour. Imagine this behaviour being maliciously demonstrated by a person who steps forward to throw stones at someone whose defences was rigorously fortified and protected? If the tables were to be turned, this person would be terrified, who wouldn't be? Since any retaliations against them would have devastating consequences as their 'glass houses' provides them with little protection from any assaults. These people prefers obscurity to reality, since in their diminished sense of right and wrong, good and evil, they only permit themselves to see half realities and are comfortable to absolved themselves of blame. So, whether we operate on full actualisations or half-hearted perceptions; can we successfully move beyond inadequate reflections?

Sheryl & Valerie

Janet & Juliet

CHAPTER FOUR

Beyond Reflection

Mirror, Mirror

Who do you see looking?

Looking back at you;

Looking back at me?

Do you see who I see?

Do you see me?

How many times have you wished rhetorically that you could change what you saw, or alter what you had just heard? There are some very exasperating actualities that play over and over again in life and one of them is when you see or hear what you had least expected. The amount of times I have stood before a mirror and thought; "Ouch, I hate what I see." Yet, as I dare to observe more closely, I recognise that the years have been kinder than I had initially thought and the grudging gaze that would have taken seconds in my earlier years, has now become a lasting, quizzical search. I am routinely impelled beyond my indistinct exterior into a deeply guarded space which stirs me to accept the image presently before me. When I take time to examine more closely and move away from the conceited edges, I sometimes find myself transported to new revelations in that precise moment of rectitude. At times, a mirror can act much in the same way as our conscience. It reflects back to us a little of what is visible to most people and much of what is hidden from all. The hidden things that we dare not think, dare not embrace, dare not live and those we dare not speak. When we speak them we are giving them power, shape and substance.

Our conscience is down to much of our social conditioning, what we learn from other people around us; what is acceptable or not, our sense of right and wrong and so on. It is from within our incisive awareness that we are able to make sound judgements for our own lives and occasionally the lives of others. In the potential dismantling of what is before me I cannot fail to be concerned that, if I set about to undo myself routinely, then I should possess the necessary skills to put all the pieces back together again. I accept that the way in which I view myself may be vastly contrasting to the perceptions held by others of me. The imperative therefore must be to seek answers from faithful and trustworthy sources before any attempts at dismantling begin.

Whenever I start to lean towards a particular belief of 'beauty' I am immediately reminded that all human beings are created in the image of a divine being and to whom all are beautiful. In Psalm 139:14, the Psalmist David is praising his fearful symmetry; "I am fearfully and wonderfully made." This is a clear indication that beauty is not a selective peripheral measurement which is exclusive to each observer but rather an artistically inspired accomplishment of the deific creator. The Scripture, unlike humans, cannot fabricate the truth since, there are no alternative truths and it cannot be manipulated to accommodate the wishes of individuals. It refuses to reflect lies to us and is powerful enough to challenge the worlds' mirrors; internet, media, tabloids and glossy magazines that transmit stories of excesses and wealth but sadly, this only represents a privileged minority. This image operates in a ravenous vacuum, feeding on the vulnerabilities of many young aspiring lives.

If we briefly explore the analysis of a mirror image from a very basic chemistry and scientific orientation we may be better able to facilitate this thought. From chemistry, we understand that a, "mirror image" is a molecule having altitudinal arrangement that corresponds to that of another image. From science, we can further develop our discussion where we understand that a mirror image is not a true reflection since it reverses everything from right-to-left, Wikipedia. So, the image we look at in a mirror is not the true person we know ourselves to be. If we are not able to see a true image of ourselves, then what do others see? Effectively, if I dismantle the question, it is simply asking, "If I don't know what the truth looks like, how will I recognise it when I am faced with crushing lies?"

When we have our own reliable points of reference and are faced with devastating lies, we must choose to rigorously defend our integrity and refuse unequivocally to be crushed by them. Of course, there are those individuals who have never seen what the 'truth' looks like and when confronted with it, they retreat to the farthest position since; they have no courage, either to stand in defence alongside it, or to take a chance on living it.

Only have eyes for you

Some years ago, I was told a story that will help to support this idea of true and meaningful realities. Apparently there was a young woman who was born blind but lived a reasonably full life with the assistance of her faithful male companion. The man was completely devoted to her and wished only for her hands in marriage but because of her blindness she was reluctant to marry him. One day the two of them were together sharing some very special thoughts and he asked her what she would like if she could have just one wish. Of course he knew what her wish would be, although his perceptions of her were not as accurate as he had hoped. "Oh that I could see, I would marry you immediately." Sometime later she miraculously underwent an operation and was astonished when she awoke and could see.

Her young companion came to the room where she was waiting, full of excitement and anticipation but only to be devastated by her reaction. "Get out of here; you are so ugly, so hideous." Needless to say, the man left the hospital completely heartbroken and bereft but after some time found the courage to write to his friend. "Take care of your eyes my dear; though they are now yours, they once belonged to me."

This story is merely an illustration of the fragility of human nature and to highlight how soon we are able to turn our backs on the very things that brought us back from existence to life. The young man was sorrowful that her blindness restricted her joy and experiences of life and in his love and devotion to her gave her his own eyes and naturally, the first thing she saw upon waking was his dark empty eyes sockets. This was clearly too difficult for her to embrace and so, she rejected him instead. In my culture there is a colloquial saying; "Sorry for a meagre dog, the meagre dog turns around and savage you." This happens to be one of the most over-used saying and at last I can understand why. This saying has its roots in betrayal and rejection.

The humiliation of rejection and the pain of being despitefully used by another is the inherent quality most moot about human beings, for it is only the human animal that would opportunely sanction another person to remove their eyes in order that they can see, then leave that person in darkness and continue their journey alone to freedom. One would imagine that if seeing enables belief, or disbelief as in the case of the young woman; then, was her belief confirmed from seeing or did seeing affirms those beliefs? If all affirmations comes by way of seeing – how is it possible that anyone should hold a belief of God and be reasonably confident in their defence of him? If every judgement is based on what a person sees, then, why was he not afraid of her blindness but she was afraid of his? Why did the reverse in their positions halt their realities? In this instance, one question is simply not the imperative. The scientific image had been reversed since she was no longer in darkness imagining him to be many things but her reality proved very different. Similarly, for those who organise 'blind dates,' when a meeting is eventually arranged, both sides are mortified when the reality is a vast disappointment to the perceptions held in absence of a true and present reality.

I am not sure whether perceptions have become tarnished with the idea of expectations over a number of years since, so many have been raised beyond what is actually achievable. It seems there are echoes of, "I can see it, so I can have it," rather than, "I don't like what I see so, I don't want it." As illustrated in my account of the woman who was blind, accepting her lover until the moment she could see, which resulted in his immediate rejection. Of course, this was a very punitive rejection and I believe wisdom must be instituted in event situation with the potential to exact a number of changes; positive or negative. If it was as simple as walking away from something I knew had the potential to exact unnecessary changes in my life and by declaring I did not want it, would indeed be a very healthy attitude to adopt. In view of the fact that I instinctively recognise when something is wrong yet, my inquisitive nature, [sinful] propels me into malevolent paths. I know I can make instinctive judgements but will not always choose to do so. I remain uncertain as to just how much I rely on my eyes to direct me but I simply would never be able to place one step ahead of the other without the directions my mind confers. It seems that in view of so many tarnished perceptions, a number of people are moving a safe distance away from the objectivity of what is discernible.

In contrast to a woman who wished for sight and got her desire, albeit by rather sacrificial and painful means, we are now faced with the idea of positive thinking. Nothing is unreachable. If we can no longer physically apprehend it, we simply imagine it there. In this age of positive thinking where people are geared up towards material success and spiritual failure, coaches of all levels are there to advise to, 'think big' for success and 'small' for diets. The way I see it is really quite simple. Success comes only by sheer hard work and dedication and similarly, if a person wishes to lose weight, they should change their lifestyle, apply discipline, undertake regular exercise and stop eating toxic waste. Human beings are not recycling bins! It's that simple. Of course I always maintain an open mind to a number of influences and although I would find it problematic to endorse a number of them, I certainly will not condemn them. There are many things that seem impossible to begin with and while I don't have a particular hope or wish in mind for certain outcomes, I definitely went armed to Pebble Beach with small expectations but was overwhelmed with unexpected actualities.

Pebble Beach: Concours D' Elegance

There have been many times in my life where I have found myself either standing or sitting in the midst of strangers. They were not strangers because I did not know their names or recognise their faces but because I could not find a place of comfort amongst them. This happened routinely over the years while attending a number of functions and meetings with my companion. The reality of not always feeling a part of social events rarely caused me undue anxiety, because I would use the opportunity to critically observe the behaviours and attitudes of those around me. In many such observations it was particularly noticeable how at the very beginning a number of individuals were often wary to approach me but as the evening progressed and their consumption of alcohol was at its peak, some would begin to disarm and consequently finding the courage to engage with me. It was during such interactions that I would gain entry into extremely guarded spaces. While a number of people may attempt to learn more about who I am, a frustrating enterprise on their part, I would in turn insert myself into the forbidden places of their lives and begin the task of unravelling past events. I suspect it is for this reason that a number of people now choose to give me a wide berth whenever such events are repeated. Admittedly, I prefer when I don't always have to feel on the margins but this was such a long time ago that it has hardly had any real impact on my present situation. There was always a marked difference when there were other people with whom I could immediately identify, with similar culture and values but overall, I would simply become redundant if there was never a challenge ahead of me at every stage of my life.

One such challenge was on the occasion of my visit a number of years ago to Pebble Beach in Carmel to the annual Concours D' Elegance. This event was the highlight of the year, televised and attended by celebrities from all placements. It was a presentation on a scale I have not since witnessed. Although I would not have made a personal decision to attend such an event, I felt I had to make a reasonable effort to show gratitude since I was graciously invited by another. As we were about to enter through the main gates, we were harassed to buy tickets for the prizes on offer that day. There was an Audi, a Mercedes and the main prize was a Chrysler Grand Cherokee Jeep, to be presented to the winner by the chief executive of Chrysler. We reluctantly purchased a ticket that I hastily filled in and adding the most unusual words in the space indicated and handed the stub back to the attendant.

It was a long day at Pebble Beach and I became weary under the glare of the sun and so went off with my son to find a quiet space to sit, pray and contemplate. I simply could not reconcile the wealth and privileges on display as though before a worthy 'god' or noble king. It is often in such places where I have had the most conflicting and difficult dialogues within. While I do not condemn wealth in anyway, I simply cannot understand the need for it to be paraded openly and with such indifference. It was in this deep state of observation that I suddenly heard my name being announced over the public address system and was thrust back to an unfamiliar reality.

I did not win the third or the second but had in fact won the first prize; the Chrysler Jeep. This was unbelievable. As I made my way to the podium I was met by television cameras and the chief executive of Chrysler who politely asked me to sit in the car as he drove it from the podium to a designated spot. This was a strange feeling and in retrospect of my earlier contemplation, I have never felt the need to ask God for objects and prizes since, in my estimation, the greatest prize that I have been awarded was the gift of life. In that moment of searching, I acknowledged a number of internal conflicts and personal struggles. The solutions I sought were not as I had expected but I know I must be prepared occasionally to be surprised by the generosity of God.

There have been so few times when I had in fact been given more than I have asked for, which affirms to me that God listens to each word we utter in faith and that the assurance of victory increases in every number greater than one. I have been surprised with unexpected outcomes so few times in my life that they remain permanently imprinted in my mind. I have searched briefly with my hands, passionately with my heart and have walked in some of the most difficult and diverse places but have always kept a daringly open mind. I have done things that would have shamed my mother, angered my father and could impact my children's children. I have walked into a room and others have walked out. I have danced with intemperance to free my soul but could not become disentangled from my chains.

I have discerned heaven and have suffered brief foretastes of hell but horrifying enough to last a lifetime. I have been on sail boats, rowing boats, large planes over the oceans and small ones through the Sahara and Namib Deserts. I have seen grown men weeping like spectres and I could not stop their pain. I have wept in secret for them hoping my tears would absolve all hidden guilt. I have witnessed 'good' men doing bad things and bad men doing virtuous deeds. I have seen wise men become foolish and imprudent men become wise. In the briefest of time, I have witnessed some of the most extraordinary events to which no reasonable justifications could be found. Whether palpable in part and imperceptible in others or perhaps, merely the magnificent beginning of my own susceptible imaginings - yet I cannot for one moment deny, I was there. How many times have you been 'present' in body and 'absent' in mind at a particular function or event, wishing you were somewhere else? How many times have you looked into a mirror and was horrified at what was gazing back at you? And how many times have you wished you could imagine or think yourself out of trouble and it would be so?

According to Rene Descartes, as long as you are able to think, you have reasonable ground to substantiate your, 'being,' but what if the thoughts that arise inside my mind are not true reflections of the person, I am? Although we could dispute that for some people, who are neither 'here nor there' and are perhaps, someplace 'in-between;' if they are able to think along the lines of prudence - does this perceived rationality gives them a complete sense of being? Okay, so, by thinking I am 'great', does that make me great? Or thinking that I am undeserving or cruel - is that all the confirmation I would need to make this a true reality, or are there other factors that hinges on such opposed assertions? If we were to consider that both internal and external factors play a role in the way our perceptions are developed, it could also be argued that our thinking and orientation could become fragmented by all such influences.

Similarly, narcotics can produce comparable effects on the minds of those who use them, a sudden rush that propel users on a, 'high.' The same or similar feelings can be generated from powerful hallucinogenic drugs, validating a person's belief in the preposterous notion they can, 'fly.' This is a clear indication that the perceptions we hold can be altered by a number of toxic factors, internal or external. This is especially true for those individuals whose views of others are highly contrasting to the views they hold of themselves.

Descartes, (Discourse on the Method and Principles of Philosophy), Most famously; (*cogito ergo sum*), "I think, therefore I am." I need to immediately expand on the process of what happens when - what I think is not who I am. For example, I Assault an innocent person for no apparent reason and believe this to be acceptable. This would be a gross under-representation of a moderate person whose thoughts are vastly opposing to her typical disposition. While the opposing asserting to that thought could be - who I am perceived to be, is not actually how I think. Some observers may take a view of a vivacious and daring individual and are embolden to speak to me in a demeaning and off-handed manner, when in fact; I am a deeply sensitive person, who deplores coarse language and patronising innuendos. Although our perceptions inform us throughout our lives, this aspect remains only a fraction of our corporeal disciplines. It is understood that our brains interpret what we see around us and it is from within the mechanics of our minds that an array of images are deciphered to increase our overall knowledge. Naturally, a number of thoughts begin as perceptions and although I am able think with my eyes closed and continue to make sense of objects and subjects, I would nevertheless become very limited if my eyes were to remain permanently closed. I attempted to highlight this thought previously in my basic 'sense oriented objectives' exercise. Similarly, for those whose perceptions become contaminated by various stimuli, will not only embrace polluted views of others but also dangerous ones of themselves. In order to limit the derisory manner in which we are informed by our observations and from where we in turn become empowered to inform others, I believe that a philosophical approach may be insightful towards this process.

For much of my life, I have been able to make reasonably sound judgements which keep me within the boundaries of safety. It is from within these specified margins that I am able to apply common-sense in matters pertaining to my sense of security and identity. The rationale behind our human objectives may not always be immediately apparent; since, it may not always be possible to remain within the boundaries of safety but I am nevertheless equipped to make decisions based upon a number of factors. I firmly believe that it is at the point where our views become tainted as we enter the outer fringes and discover their baselessness, both morally and ethically. The loss of meaningful perceptions surrounding identity and values often occurs on the fringes of society. When this occurs, we are no more able to hold morally right assessments of ourselves, much less others. In the search for my reality over a number of years, one underlying truth continue emerging at each stage of my quest, that no sooner I move to a different alignment, my reality oscillates and the moment I accept one orientation, the moment has already passed. I suspect that there are a number of realities and they are not confirmed simply by a mere thought but also by what is meticulously observed. In view of my methodical analyses of the perceptions held by others as well as myself, if I were to attempt to redefine Descartes principle, naturally in retrospect of my own physical experiencing of reality and being; "I saw, therefore I was." Whilst this thought admittedly is retroactive in origin since, seeing meant that I was there and being there, neither diminished my reality nor has it enhanced that of another person's.

My reality nevertheless, remains a true and meaningful assertion since; it is neither past nor future, but present. Suggesting that the immediacy and palpability of life cannot be suspended and although

Descartes gives a level of proximity and presence, the tangibility of what is seen far outweigh that which is only an incoherent, internal thought, since the objectivity of seeing allows it to be substantiated, "I think, therefore I am"- there are no reasonable measures to validate the essence of thinking, thus its ability to define a person's 'being' serves merely as a platform to articulate a 'state' and not a sense of being as in identity and values. Perhaps I could expand on this thought briefly.

The task of the mind is to transmit data from one orientation to another and is maintained within short and precise periods. Humans simply cannot keep excavating the same thought patterns and maintaining an inflexible position as held at the outset. The contours and direction changes and the thoughts become more or less effective as the proximity of the moment contracts. Much of human experiencing comes by way of visual contact with objects and subjects and one can never dispel the palpability of the human senses, as effect is always at the very point of contact. Once the impulse has passed, the human senses tend to recoil back to their original posturing and effect is no longer with propinquity. If much of what is believable in our universe is based on what is seen; 'Feeli kadochi', a colloquial saying in Ghana which simply means; seen with my own eyes - can the vastly unseen dimensions of faith ever become the trusted apparatus of change in the lives of those whose eyes inform them every step of the way and where the idea of 'faith' is a mere illusion for those whose lives are suspended between the invisible gates of heaven and the visible earthly realms?

Faith and Sight

There is state of belief that impels a believer beyond the boundaries of all known fears - faith; "For we live by faith, not by sight". 2 Corinthians 5:7. Faith is the position from where each person becomes enabled to run with their eyes shut tightly, and their hearts wide open. It is the reassurance of what is hoped for tomorrow, but is present with us today. Faith is the suspension of every dread that potentially disables the fragile human spirit and it is in the uniqueness of this gift that a person forms an unbreakable alliance with God through his Holy Spirit. Jesus said; "With faith you can move mountains," naturally, mountains, such as Everest, are perfectly placed where they are and I suspect this was not the only intention behind the words of the Lord but effectively, we were being assured that there is absolutely nothing that would hinder a person whose faith was a big as a mustard seed, for faith is different to power. With power, one wholly believes in own ability and potential. Faith on the other hand, is assuming humility and seeking the presence of God and allowing his influence and grace to be the all-consuming and transforming power within our lives. The Bible is never silent on issues that really matter to people, for whatever concerns them, matters to God. The words of God elucidate our fragmented lives and it is from them that we are healed and transformed. These words, when applied are able to repair fractures, bind wounds and restore brokenness in every life. It is also from where the destiny and direction that many seek is to be found. In 1 Samuel 16:7, we see God instructing Saul not to look at David's diminutive stature.

People are often pre-occupied with the outward appearance of everything. God on the other hand is only interested in hearts. There is so much emphasis placed on what is seen in preference of what is not. Yet, it is God's desire that men and women possess internal qualities that should surpass the meagre perceptions to which many have become slaves. A majority of my generation are simply not interested in morally right perceptions, as everything seems to concern the view of wealth and privilege. Everything has been reduced to measurements; how big, how high, how wide, how long and how fast! It's no longer considered a quality to be attached to a companion or friend whose virtues outperform their status but as long as they are deemed 'beautiful' outside, the internal attributes remains unimportant.

In recent years the most prodigious and chic possessions are those that validate the view a person holds of themselves and affirm those held by others. The days have long passed when a man or woman was considered beautiful because of their compassion and care towards others. It is noticeable that much of our assessments today concerns - the prettiest woman, the most streamlined cars, the biggest houses, the finest suits and the most impressive salaries. We have become engrossed with status and wealth – those who possess such things are sinking with the load of their excesses and those whose aspirations are fuelled by them, are diminishing for want of them. The perceptions held by humans are often contrary to the insights of God. It is for this reason the Bible is very clear on how we ought to live. In the instructions given to Moses we understand that our perceptions unwittingly lead us to trespass and it is only by faith and perseverance that we can choose alternative directions.

The Ten Commandments are God's standard of righteousness - a righteousness that demands, spiritually, morally, and ethically, 'right' actions in all our relationships. If there were no laws from where values, principles and issues surrounding conscience were drawn, the human race would be virtually redundant. Although a majority of people are law abiding and respectful individuals, there are a minority whose view of the law is as twisted as their overall perceptions. Yet for me, in every instance, as much as I hate many aspects of the modern judicial system and its woeful interpretations, or lack of them; I obey it because it is an act of respect on my part and to disregard it, would show utter contempt and a lack of regard for others.

Our identity is partly framed within the fabric of laws that are upheld by the state since, in them we are reasonably free to choose to become wholly autonomous beings. If there is no law, there is no foundation for truth in any society or its people. Of course this is another one-sided aspect since, I have no measurements for the truth, nor am I able to discern the number of sides it possesses. I am merely defending one particular truth in this space even though I suspect the number of opposing truths based exclusively on perceptions, would make liars of us all.

One particular truth that promotes my freedom is my rigorous application of the law; God's law; admittedly, this may be bondage for many others. Of course I exceed the speed limit occasionally and I might even refuse to be cooperative where matters of principles are at stake but I refuse to covet; the life, the wealth, status or privileges assigned to others. The word covet shows a deep resentment that, when left to fester is both incapacitating and asphyxiating. Scripture is never silent on a matter that consumes a person and it is for this very reason the laws were given. In Exodus 2:17; "You shall not covet your neighbour's house. You shall not covet your neighbour's wife, his male or female servant, his ox or donkey, or anything that belongs to your neighbour." In spite of knowing fully the desires of God concerning the way we should live in healthy relationships with each other, we seem to continue along ambivalent paths.

In Matthew 6:23 we read, "But if your eyes are unhealthy, your whole body will be full of darkness. If then the light within you is darkness, how great is that darkness." The ephemeral nature of human existence is inescapable and no sooner that a present reality is outworked, another becomes apparent. If we have no reasonable means to differentiate between light and darkness, we continue to operate on the fringes somewhere in-between. Christ speaks of a darkness that has the potential to incapacitate our world, either in part or entirely but when I apply the truth of his law, the darkness is absorbed completely. In life, there are two definitive pathways; the way of Christ and the way of mankind [the world]. The way of Christ is a single cross and the way of mankind, many crosses. My life as a Christian is by no means free of complications but I am confident that through each phase there is an assurance of victory. Psalm 34:19-20, "The righteous person may have many troubles but the Lord delivers him from them all. He protects all his bones, not one of them will be broken." For much of my life I have been escaping a number of hurdles placed before me, or trying to remove the malicious labels attached to me. This action of running reminds me of my early life, my mother training me to run with no shoes, since in her prophetic visions she must have been aware of the number of dashes ahead of me. I could never adequately define my life as triumphant without challenges.

In my continuous action of running through hurdle after hurdle, the operative word for me is no longer 'hurdle' but 'through.' I was determined not to succumb to fatigue, to become down-hearted, neither was I prepared to fall and stay down. In almost every instance God has brought me through since, I depend completely on his unfailing love. My life is not dissimilar to that of many of my contemporaries though my beliefs are vastly opposing. I believe that my real definer [faith], in every instance is the rock to which I cling. In every situation, perilous or harmonious I am able to reaffirm the core of my distinctiveness.

A number of experiences have taught me, that whenever God is wrapped around the centre of one whose faith depends on him, perceptions not only change but are also revivified. I have walked into some of the biggest objects directly ahead of me and have identified microscopic ones in advance. The significant turning point in my life was not the day I ceased to care about the perceptions others held of me but the day I began to care deeply what God knew of me. In this moment of renewed acuities, an action instituted by faith, I no longer dread failure but anticipated success. My life has become one of freedom since, although I fell through pride in full view of thousands, I rose in humility in the presence of just one. Proving that it's not the height or persistent nature of the hurdles but it is a fact that, there is always assurance of victory in every number greater than one.

The judicial system serves a purpose in all democratic nations. It upholds truth, defends the innocent and prosecutes the guilty. My fear surrounding this motif of justice is not its obvious principles but its practice or visibly lack of them. I believe a vast number of judges are themselves under judgment. This stems from the contamination of their values and perceptions, issues of nepotism and bribery. The law cannot be effective as long as those who are its guardians continue to lose sight of its origin and integrities, for when this occurs, it is no longer just one who is under attack but an entire nation is under judgement.

September
2012

Sheryl Sophia
1988

CHAPTER FIVE

Sub Judice: Under Judgement

Just over two thousand years ago, a man stood in the world with a voice - succinct and powerful and his was the voice of reason, mercy, compassion and humility and demonstrating at every level a type of human being who has never been hitherto present in the world. This inspirational being was a light in every dark place, courage in hopelessness and one possessing words of truth, insight and wisdom and who also possessed the power to transform lives. Christ most definitely did not come into the world for self-elevation but came that the name of God be worshipped and lifted up; a God he taught all men and women to simply call, 'Father.' Father was both in heaven and on earth simultaneously; Jesus answered, "Don't you know me, Philip, even after I have been among you such a long time? Anyone who has seen me has seen the Father. How can you say, 'Show us the Father'? This loving Father recognised the abyss underneath humanity and so, sent his beloved son to be humiliated, brutalised and nailed upon a cross to die a painfully slow death as a common criminal. A most ignominious end to the hopes of mankind, yet it was not, for it was to be mankind's endless hope. It was through the act of Jesus's dying and resurrection that the hopelessness in which all human beings had become enslaved was given freedom to enter into the realms of God's endless hope and grace. This is highlighted in the Book of Matthew where Christ was brought before Pilate and for some observers witnessing the degradation of God, this may have confirmed their worst fears or inveterate their joyous hope. This was not the end of God's reign with mankind but was in fact, only the beginning.

In Matthew 27:22 we read; "What shall I do, then, with Jesus who is called the Messiah?" Pilate asked. They all answered, "Crucify him!" "Why? What crime has he committed?" asked Pilate. But they shouted all the louder, "Crucify him!" At this point I must hasten to relinquish any conjectures and judgements admittedly, a difficult thing for me to do and must therefore assume that during that period in history, there was a calamitous vacuum of reason, mercy, compassion and humility; centuries removed but the same motifs as our world today. For it was the very nature and mind-set of those upon whose callous judgements Christ was crucified. The rulers who elevated themselves above every person in society, appearing 'faultless' and 'perfect' and so, giving legitimacy to their practices of ruthlessness.

The New Testament in particularly is very vocal against harsh judgements being passed from one person to another. "Do not judge, or you too will be judged. For in the same way you judge others, you will be judged, and with the measure you use, it will be measured to you." Matthew 7:1-2. This passage is well known, even amongst non-believers of Scripture and could reverberate at any time in their lives. It is so easy to pass harsh judgements about those we do not recognise. I understand that a number of people are authoritative on the lives of others to the point of annoyance. If however, they were to be asked the most minor details about their own lives, they would simply have nothing to say. Admittedly, I am a guarded person. If I don't know an individual I refuse to invest my privacy in them. This is one of the more difficult lessons I have had to learn through the act of a number of painful betrayals. In the past, I only informed people what they needed to know about me and anything else, they could either guess or imagine. My laconic nature is nothing to do with secrecy but overall, I have a strong belief that far too many people are intrusive for menacing reasons and have since learned to speak only when I am being paid or giving praise and remain silent at all other times, for it is often in my silences where I have gained the most wisdom and strength.

I remember a number of years ago I was driving to my work and as I idled in traffic another driver was very aggressive towards me. He was poor at his judgement to manoeuvre but of course being male and I a woman, it was naturally my error. I was gracious to him and continued my journey, unaffected by his behaviour. I arrived to my workplace and was about to start my afternoon shift when one of the staff came to inform me that someone was waiting in the foyer to see me. I asked that the person be brought to my office and was pleased to see the very man who had behaved so irrationally towards me earlier. The pleasure for me in coming face to face with my nemesis is that, there is a hope I may be given the chance to reprove a particular behaviour. He was a salesman coming to impress me with his banter and cut price merchandise but of course he had already left a different type of impression upon me earlier. I spent time with him because he was both charming and polite. At the end of our meeting I had saved my company a considerable amount of expense and he had earned his bonus, not for his earlier attitude but for his confidence and assertion. It was never my intention to assault his integrity; instead I gave him the opportunity to substantiate it. I could have invited him to come alongside me with the belief that I would be entering an agreement, then rescind in spite. The way to highlight his aggression was to excuse myself half-way through our meeting and to get my car from the garage and park it alongside his. After all the agreements had been signed, I walked outside with him and seeing my car, he suddenly realised I was the same woman. Needless to say, his humility was evident and it was for this moment that I had most eagerly waited.

It has always been my hope that if I suspend my judgements of others, they in turn will do the same for me. I know from past experiences that whenever I have been too swift to judge, that I also was judged and condemned. My conscience continues to guide me along and although I have not always harnessed its wisdom, it has nevertheless remained faithful. I understand the majority of things that are of value to me and some that appear pointless to others. I understand that while a number of people continue to rise, the majority will fall and that in my inevitable rising, a number will undoubtedly decrease. There would simply be no point to my life if I did not rigorously defend my own beliefs and values and promote the right to life for others. My conscience, though far from maturity and perfection, permits me to hear a number of voices around me. I have admired a number of men for their effortless wisdom and service to others since, service to others can be the most rewarding aspect of wisdom. Gandhi, in particular was both piercing and brutal with the truth, especially those concerning conscience, "That the human voice cannot reach the distance of the still small voice of conscience." Mahatma Gandhi - (Quotes of Gandhi p.43). I have often wondered what it is that allows one person to love and another hate, or one who protects while another abuses. There is simply no rationale behind a number of unacceptable behaviours, yet a majority of individuals appears wholly unaffected. If it is our conscience that guides us into morally right paths – what happens when a person deviates from these? No one knows what a conscience looks like but its indifference can impact the world incalculably.

I remember a few years ago being faced with, not only issues of conscience but also those concerning values, morality and propriety. In view of my beliefs, I tend to make decisions slowly, especially those with the potential to unhinge my life. Conscience is a most peculiar quality, for although a majority of us possess it, or vague traces of it, very few of us, at the least are able to apprehend it and at the best, institute it. This situation demanded a solution but I simply could not bring myself to make the decision that I knew would ultimately set me free. Instead, I traversed back and forth for years; searching for the answers in others, I knew was present within me. I had married my first love; the man I believed would be able to safeguard my dreams. He was intelligent, amusing, inventive and resilient. His family's background was steeped in Christian values and although he was not deeply spiritual, there was a least a foundation from where we could build. He brought laughter, balance and a new confidence to my life which was indescribable.

The thing that halted us in our track was not the fact that we had changed but two people effectively became one through the union of marriage and sadly, reverted back to two through the act of betrayal. Of course there are different levels of betrayal and there is nothing that is unforgivable since, one person cannot seek forgiveness in isolation and it must be acknowledged that, in all issues of a violation of trust, two people are occasionally as guilty as one. I have never learned how to leave someone because; it was always others that I have loved who had habitually left me. The challenge now facing me was compounded by a number of opposing values since; I could not reconcile the fact of being the first in my family whose marriage had failed. My mother's marriage lasted almost fifty years until my father's death. My sisters, Carol and Natalie both married their 'first loves' and have amassed an incredible forty years between them. So, when I gave my hand in marriage to him, this was to be an unbreakable union. I gave him my heart and my hopes, for in this cooperation I was only too pleased to also share a number of my dreams with him. If I left, just how much of 'me' would be left behind? Of course I found the courage to leave; my first step was to open a door that took six years to finally close behind me.

To be betrayed by someone close can be unforgivable, although with hard work and effort is totally achievable. In my sporadic sense of right and wrong, my conscience allowed me to refocus and acknowledge a morally right position over a number of unsubstantiated denunciations. I cannot say that I have never uttered a lie in my life as this would be another lie and that I have never wished for my enemies demise would be further untruths. I believe in my principles alone and not those of others. At the inception of all my relationships my vulnerabilities are partly exposed, not because I wish them to be so but relationships are only possible because we able to disarm. In our act of disarming we may unwittingly surrender a number of our principles and values and embrace those of another. The number of times I wished I had been wiser in retrospect but wisdom emanates, not ahead of our trespasses but must follow on behind. It is this lack of wisdom that has instigated a number of errors in my life but I recognised them and appropriately amended them. I cannot judge another person for being hurled into disagreeable places since I have traversed a number of my own accord. It is in such dark places that my conscience was most stirred and as hard as I tried at times, I could not be released. My human nature was designed around the blight of sin but my character is being continuously developed around God's righteousness. I understand that like me, a majority of people will suffer greatly – from weaknesses, addictions, malevolent associates and betrayal. I know that people have to suffer in order to recognise the signs of victory and I simply cannot complaint since, if Christ suffered: who am I to lament?

I continue my motif of victory in suffering since my unending inspiration is Christ. The betrayal he suffered became the turning point of human conscience since, in his death all were raised to new levels of consciousness. Admittedly, Christ was aware in advance of his betrayal, not so with many of us, we can only witness the outcomes as they develop before us. Naturally, there are many levels of betrayals and all are inexcusable, although not all are as disturbing as the betrayal of Christ. Imagine being chosen because you are weak, selfish, unpredictable, materialistic and uncompassionate? Judas was chosen because of his nature and just in the same way a number of people will choose their friends, workers and associates for the same or similar motives. Judas was overwhelmed with remorse when he was faced with the enormity of his actions. It was his visibly lack of conscience that allowed him to fall, resulting in him fleeing to the wilderness in shame and choosing to end his life.

It is all too often that our actions determine our destiny and just as my father used to say to me, "If you bawn fi heng yu cyan drown," [if you were born to be hanged, you cannot drown], meaning, whatever your destiny, it will be fulfilled. I continue to search eagerly to determine where my conscience starts and my potential for duplicity begins. I simply have to accept that in the absence of human perfection, I possess the potential to do wrong. At the inception of each impending action my one question imperative is now inclusive and no longer exclusive to one, "Another person may forgive me but can I forgive myself?" I believe that the act of forgiveness begins in the conscience of all, for it is a reasonably assertion that we may not always understand why we forgive but we nevertheless embrace the freedoms it bring. This freedom in forgiveness is not exclusive to the ones we forgive. I am so aware of the times I have been forgiven of major errors or minor irritations and was met by instant relief. I suspect that when we have been forgiven, our forgiveness is meant to enrich our lives as well as the lives of others. Of course not everyone will want to boast about being forgiven as they are afraid of appearing imperfect, yet I am sure the thief hanging on the cross beside Christ, found his true identity in the humility of seeking forgiveness.

Jesus once more exemplified the idea of suspending judgements of others and granting pardon to one whose action was about to end his life. Of course the one that was too proud to seek forgiveness languished long after his lifeless body was removed and placed in a grave but the one whose humility propelled him to ask – was saved beyond the grave. "This day you will be with me in paradise," yet, far from the noblest act of Christ in his dying moment. The most moving act of Christ in his final moments as his life ebbed away on the cross was the instant he turned his face to heaven and begged God to forgive those who had dehumanized him, "Father, forgive them for they do not know what they are doing" And they divided up his clothes by casting lots. Luke 23:34. I have often wondered just how many people would find it possible to forgive their enemies, the ones who had caused unbearable sorrow as they were about to die? Christ on the other hand, could so easily have asked for judgements to be passed against us but instead, he asked for pardon. A number of perceptive people will automatically recognise the 'good' present within others, while others may never be able to discern it even at close proximity. Jesus, admittedly, bypassed the feeble exterior and was aware of the thoughts and conscience of both thieves. Admittedly, I no longer place myself under unreasonable obligations to others, especially those from whom I may never need to seek forgiveness. The thief who was granted pardon did not languish because he could not gain absolution from those whom he had directly offended since; there was one greater alongside him whose ultimate pardon superseded that of any other.

Although I am attempting to become a more broad-minded person, I shall nevertheless remain a judicious one and continue to steer my life away from intractable judgements. I understand the power of forgiveness, not because I enthusiastically forgive but because I have been forgiven much. I believe that forgiveness is possible in the absence of all judgements since, it is from here that morally right paths can be best directed. The number of times in my life that I have gazed into the path of the wrong accompanied by the impossible and knowing that, no amount of imagining will alter the way ahead and so, retreating became my only option. It was often at such times that I was most susceptible and would find myself yearning for the freedom and relative innocence of childhood. Admittedly, the place of our greatest freedoms can also be the place of our greatest pain. Even though the misery of traversing back can be unbearable yet, it has often been here that I have gained the most strength. It is for this reason I longed for red dirt lanes, the colourful humming bird darting from flower to flower but not nearly as much as I long for George – one of the few places, I was unquestionably safe.

George: A Beautiful Memory

In my culture children are taught from a very early age to be industrious and independent, in both their actions and thinking. Since, the worse situation imaginable would be for a young girl in particular, to be completely incompetent and was unable to become a responsible wife and mother. From as early as I could remember, I was doing 'women's work; washing, cooking cleaning, shopping, planting my flower garden, feeding and caring for the animals, in addition to going a considerable distance into the hills to fetch fire wood. I would raise a batch of chickens to maturity, loving them, then catching the least favourite, chopping off its head and putting its body under a bucket while I sat on the top until the poor bird stopped wriggling and would sit for most of the day, plucking it for a tasty dinner in the evening.

I had responsibilities but there was also unconstrained freedom. I simply played for hours, refusing to pause until sunset. From what I have observed of children's upbringing in Britain, I am grateful that my formative years were spent in a place where values and beliefs were vastly opposing. I supposed if unreasonable judgements were to be passed against my culture, it may be viewed that children had far too many 'adult' responsibilities but in defence, I would assert that since, childhood is for such a brief spell, that it is far more productive to teach children to become what they should be for the majority of their lives – responsible adults. Of course the flip side of this argument could suggest that, since childhood is so short, children should be children for as long as possible. I believe this a fair appraisal in some cultures, my own included but I am a pragmatist who evaluates the merits of discipline and fortitude and would much prefer to see balance in every avenue of people's lives. I was often told that I was being trained for victory, not failure and my mother's favourite saying at this time endorsed this thought, "Ben de tree when it young, when it is old, it wi bruk." This was adopted from the Book of Proverbs, which simply means, to train a child when they are young, to enhance their potential to become responsible and conscientious human beings. Of course it was this idea of responsibility that saw a number of Caribbean families being devastated by numerous separations in order to secure freedom for some and raise the socio-economic bar for others.

My father was no exception; he gained a work permit and duly left wife, children, home and livestock, making his way to London with the expectations of a better life. My mother did not travel with him initially but made subsequent visits on other occasions. My father was able to make the transition from a relatively stress-free life in the Caribbean to a demanding British one. My mother on the other hand, found this virtually impossible and was torn emotionally in view of the children she had left behind. Her health began to deteriorate and a decision was taken for her to return home. With my two year old brother in her arms, heavily pregnant with me, she made the long passage back to St Elizabeth. This proved a difficult time for her and naturally, when everyone was leaving she was returning; many judgements were passed once more. I don't believe for a moment that my older sister and brothers gave a thought to the judgements that were passed by others. The fact that mama had returned when they thought she may not, must have been the greatest feeling in the world. I have never been afraid of past events, neither am I afraid of future revelations but I have come to a place of acceptance that the first eight years of my life were in fact my happiest.

I know that a number of observers may doubt the integrity of my ability to recall events in such painstaking details but one thing must be made abundantly clear - as children we simply had no distractions. There was no television, music centres or even a radio in our home. Everything that brought pleasure to our lives was a joint invention by us all. We were creative, not because we were born that way but because we had to be so. It is for this reason that I am able to recall events with such precision; there were simply nothing to contaminate our precious world. The only thing missing, conspicuous by his absence was the father I dared to imagine, as an exceptional human being. The first time my father met me, I was four years old. The first time I met him I was twelve – where do I begin? I could not call him father since his absence had created an imperceptible wall between us and with everyone calling him, 'mister,' purely on the grounds of respect, that was a good enough place for me to begin. It must be understood that in my culture, all children must address men as 'mister,' since this is the norm and although I would have preferred 'dad' or even 'father,' these terms however, felt much too awkward. The very first time I recognised my father as 'father' was the day I stood as a woman weeping at his grave. I was weeping for the father I had, but could not apprehend and was bereft because his death halted all future prospects for change. I cannot fully understand the mechanics of grief since, its origin begins in desolation and sorrow and since sorrow concerns loss, I never grieve for what has been taken but only for what remains. One thing which is remarkably clear to me is that, when I am in intense pain, I can appraise more clearly my fragile world.

It was during this period that I was able to draw comparisons of my friend George; too painful to remember and too beautiful to forget. Since it was through his death that I was able to accept that life may be accompanied by the occasional rudimentary manual but there are never any guarantees. George was exceptional. He was handsome, kind and mischievous. Even though these were amazing attributes, they are still a long way short of what I believed to be his most outstanding feature. The alliance created between George and I are to be acknowledged for a number of reasons and the most notable one was the fact that - I was a girl and my best friend was a boy. This, though not unusual in my culture was not an everyday occurrence.

I was the youngest of five children and the three immediately ahead of me was a trio of interfering boys and even though I was loved and protected by them, I had to learn to be strong and stand up to them as well as against a number of difficult opponents. It was my brother's intention that I should be the most formidable girl in the neighbourhood and so made it their on-going commitment to train me for battle. I would be routinely given an aggressive male opponent who I had to dismantle as though in a boxing match. I became all too aware that losing was not an option since; if I dared to lose I would be further chastised by them. It was partly for this reason that George was my shelter, for in addition to his aforementioned qualities, he was an incredibly gentle soul.

George's grandmother was blind and he was her eyes in almost everything and I was my mother's ears. Admittedly, my mother's deafness although not profound at this time, was becoming increasingly challenging for us all. The unpredictability of life, the seemingly unchanging days which runs concurrently into each other and bringing a sudden halt. It was at this point I knew my world would never be the same again. It started out like any ordinary day but ended the life of my friend and shattered the hopes and dreams of an entire family. It was a morning just like any other and George had got up to get ready for school. After breakfast he set off down the lane and as usual, started whistling on his way to school.

George was a prolific whistler and he and I used to compete to see who could whistle the loudest. He was a few minutes into his journey when he realised that he had not prayed before leaving and so, made a U-turn for home. During his brief walk he saw a fencing staple on the ground and for some unknown reason picked it up and placed it into his mouth. Obviously, an unnatural and bizarre thing to do but this is not an exercise in logic. He rushed into his room, knelt down by his bed and began saying his prayers when the staple slipped down his throat. He managed to summoned help before he collapsed in agony as the staple started to restrict his airway.

George was rushed to the best hospital at the time but there was no doctor wise enough nor was there any equipment advanced enough to save his life and so, he died the following day - he was eight years old, just like me. One of the greatest privileges of being a child is that I could ask the questions that seemed to paralyse all the adults. This was the starting point of some of the greatest challenges that I would face in my life. Of course there was pain but there was also a lot of anger. A number of George's close family, his mother included were living and working in New York at the time of his death and were about to buy and ticket for him to join them. The day of the funeral was the first of many dark darks ahead for me and although I gained comfort from my tears, I knew real consolation would take a number of years. Our grief is not purely down to loss and lack of understanding, because grief is never attributed to wisdom or strength but is wholly connected to suffering in the human family. I understand a boy being faithfully committed to his principles and belief in God. George, like me was taught to pray on every occasion and I would sooner lose my life praying, than to lose it laughing in the midst of uncertainty. I have given worthy things to unworthy people and have become impoverished through a lack of knowledge. In this instance where I can choose to make a real difference, I will honour the boy who was an exceptional friend to me but was simply never given the chance to shine:-

GONE

Gone is the face so sweet
The whistling, laughter and mischief
The childhood friend with whom I'd share
The ups the downs, the burdens the cares
Your life ended much too soon
There was never a chance for the man to shine
Except as the little crowd of stars come tumbling out
In God's celestial heaven, calm and sublime
Heaven had briefly lent you to earth
To use your eyes to guide your grand-mother
And to make you a living example to all,
A lasting testament to everyone who in Christ is a brother

I believe from the moment I overcame the fear of death I was able to assume my place in life's mainstream. Naturally, the idea of a stream is that, it flows in a direction of its choosing and whether up or down, I must become adaptable to flow with those changes. My resources, whether physical, emotional or spiritual, cannot continue to allow for depletion and it is for this reason I concern myself only with those things that are inter-changeable. In much the same way where I take an optimistic view of a number of things in my life, I hold and nurture an equally optimist one of death; I refuse emphatically to allow it to create a chasm in my life. My one question imperative will further illustrate this. "How can death create a gaping hole in my life when nothing has been breached?" Of course this may not be a true assertion in some instances but for a few, is a definite reality. I have never feared death only the injustices I have found in living, the very ones which occasionally impels a person to end their own life.

I simply cannot reconcile the sorrow which allows a human being to make a decision that will end their life. Even though I struggle to accept a number of vastly opposing values to my own, I simply cannot condemn them. My chief concern regarding our human complexities and continuing search to reduce our failures and increase our triumphs, is that, none of this will be possible until we are able to disarm our affectations and show vulnerability and transparency. So, whether, if in our minds we are facing fictitious or real opponents, in a boxing ring or on the top of a mountain, our victory will only be secured, in every number greater than one.

My Chief Concern

I have rarely craved adventure, yet there is an overwhelming desire in me to gain increased wisdom. I am simply not a woman who seeks explorations and daring to stimulate a revitalisation of life since, for me nothing but pride has died and I wish it to remain permanently so. Yet, a visible lack of wisdom propelled me, if only briefly into a malevolent pathway that would not so much change my life but drastically altered its purpose and direction. It was on the evening of the 5th of November two thousand and five that I first met Michael - the police chief, whose position was not really a chief concern to me but it was in fact his personable manner that allowed me to engage with him. Michael was one who initially appeared to be as full of life as life was full of him but ultimately failed to grasp its significance, triumphs and freedoms.

I am a mindful and extremely cautious person who takes time deliberating for weeks, months and even years when I am faced with life changing decisions. I simply prefer to live my life within its pre-set limits of what is permissible and continue to assert my influence over those things I hold as trustworthy and indispensible. I have never once entertained the idea of surreptitious liaisons with another person whilst being committed to another; this is counter-productive, wicked and a disrespectful enterprise as far as I am concerned. When a person is in possession of everything which validates their life, making it honourable on almost every level, to pursue anything else is a cruel and extremely selfish act. I have always held firm to those things I value most and to forfeit them would be almost as severe as to lose my soul. I cannot comprehend the ideologies of some people whose overbearing desire is simply to have one aspect of another human being and once satisfied, disregarding the other attributes.

I can never find the logic behind this methodology and regardless of how much I pursue wisdom to work out this mystery; it has continued to elude me on every possible level. If I chose to buy a car, I would simply not purchase the steering wheel alone; I would naturally want the whole vehicle and all the power of its engineering dynamics which allows it to be comprehensive and workable. Just as in the same way no one would buy a house which was incomplete and had all the windows and doors missing or the roof unfinished. Yet, there are so many individuals [men in particular], who simply wish to devour the most primary aspect of a woman and what is largely disregarded is often the most compatible elements but would unquestionably require far too much time and effort to impact realistically and meaningfully. I have never had a cathartic desire to be consumed by alpha males of particular unsavoury dispositions since, this behaviour to me is bordering onto 'cannibalism' and I simply cannot function effectively when my members begin to be disbursed. There is nothing worse for me than to be in the state of suspension from where I cannot procure a continuous sense of identity, purpose and destiny. If I am not desired and wanted in full, I refuse to be dismembered in part. I fail to see the rationale behind a man's desire for the 'contents' but ultimately condemns the 'container.' My simple philosophy is, 'it's either all or nothing' and I have nearly always chosen nothing over a fraction of a derisible something. I simply do not want it and refused to become entrapped by it.

I am always approachable and friendly and because I appear so confident many people have held wrong perceptions about my over-all character. Michael was someone I had not met previously, neither was I familiar with him as a 'public figure,' for in my life, I pay attention mostly to those things that are its fundamentals and will only give consideration to the lives of others where I have been invited to do so. He was introduced to me and a small group of friends and we immediately conversed as though we had all known each other for some time. I do not care in the slightest about the status or indefensible positions of particular individuals. As long as they demonstrate a high level of regard for others and humility for self I believe I am well inserted within pleasing company. My on-going difficulty has always been that I can immediately by-pass all those titles, badges and prestigious awards. I find piercing through the outer barriers and going deeper allows me into a space which is largely impenetrable for a majority of people. This 'gift' has been a blessing and a protracted curse at various points throughout my life. I saw a man the size of a 'giant' standing in front of me but I knew at some point in the very near future, he would invariably fall down; of course he fell down, for there was absolutely no one there to 'catch' him!

I often have this analogy in my mind of a train, [the train being Michael] hurtling out of control spitefully derailing itself in protest at being made to travel on an opposing line to its preferred route -

naturally, disaster is the inevitable outcome. One of my philosophies has always been to maintain right over wrong and truth over lies and to never compromise my principles and values. It would have been so easy to breach the trust of everyone and go against what I hold firmly as morally right but in spite of being amused and fairly pleased at his attention, I was by no means about to throw myself into the path of this felonious 'train.' I was reasonably obliging to exchange contact details along with the three other people present but to this day remains one of my most regrettable actions.

During a turbulent period of two years and four months and several dozens of emails and text messages later, all bearing the obvious reminder. I have never 'fought' so much with a stranger. This was one of the most bizarre encounters imaginable and the number of words said during that period of time was unquantifiable but they ultimately reiterated the same thought along the same repeated pattern: "Michael, I am married and so are you and I am never coming to meet with you unless of course it was your last day on earth." The incredible power of words and how they can return to haunt us at an unsuspecting hour! I had often visualised many aspects of Michael's life, his nature and character and everything that was becoming so disconnected and fractured around him but I was never invited into his private space for those reasons, and neither was I prepared to compromise and willingly insert myself into the beginning of what was to become a spectacular nightmare. Instead, for two years and four months I 'cared' for him from the safety and distance of my home – this has always proved the safest way in which to care for a number of people, men in particular.

Naturally I have many regrets concerning my life; regrets at being separated from my family at the age of ten, being emotional and physically abused as a child by members of my own extended family. I regret being an observer rather than a participant in many of the plans and schemes of life and feeling an incredible sense of failure and disappointment in a number of resourceful endeavours. The failure of my first marriage, the failure of businesses, the failure to find genuine kindness and real love in all but a pitiful handful of human beings. I have nevertheless, arrived at a place of trust and safety from where my beliefs surrounding issues of failure have actually become my enduring strengths. I am now much better equipped to devise my own standards of freedom where the motifs continue to work harmoniously within the scope of every new and meaningful possibility which is created within my life.

Admittedly, what a number of people fail to understand or what they choose to overlook concerning the lives and circumstances of others is due largely to fear or a gross lack of respect. If we were to briefly scrutinise society's worst offenders, [media, tabloids and the internet], who are self-appointed judges, we would in fact be appalled by their own low morality and diminishing principles and who are themselves embroiled daily in the defence of their gross lack of respect and overwhelming absent integrity. If it were at all possible to gain unrestricted access into the lives of these seemingly 'noble saints,' their storehouses of transgressions and their closets of conceits would be so bursting with 'skeletons' that many terrified observers may believe themselves to be in the midst of acres and acres of primordial burial grounds! I remember Michael's pleading and asking on that fateful evening in March, on the occasion of my birthday and against all reason and logic I disarmed and agreed to meet with him but not at a place of his choosing but one of mine, which was a public place. At the last minute he informed me that he had been drinking and was unfit to drive and therefore asked me to meet at his preferred location.

Reluctantly, I agreed against all my better judgements and entered his postcode into my satnav and set off. I was sent around three text messages in a very short space enquiring how much further away I was. Of course I could not answer that since, I had no idea where I was going. He saw the humorous side of this sometime later on. I simply could not believe the reception which awaited me upon arrival, I was met at the gate, which was opened remotely and as I climbed down from my car I was greeted by the warmest and most sincere of embraces. Given that I had only met this man in a very formal setting over two years previously, I was speechless at his welcome; his words even more profound; "Welcome home." That evening was one of the darkest and most disturbing incidences I have ever encountered in my life. Was there tears? Far too many, was there loss of self and identity? There was an undeniably loss of direction and purpose and far too many regrets. The answers sought simply could not be found and if they could have been found they would have been apprehended way in advance of this evening but there were no answers simply because the morally right questions were ignored at the inception.

Did I love Michael Todd? Perhaps - but since love was never the imperative question, neither could it become the desperately pursued answer. But undeniably, there was a resolute determination on my part not to lose sight of my fundamental values. And although I was immediately aware of a number of underlying concerns, I knew instinctively that I would find it impossible to compromise my unyielding and untrusting position for a long time in the foreseeable future. I have spent a great deal of my adult life trying to comprehend the intensity of love and hate – and needless to say, I have recently discovered them to be the same 'demon,' occupying the same space but the one major difference between them both is their closing sacrifice. To love is agony, to hate – a deeper anguish; so, what's the difference? None, Love releases and engenders freedom; hate simply enslaves and brings bondage but both crushes the human spirit when instituted recklessly.

Everything which applies to love is the reverse of hate but since I have such little understanding of hate, I will briefly explore the ideology of what I believe love to be. For me, love must be established around trust, mutual respect and friendship, even before a handshake is permissible between me and another human being. In the aforementioned instance none of these were present and so, there were no foundations on which such an assumption could be substantiated or upheld. I was not 'in love' with him, for I simply cannot rationalise a concept of being into a 'verb,' love is not an object, nor is an opportune covering where one shelters from inclement weather, [though some may choose to argue this point] but for me love is getting my hands dirty, my eyes wet with both tears and laughter, it is everything that I do for myself but is a marked improvement when I do it for another. I believe I display a high regard for others in my life but it is a two way process, demanding a mutuality of respect and understanding. I simply do not have an inexorable amount of love to give without a thought. The idea of being totally 'in love' today and 'out of love' tomorrow is absolutely alien and foreign to me. Love does not come by means of 'in' and 'out' nor 'up' and 'down,' but is rather an all-consuming action of will and intention, steeped in pain and sacrifice. Love is simply a giving 'up' of self and surrendering to another but this action was never going to be possible here and those rhetorical echoes of morally right questions would continue to impinge upon my every thought and action for the anticipatable future.

For me, pure love can be likened to one person being wrapped in fine silks and linen, while another is stripped bare in shame and nakedness. Love is when the beat in your heart stops and words become inexpressible. It is when you walk into a room with a million words on the tip of your tongue, only to become mute in the presence of the one your heart is beating for. Love is the only verb that stirs your heart to beat in line with another, then stops suddenly and fades away into the stagnant darkness. Love is what holds one in high esteem, then turns around and leaves that one all forlorn. Love is indefinable pain of both rapturous joy and bitter sadness. Time can never erase its touches, for they are engraved deep within the soul, there is nothing greater and better than love that understands itself in every moment of fear and complete disapprobation. Love is everything in life, love is stronger than death. This thought is unequivocally supported in Songs of Solomon 8:6-7; "Place me like a seal over your heart, like a seal over your arm; for love is stronger than death, its jealousy unyielding as the grave. It burns like a blazing fire, like a mighty flame. Many waters cannot quench love; rivers cannot wash it away. If one were to give all the wealth of his house for love, it would be utterly scorned."

The perfection of love begins and ends with God naturally, for God is love and I cannot imagine the thought of God's love swinging ominously on a pendulum, 'for' and 'against;' when he is sincerely pleased the 'for' scale is at its highest point and when 'against' us descending beyond the reaches of hades. Love is a gift between God and humankind and we are in turn enabled by God to love and demonstrate a high level of care and regard towards each other. I bear no guilt or shame of loving a fragile and suffering heart, those hurting and lonely and those who remind me of my own struggles to freedom to gain respect and becoming safe in the places where like me, they too have placed their trust.

Michael had nothing substantial to underpin his life. The fragile nature of each person often asphyxiates under intense pressures, especially those surrounding fears and humiliations. I knew the time had come to leave and that I would not see him again, for this was 'farewell.' My parting gift was a bottle of champagne that caused our final disagreement. Michael reluctantly took the bottle from me and asked me to have dinner with him; somehow he knew that he would never drink that bottle of champagne alone nor with me. As I pulled away in my car he held his head in his hands weeping. This was distressing and confusing for I did not know him and had no previous points of reference and although he was overly distressed I did not begin to feel a sudden urge to call some unknown source to intervene, since it was neither my position nor my place to do so. Naturally when I left him that evening I was deeply saddened, although a little wiser, but not nearly wise enough! Michael asked me faithfully before I left to contact him and let him know that I was safely home and not in too much difficulty and that was exactly what I did but I also realised that the picturesque landscape that was my life was about to change beyond recognition. On the eleventh of March Michael was found dead on Snowdonia and much television coverage followed, with every single aspect of his life being excavated; good and bad. There were so many terrible accounts of his behaviour and what he had done with whom and where they had done it that it became as farcical as an out-dated soap opera. But I simply did not care what he did to whom, where or how often they did it; I was simply concerned what he had done to himself and his family in this extraordinary act of despair. My heart was broken in part because this derailed 'train' was way above my strength to halt and for once there was nothing tangible to secure just one tiny flicker of hope.

Sadly, this minuscule flicker of hope, [as envisioned and articulated by Michael to me earlier], had now morphed into utter hopelessness and if he thought for one moment that the courage that he had so desperately craved was present within me, he was dreadfully wrong, for my boldness is not engendered from myself but from God who continually strengthens me. I am equally as fragile and hopeless as the next man or woman without the restorative power of the God in whom I have placed all my love and trust. I remember a number of journalists attempting to contact me in the days following his death and there was one in particular who pursued me intently. I was curious because this man seemed less dishonourable than the others and I decided to speak with him briefly but was alarmed by the last thing he told me before I terminated our conversation. He informed me that such was the embarrassment of Michael's association with me, that the 'establishment' would have preferred if he had spent his final evening with a dog, for this would have been far less humiliating for them.

Of course I am not a dog - I am a woman with a heart of flesh and not of stone, I am compassionate and kind to everyone I meet and I simply refuse to judge others when there is every discernible reason to judge them and the only thing that is comparable between me and a dog is my abiding loyalty, my tender-hearted nature and my enduring faithfulness. Michael must have seen something in me that was not present in those people around his clinical environment and for one brief moment was prepared to disregard protocol. One enduring question remains for me in all of this and perhaps I don't wish to discover the answer, for maybe I would not be able to live it in the present nor into the future. "Of all those 'thoroughbreds' around him, why did he chose to spend the last evening of his life with a practical stranger he had met only once previously?" I simply don't need the answer in order for my life to continue along its pre-determined course and at no time in the present or the future will it become derailed through fear, malice or a lack of compassion for others. It is for this very reason that I dedicate this poem to the man whose name was chief to some, reckless to others but will remain affectionately; Michael to me.

38 to One

He spread his wings like an eagle to fly
But alone on a cold mountaintop he suffered and died
He died in anguish but not from the cold,
But died in anguish from a broken soul
A soul so wretched that none could see
Not even the closest of his family
His final days indeed was a mess
What wretched untruths what bitterness!
For it was better that it was all polished over
And not a citizen in the land would be any the wiser
The corruption and dread that bore down upon him
Drove him beyond the edge to win
He spoke of poison he told of greed

He censored nothing as I listened and heard

I saw a giant, a rock of a man

Crumbled like paper and sand in my hands

His face was fearful and his voice was weak

He talked of leaving; I was confused but sought

With my heart to show him a way;

To find a new path to make him stay

His troubles had overwhelmed him to the core

He had made up his mind to take no more;

No more of the pain deep within his heart

For night after night his demons he fought

He wrestled for years to overcome

But this final battle could not be won

A stranger to me for how could this be?

A man I had met just once before;

They say there were 38 others he could have called

But oh God of God's, it had to be me that he met!

I was met by a man broken and stricken with grief

Whose pain and suffering was beyond belief!

I was out of my depth I had not a clue

I had no idea I did not know what to do

In others pain and suffering one should lend a hand

So I offered a heart to seek and understand

Understand just what he was going through

But oh God of God's I knew not what to do

He spoke of love through his many tears
He shared his accomplishments through the years
He recalled past times of happiness
But somehow strangely, I was really perplexed
He was in the past and not the present
For he could not see beyond this day
I hoped for him a new truth would come
But blindly, I failed to see his days on earth was done
For he was weary in body and broken in mind
But in true 'British spirit', a little courage to find
To dispel the myth the unfounded truths
But the rhetoric he spoke, just mirrored his youth
In the earlier days when life went wrong
When he pursued a career with a wish to be strong
But the force that he had so proudly lead,
Abandoned him on a mountain until he was dead
No surprise for infallibility was not to be compromised
For all public figures in high office are to know
That the powers that be all control
Their lives in centimetres, inches and square
With no compromise for unwarranted fears
Oh that comfort was offered or that help had sooner came
His name now omitted from future accomplishments and history;
One who would have exceled and gone from strength to strength.
A father who spoke so tenderly of the love within his heart

A giant of a man now weeping with a stranger as he walked

The brownness of my face did not scare him

Neither did the pink braids twisted in my hair

For it was this difference which drew him unto me,

A getting to know and a setting free

Oh that I had more wisdom and that I had known

That this man now speaking in riddles

Was already dead inside, but only stood to show;

That he was essentially good in his heart within

And this final moment was to disarm and forgiveness bring

But I was a stranger and nothing seemed out of place

A wounded heart choosing in his final hour;

For not a single observer could comprehend

How two total strangers, who are barely friends

A simple connection not borne from ambition or greed

But one which simply met a need

And from the distance and safety

Of my home far away, I prayed with all my might and power

That God upon him would shower

The peace he sought in his wretchedness

And release the chief to a new type of 'happiness'

For there is freedom in death, but constraints in life,

The commitments, woes and every bitter sacrifice

The chief is now at peace and completely set free,

Free from suffering and misery

But I thank God in the strangest of ways
That the lessons that this situation brought to me
For the chief in a strange way when he died;
Closed my heart, and opened my eyes.

The enduring spirit of each human being remains undiminished when those things that underpin our lives are always at the forefront. Admittedly, those events forced me to take a very exhaustive view of myself and redefine who I was in order that I may find the courage previously lacking. When we are able to do this we are also granted the release we seek from hurtful past events that would have otherwise kept us in bondage. I have lived a most unremarkable life on one hand, yet on the other, I have witnessed a number of actions that have undoubtedly given meaning to some of the things that I have come to value most of all. I remember the evening we almost ran out of oil in our table lamp and was about to be plunged into darkness throughout the house. My mother, as resourceful as ever, got a bottle of highly flammable spirit, the one she used whenever she administered insulin to my diabetic brother and began pouring it into the depleted oil lamp with the wick still glowing. She was immediately engulfed into a fireball and began to burn to death in front of us both. We were too young to do anything to help her except to scream at the top of our voices and I thank God our screaming worked, because it drew the swift attention of my older brother and his friends who came running from a short distance away and was both wise and calm enough to get a large blanket from the bed and threw it over her and saved her life. My mother sustained burns to over thirty per cent of her body but refused to remain in the hospital. She immediately discharged herself after she was bandaged from head to toe and returned home to care for us. I remember as my brother removed the blanket from her body, she was draped in a corner of the veranda unable to move and sobbing helplessly like a little child and the smell of her burnt flesh has stayed permanently fixed within my memory.

I also recall the Methodist priest, the Englishman who was in charge of the parish of Mountainside, I remember in particular his cold eyes, blue as ice and his dark heart as repugnant as the devil's and his greying blonde hair swept back from his dishonest face like a show room dummy; without real emotion. I recall my father always saying; "No care how hog try fi hide unda sheep wool, im grunt let in down," meaning, it does not matter how much a hog tries to hide under sheep's wool his grunt will betray him. This simply means that it is impossible for a person to conceal their true character for too long. With this thought in mind, I became very concerned the number of times this priest drove his car to the gates of my primary school and brought sweets for my young friends but especially concerned the number of occasions where he bundled two or three at a time into his vehicle and brought them back to the gates at the end of the day. I remembered how afraid I was for them and knew I had to find a way to protect them from this degenerate excuse of a human being.

My great sadness to this day, was the fact there was not a single trustworthy adult in whom I could confide this dreadful secret. If I dared to tell anyone about the priest's perverse behaviour, I would have been beaten senseless for maligning a 'respectable' Christian man from England. I simply could not justify a beating to save my friends at this time and so, I decided I had to find a way to halt their routine trips to his home. I was smarter than many of my peers but not nearly smart enough, I was stronger than some of them but at the age of ten years, how strong should a child really have to be? One day as he came by and bundled a number of my friends into his car, I frantically went looking for one of the older boys with whom I was reasonably friendly and he and I formed a plan and followed behind them. It wasn't too difficult to gain access to his home since, people mostly called by when invited to do so and it was reasonably open and so, we climbed up onto the veranda in a hope to catch a glimpse of what was happening. That day I learned of a new type of evil that can never be washed away; not in a bath, a pool nor a tub. For that perverse man had never been transformed by the blood of Christ but was masquerading under the banner of 'religion,' the foulest of all known evils. This was the first time in my life where I was able to outsmart an evil beast of a man and allowed my beautiful friends, Lorraine and 'Brighty' to escape from his clutches to freedom. They were young and innocent and were simply not aware of the perverted nature of the man in whom they had placed their trust for that moment.

For the first time I saw real evil and recognised it, I hated what I saw and was so repulsed by it, I became determined to halt it in its track; and we did, we all did. I knew if I did not find a way to halt this evil, many innocent lives would be devastated by his actions. Of course he was never seen at our wonderful school gates again, in fact, I never heard mention of him from that time on. This highlights the fact that, in matters of principles and morally right actions, it's not the size of the person that matters but in the end it comes down to the strength of character. This period in my life was a time of many 'first' encounters. My friends and I had a secret and although I find secrets in general an abomination, I have come to recognise that not everything needs to be acknowledged to another, especially when there was an excellent outcome. This was the first time I recognised the power of knowledge and its effectiveness when used positively and began to grow more confident of the fact that; there is always assurance of victory in every number greater than one.

I also remember the man who committed the most dreadful crimes against others in my community and when everyone was incensed against him, he disappeared into the night and was found hanging from a tree the following morning. I remember as a very young girl looking up at his dead body hanging in the tree, I felt neither sadness nor regret and the unbelievable stillness of those standing gazing at his lifeless form with an undeclared morbid approval in their eyes that he had done the right thing. I have seen many men gone out in rough seas fishing and their corpses came back one by one. I was propelled with curiosity to view their disfigured dead bodies, at times headless, armless and beyond recognition but would later regret my actions as the darkness descended upon me during the long watch of the night, constantly reminding me of the fragile nature of my own life. I have been cognisant of a number of men who raped and violated scores of vulnerable young girls but were never brought to accountability. I have seen men killed other men because they were angry or simply because they were hungry. It is for these reasons that I have sought unremittingly to find men in whom trust on my part could be genuinely inspired. Whilst I do not possess an intense dislike of men in general, trusting them is something I have never learned to do. I have nevertheless discovered generosity, confidence and loyalty in the one who has chosen me as his companion and who has unquestionably walked alongside me every day in my shoes rather than compelling me to walk alongside him in his own and without a jot of doubt has remained my most faithful and trustworthy of friends.

There are however, a number of exceptions to this rule and I remain grateful that in recent years I have found kindness and integrity in four of the most remarkable men I could possibly know. There is Thomas, [Dr Tom to me, aristocrat to some and egotistical to others] and Peter, the last boy scout, [both German], Kaine, [British], Peter [British], all possessing an unequalled spirit of decency and open-handedness.

Thomas is remarkable in his intellect; a genius of life in every sense, his major claim to fame is of having read fifty thousand books. I suspect this is probably a little far from the truth but as a doctor of economics his knowledge and skills are very telling. He is successful by the standards he has created for himself and pursues a life of excellence through accomplishments. His zest for living remains undiminished and although I cannot understand his need for such excessive affluence, I refuse to judge or malign his character. Any man who has an overwhelming desire to possess a dozen or more of the rarest Rolls Royce's ever produced, numerous other unusual and exquisite cars, homes in the Middle East and in a number of major European cities, is simply beyond my understanding, yet remains above my judgements. His generosity and care are qualities I have rarely found.

Peter on the other hand is the uncomplicated one whose computer programming skills has placed him within one of the largest firms in the world; and yet, he never speaks of it; his wife Susanna is equally straightforward and pleasant. Kaine, also a computer programmer is a remarkable and respectful individual who possess a deep sense of social justice and integrity. Peter, my father-in-law, from my first marriage – how I love this man! I have found in this gentle man, a warm and generous heart, a Christian whose life has been exemplary in every sense. Peter is a genius, although I don't believe he knows it. He began playing the piano by ear at the age of four and swiftly developed a gift for music. He has played on a number of occasions at prestigious events in major cities but has played tirelessly at various churches for almost seventy-six years; this truly has been a life of obedience and service. Life would simply not be the same without these four individuals in whom I have been permitted to invest a great deal of trust and mutual respect.

When I consider such wealth and privileges in contrast to having gone to bed as a child with only a prayer to keep me alive until the following morning, I simply cannot reconcile what the fundamental values of others are. I remember on a number of occasions standing in line for food during one of the most repressive periods in my country's history and not knowing whether my tiny stature would disadvantage my position. I have ran many miles in barefoot to please my mother, [not because I had no shoes, but simply to preserve the only pair I owned], because she would sit and time me for excellence and I always wanted to beat my previous record. I have buried, I have unearthed, I have dreamed and awoken and was wretched because nothing that I longed for had changed. I have fallen through fear, through neglect, through pride and physical abuse. I always found a way to recoil back and stand once more. I have remained standing, not within my own strength but within the strength of my God who steadily and compassionately empowers me through each dreadful period.

I have watched my older brothers and sister baton down the hatches waiting for a hurricane to pass, hoping that we would live through it all. I have been rigid with fear through the terrors of the night from the childhood stories we were told to keep us from going out after dark. I have buried my father after his death to prostate cancer and six years later buried my beautiful and unforgettable mother, whose slow and painful death from bowel cancer was the ugliest and most agonising thing that I have witnessed in my life. I have buried my friend's infant who, after being born pre-maturely, died at the age of thirteen months in her arms; his death could not be explained. I have witnessed Chantal's strength and her dignity, the type only to be found deep within the heart of a grieving and loving mother. At each difficult point in my life I have recognised the two things that are way beyond the control of anyone; death and the evil done against others.

My father was full of many words and possessed a saying for every eventuality in life. He was at his most vocal when contrasting life and death. His two most over used sayings were; "Death is shared equal" and that it also "Respected no man," and our only defence against these devastating forces was to accept them in order that we do not become consumed by them and that no amount of wealth or status can halt the inevitability of dying. I don't believe for a moment he was advocating that evil against other human beings should be accepted. I simply believe he meant that, while we are relatively impotent to effect any real changes in the behaviour of evil men and women, we must simply chose alternative paths within our own lives in order that we gain distance from evil and are able to seek good in all our undertakings.

There are so many men and women who wish that they could be good but I believe that they simply do not know where to begin since they have no genuine points of reference from where goodness can be harnessed in a world of vice, greed and selfish aspirations. It has become so easy for 'good' men and women to do the most heinous and abominable acts against others and once more I am finding it increasingly difficult to recognise the angels from the demons. Naturally, I am not alone with such grave doubts and while I may not have a visible platform from where to articulate them, there are many decent human beings who are dying every day under the banner of truth and oppression, simply because they refuse to surrender to vast untruths and injustices.

Whenever I was able to see beyond painful challenges, I began to recognise that suffering is in fact a facilitator to growth. This is supported in Romans 5:3; "Not only so, but we also glory in our suffering, because we know that suffering produces perseverance; perseverance, character; and character, hope." It is through this hope that many of my fears were confidently relinquished and where I was better equipped to motivate others into direct action as opposed to an indifferent reaction. In many instances, the action of compassionate and responsible individuals can strongly challenge those who elevate themselves above others with the sole purpose of passing judgements and to condemn by way of exclusion, manipulation and ghettoization. I have no idea what a ghetto is since its context and values are wholly alien to me. If someone was to tell me, "You are an alien," the onus of disproof would not be attributed to me but rather for them to prove their ludicrous assertion of me. Admittedly, for those people who are actively living damaging stereotypes and labels that have been attached to them continue to raise my levels of anxiety to troubling intensities. Those who are unable to embrace an optimistic approach towards meaningful realities should cease to think at all. I have been met with open hostility and with incredulity and whether these were in fact attributed to my notable difference I simply do not care. I am delighted my difference was not overlooked. One of the most terrifying realities for me would be, if I was to be transported to a place where everyone looked exactly the same as me! I would not want it neither could I live it.

Whenever I have been maliciously and unreasonably judged by those around me, my one question imperative was immediately instituted. Since, as soon as I am able to understand the charges against me, I stand a far greater chance of a robust defence leading to my acquittal. Of course I don't actually care what the world thinks but I nevertheless, care how it thinks. I am confident that if everyone was permitted to think exactly as they choose, the planet would have more of its inhabitants in purgatory than on its surface. Although a minority of people are unnecessarily cruel and unjust, there is still however a large majority, who are generous and warm and who become deeply affected by injustices against others. There is a moral transformation for those who are willing to move past the boundaries of their irrational fears.

This transformation begins to occur when judgements of others are permanently suspended since, all are inadequate aspiring beings. It is only from here that all are able to move from darkness to light and from many faults to a credible perfection.

CHAPTER SIX

Fault to Perfection

I am confident there is no such thing as a perfect man or woman, a human being absolved of all faults and blame. It's a fact that every person possesses the potential to be both good and evil since, both must co-exist alongside each other. The universe simply could not be a continuum without good and evil on opposing spectrums. This is the reason God incarnate, [Christ], came into the world to redeem mankind from the place where they had fallen and raising them beyond their pitiful seats of misery, fault, blame and suffering. The fall, accredited to the very sinful human nature and from where there was no means of escape, except in the redemptive act of Christ where he restored lives back to purpose and in the fullness of their intended image. God, the complete embodiment of perfection and the only one perfect enough to make a sacrifice on such an immense scale because God is perfection exemplified -both in practice and principle. Perfection is the highest degree of excellence; but whose excellence? If mankind has no meaningful ways of measuring the length, breadth and depth of absolute perfection- can they have a valued argument for or against it? Admittedly, this argument may not be plausible since, God's ways of measuring are highly contentious to the measurements of mankind and the reference points that they create are based loosely upon the feeble methodologies from which many such judgements are drawn.

On the basis of this brief thought, one recognises further that, in the absence of good, evil is the dominant factor, possessing the inner man or woman and in the absence of evil, good is the state by which many people become essentially constructive beings. In contrast to the many faults over which a person appears to wrestle for much of their lives, there is the seemingly unattainable virtue of perfection. No one can be perfect all the time but can continue to strive to achieve aspects or moments of perfection. In order to understand what human 'perfection' looks like, we were given a very clear example in the book of Job.

In Job 1:1 we read; in the land of Uz there lived a man whose name was Job. This man was blameless and upright; he feared God and shunned evil. One immediately explore the idea of a 'faultless' human being, one of whom God boasted to Satan. Then the Lord said to Satan, "Have you considered my servant Job? There is no one on earth like him; he is blameless and upright, a man who fears God and shuns evil." From this opening verse in Job chapter one, we are acutely aware of the nature and character of Job. God was not boasting merely to annoy the devil into retreat but he was boasting to provoke a reaction. As the story in the book of Job unfolded, we begin to understand in greater detail the bedrocks which underpinned Job's life, his immovable faith in God, his determination, his indomitable will and his enduring love and trust in the God of his people. Job clearly was a man whose life was pleasing before God and who possessed a healthy and natural fear of God which allowed him to endure his suffering graciously and to look to God hopefully. It was quite a momentous narrative; a discourse which took place in the presence of God, angels and that demon; Satan. This highlighted one particular point that, God is pleased when a person pursues him and is blameless before him.

In most of the Bible's narrative God was in direct conflict with prophets, priest, Scribes, Pharisees and his people Israel. There were so few occasions when God was sincerely pleased with a human being. The one other instance which characterised the nature of God's pleasure in relation to absolute perfection was the moment where Jesus was baptised by John the Baptist in the Jordan and as he was coming up out of the water a voice from heaven said; "This is my son, whom I love, with him I am well pleased." Matthew 3:17. Just as in the same way as God was sincerely pleased with Christ, he is equally pleased when the lives of men and women pursue his perfection. God did not call any human being to live a 'perfect' life; instead, he called each person to allow him to live a perfect life in them through his Holy Spirit. In human terms of what is achievable or not achievable, the standards of mankind could never be set against those of God since; God's infinitely surpasses all aspects of human beings. We must however, have a point of reference, a place from where we can begin a reasonable journey of faith, where God will travel with us step by step of our voyage and continue to inform us daily through his Holy Spirit. This perfection is concerned with inward transformation and although seldom visible to those around us, it can never be hidden from God. God undoubtedly is the only one capable of transforming lives completely and equipping all to live meaningful realities, not only before him but also before each other.

The idea of perfection for me, begins with a deep knowledge and love for the deity. And as we understand from Proverbs 1:7; "The fear of the Lord is the beginning of knowledge." This is highlighting the desire that God has for human beings to understand His holy and righteous admonitions. Since, it is in the outworking of God's Holy Spirit that a life of perfection is made possible and each person is fully able to discern God's divine purposes. In my pursuit for moral perfection through various enumerations; humility, justice temperance, order, resolution, moderation, and chastity, I have spent a great deal of time discovering the principles that impact and govern my life. If I remain unaware of the bedrocks which underpin my existence, I would be no nearer to eradicating those major annoyances that hinder my growth towards transformation and freedom. I find that a process of re-evaluation becomes necessary in order that I may know the things I value, the ones that are insignificant and to understand those things that either strengthens or weakens me. Whenever I am faced with adversities that bring me into the path of conflict either, my faults increase thereby, or I will simply be guided towards moral perfection.

So what is moral perfect and does a person ever really become perfect? If I were to consider the idea of 'moral perfection' and what it means in human terms, I simply would not have a viable and credible source from where I could seamlessly align this thought. When I look at Scripture however, I am immediately aware that the perfection of God surpasses all others since, man's ideologies are God's realities and all feeble human aspirations have been met and exceeded within the Godhead. God would simply not continue reproaching men and women to live holy and pleasing lives before him if there were no reasonable hope of this being a definite reality. He would simply never ask a person to become what he or she was incapable of becoming and it was for this reason that the gift of the Holy Spirit, also known as the 'enabler', was given to all. This seemingly ideal life, whilst highly possible, is not one that is easily achieved since, it is affiliated with suffering, separateness, sacrifices and at times being ostracised by those closest to us. This life of perfection requires a faithful and steadfast spirit and one that should be highly enterprising and adaptable to change. I believe a life in the spirit is the most authentic experience one will ever know in their pursuit for perfection. This ideal cannot be matched to any other value known to human beings.

Of course it is so much easier for a number of individuals to appear in control by their portrayal of a 'perfect' existence to their contemporaries when in fact, they are assaulted daily in their lives. It is partly for this reasons that so many of us would rather appear 'full' rather than 'empty' to those around us. My mother used to remind us as children, "Empty barrels make the most noise." Naturally, people dispossessed of morals, scruples, compassion and empathy for others and who are living deceptive lives, would sooner continue their woeful pretence than to address the faults that hinders their attempts to move to a credible perfection.

The Bible speaks the truth on many subject matters, some difficult and contentious issues and others where just a brief measure of common sense will allow many to work out what the intentions are behind them. In Luke 16:15, we see where Jesus was having another confrontation with the Pharisees; He said to them, "You are the ones who justify yourselves in the eyes of others, but God knows your hearts. What people value highly is detestable in God's sight." There are many such incidences where Jesus was in direct conflict with the 'righteous' Pharisees, who by their own admission observed the letter of the law and that, their pursuit for perfection was to be found in this rigorous application to the law and their righteous living and fear of God but was clearly not reflected in their treatment of others around them. Jesus continued to be dismayed by their over-zealous attitude in all their visible actions. They were only too pleased to display their overtly 'perfect' attitudes to a number of habitual observers. Those hypocritical men were merely masking dark and sinister intentions that were deeply troubling and had their roots in greed, lack of compassion for the poor, orphan and strangers. Their attitude boasted of superiority over all other 'holy' persons; Jesus included. Since humility was not an underpinning virtue of the Scribes and Pharisees, it was no surprise the approach they adopted, for while they boasted about their 'perfection', underlying hidden faults thrived and festered which was displeasing before God. According to Gandhi; "There is no one without faults, not even men of God. They are men of Him not because they are faultless, but because they know their own faults, they strive against them, they do not hide them, and are ever ready to correct themselves." It is only in the admission of one's short-comings, faults and sinful desires that one becomes empowered to effect lasting change and transformation. Admittedly, a person can only begin by acknowledging those aspects of their character which is lacking in both morals and principles. It is only when the desire to change exceeds the need to remain the same that a way forward becomes possible.

Whenever I recognised a need for change, I would institute it swiftly since, revisions have proved to be the most beneficial way to exact necessary corrections and allow myself to become the autonomous individual I crave. From this point I was able to overcome the same mode of conflicting behaviour patterns in which I had become lodged.

One of the most difficult exercises for many people is identifying virtuous qualities about themselves and yet, if many were asked to make a list of virtues and faults, the list containing faults would far exceed the one with virtues. This is a natural response since, so few people are able to discover any virtue within them. It's hardly surprising that the minor faults witnessed in others are always easier to highlight than the huge liabilities in a person's own life.

A man or woman whose existence is always operating between the defences of fault and blame, often fail to recognise even the faintest hint of goodness in another, if something is unknown it simply cannot be given shape nor purpose. I am aware that evil can overtake a person who was previously judged as balanced, trustworthy or even compassionate. Every person is capable of violating the boundaries of another and it is for this reason that I remain cautious and observant at every stage of my life. One of the worst possible outcomes that I could imagine would be, for a person who had spent the majority of their life undertaking malicious actions against others and dying without making the necessary expiations. It is for this reason that I have made the decision on a number of occasions to go back to the place of hurt and suffering and although never taken lightly, has nevertheless proved, the most seamless way to expedite morally right actions. Understandably, it is helpful to gaze back through the window of the past from time to time although one should never linger unnecessarily, for although life must be understood backwards, it must be lived forward. Soren Kierkegaard, (1813-1855).

Seven Departures: One Arrival

I am a person who believes in simplicity not duplicity. I have never felt an overbearing requirement to have my life influenced by either, dishonest or challenging people who will cause me undue anxiety. Of course, much of this is a direct result of my mother's and father's numerous admonishments in my earlier life. I believe I was determined and organised as a child and would speak my mind on a number of issues but was also a source of confidence for many who entrusted me with a number of private matters. Naturally, as I have grown, I have maintained this position and will remain defiant in its defence. It is hardly surprising that I take a pessimistic view in almost every instance on human nature since, the majority of my experiences have highlighted a number of malevolent and reckless individuals, who in their dispensation of 'justice,' went way beyond the remit of what was deemed morally acceptable.

In western culture, Britain in particular, there is a rigorous network aimed at the defence and support of the most vulnerable in society; children, the elderly, those on the fringes and numerous others. Admittedly, it has failed spectacularly on a number of occasions but by and large, the fact that there is accountability, means a number of people will consider the consequences before any attempts are made to breech any boundaries. In every society children remain the most valuable but most vulnerable members. This vulnerability demands protection, support and cooperation from those fortunate enough to be gifted with lives that are to become the future and heart of every nation.

Undoubtedly, children are my greatest love. The ease with which I am able to feel accepted and valued amongst them surpasses that of many other feelings. I wanted children for two reasons; first, to enhance my potential as a woman and secondly, to demonstrate what a supportive mother can do when she stands alongside her children from conception, through to the fulfilment of their lives.

It is for this reason that I cannot walk pass a child without wondering whether they are loved, nurtured and protected. I simply could not imagine having children and leaving them behind. Of course culture and economics plays a vital role when such decisions are taken but I would sooner die in poverty and want protecting my children than to send photographs and parcels routinely from a distance. Children simply don't want to see a picture of their mother; they need to touch her face, to be embraced by her night and day and be made to feel loved and secure in her presence, rather than longing for her due to her absence. A number of people succumbed to the idea that of a better way of life with promises of vast improvements to their economic situation, thus forfeiting family and traditional values. This sadly, took precedence over a majority of other principles.

In my culture particularly, a great number of children have suffered unduly in their parent's quest to elevate their standard of living. It is virtually impossible to raise the socio-economic bar without lowering a majority of philosophical ones. Of course I am a habitual thinker, one who attempts to rationalise events in a hope of making a number of meaningful evaluations. There are some however, that are compounded by their sheer weight and intensity and what transpired finally was that, no amount of rationale would elucidate the darkness surrounding them. It is for this reason that, as painful as it is for me, I have made the brave decision to step back briefly into a very large space in order to gaze tenderly on a small and extremely vulnerable girl.

I was ten years old when I found myself clinging to my mother as she was about to leave me with a distant family member and board a flight to Manchester. For a child who had spent the majority of her time either by her mother's side or on her knees, this was impossible. The other side of the fence was as far away to me as the moon and

Manchester, well, at this moment death seemed nearer. I feared that I may never see her again. Much of my memory about that wretched morning is still a blur but I have had the event played over and over again by those adults who witnessed it as I grew older. That was the second time I died. The first time was a year earlier when in the same way, I was clinging helplessly to my beloved sister Carol as she boarded a flight to Toronto. This was the moment my family started to be dismantled. It was everyone's belief that things were going to be better but not for me, everything became worse, much worse. I was terrified of the darkness ahead me and fearful of the disintegrating identity behind me. Although my two year old niece Desha was left with me at this relative's home, I was unable to gain an ounce of comfort from this at the height of my suffering.

Miss Linda, as she was known, was an authoritarian, a seventh Day Adventist and of course, attending church every Saturday was a prerequisite. Miss Linda was old, perhaps not that old, but she seemed really old to me. She had been widowed a number of years and had six grown-up children, four of whom were professional people in positions of teaching, banking and with the government. In every family there are exceptions and in this one it was Beverley and Roy who both suffered from mental health issues. They were the most inoffensive people imaginable but routinely spoke with Desha and me, trying to make us feel welcome into our new 'family.' In contrast to many other families, Miss Linda was seen as reasonably wealthy, a good Christian and an upright member of the community. I am used to hard work and of course in a new environment I knew I had to work even harder to justify my care. I was not however, prepared for the hen houses! This was Miss Linda's most viable source of income: the hen houses that outstretched six football pitches! It was my job each morning before school and again in the evening to collect the eggs and washed and prepared them for market. I found this task arduous and lonely and those hens - they were uncooperative every time.

Somehow I was coping. I was finding my way into this stranger's heart and home. She would read with me when the chores were done and would spend time braiding my hair in such a loving and affectionate manner that surprised me on many levels. She seemed a kind and considerate woman. Although she never permitted me and Desha to return to our family home, just twenty minutes away on foot, she did however, allow my brothers to visit me on a few precious occasions. Of course this was the best days for me since I was able to feel like a real family again, however brief the moment. Time seemed to begin to ease the sting out of my mother's departure and with regular letters and telegrams from her; the day of my arrival was now some distance behind me. When the weather is about to change we know since, we can see the clouds getting dark and heavy and the wind changes course from a westerly direction to perhaps an easterly one but there is an unpredictability that is human nature and no amount of calculation can ever determine its final path.

One day as I returned happily from school Miss Linda marched over and apprehend me by my arm and without uttering a word, marched me through the house and threw me fiercely into my room, locking the door firmly shut behind her. This fearful imprisonment was my reality for a number of months. The door was opened twice a day; once in the morning and again in the evening to bring me what they interpreted as food. Although I was too distressed to eat, I realised I needed to survive and would eat only enough to keep me alive. I simply had no appetite for food, only for life.

My ambivalent attitude towards food for much of my life has part of its origin here. I have rarely found pleasure in eating as much as I should and my view of it is that, it is merely an aid to the continuance of life. To say that this was a distressing experience is a gross understatement, it was beyond terrifying. In the moments of silence I would try to logically work how I was transported from the gates of 'heaven' to the pits of 'hell' in in such a short time. In my basic rudimentary analysis, I simply could not understand how a perfectly gentle woman could be transformed into a monster and virtually without warning. It was during one such moment of searching that the door was flung opened and in walked Gordon with Miss Linda following sharply behind. He is Miss Linda's eldest son, the head teacher of a local secondary school, an upright and respectable man when adorned with his fine linen suit. Gordon is a giant, over six feet tall, with the girth of a muskox and a face to match.

I remember this day remarkably well, in fact, it is one I remember better than all the others. In this moment, the terror which gripped me was almost as overwhelming as Gordon's powerful arms. There was an expression on his face that was alien to me and as he grabbed me and started to beat me, I feared that every strike would end my life. When it was over, I was impassive with dread. Gordon and Miss Linda proceed towards the door and locked it behind as they left.

I remember whimpering, though barely audible. I realised there was no point in screaming because, there was no one around and if anyone heard me, they simply would not come. I remember curling up in the corner of the room and the intensity of the beating was made worst because I was wearing a nylon nightdress, making the tough leather belt finding its target of my back that much easier. I must had fallen asleep sometime after and remember waking up a few hours later and attempting to remove my night dress since it was covered with blood. This was too painful because the nightdress had now merged into the wounds on my back and had stuck fast to them making every effort to remove it agony. I made a sensible decision to leave it and just allowed everything to take its own course.

This period appeared endless. I simply had no idea how long it would last. I don't believe my brothers were aware of my plight since, I was confident they would have come to my assistance. Days merged into night and nights into day, nothing made sense to me at the age of ten. I was repeatedly asked before subsequent beatings to confess of money or goods I had taken but I had no idea what I was being asked. I know that I was always given permission to make eggs for my diabetic brother on the few occasions he was permitted to visit me. I would have fed him from my own plate than watch him perish in front of me. I simply could not understand how Miss Linda and her children had arrived at this ludicrous and unfounded assertion. Admittedly, as difficult as it has been to forgive the woman who stood by and watched as I was beaten for something that she had done, I have forgiven her since, I could see no other way to show an alternative path.

Throughout history, a majority of people have been complicit in the pain and suffering of others and have been impotent to make a difference. When this suffering, is a direct result of their wilful and malicious actions, then it is time to take an exhaustive view of the purpose of their humanity. The fact that I forgave her allowed the generosity of her grand-daughter to impact my life twenty-five years after that dreadful incident. I was dehumanised because she was greedy and possessed a callous heart that would rob a widow. I was punished because she knew that as a child I could not be made accountable but if she confessed she would face the judicial system and her own young children would suffer. I love Shania more than any other child in Newcombe Valley. She fills me with both joy and hope of what each human being is capable of becoming. In her I simply could not ask for more in terms of her care and regard for me and my family. God has a way of bringing our enemies back but recycled as better people in their children and grand-children occasionally. When this happens, it is nearly always tinged with an added measure of sweetness; to God be the glory!

I am not sure whether, 'rescued' is the right word but after the darkest period in my life a light did eventually shine. The unexpected happened, my auntie a magistrate and wealthy landowner, came with unquestionable authority and this period finally drew to a close. I was pleased to be returning to my own community and naturally, life would be very different since my aunt and her husband was even stricter than Miss Linda, this appeared the least of my concerns at this time, I was simply overjoyed to be free once more. Apart from my mother and sister Carol, my aunt was the woman I most loved. It's interesting that in addition to loving her, I had a secret admiration for her. She was intelligent, educated and was in fact one of the first women in our district and beyond to drive and own a car. She was an accomplished and highly envied individual and she knew it. I did not mind that because she was my mother's only sister and everyone were afraid of her wealth, but especially her wrath.

I believe myself to be a very adaptable person, I had to be. I learned from an early age to exceed the required standard in almost everything since, this excelling, either averted a beating or unkind words or if fortunate, may even merit a tiny amount of praise. My aunt's house was the biggest for miles. She was an extremely busy woman, travelling the length and breadth of the island on a weekly basis with her authoritarian husband and so, employed a number of young people in her absence to take care of the cattle amongst a number of other jobs. Audrey was the fourteen year old girl who was one such person. Admittedly, as I child I had no idea how young she was because the way she performed her daily chores was like that of a builder. She cleaned, washed, cooked and cared for Alicia their four year old grand-daughter.

Audrey was rescued from poverty, I was rescued from pain and it was seamless forming an alliance. We had a great routine to get the chores done to limit complaints but the most notable aspect in all of this; she was now my dearest friend. Audrey was four years older than me but decades wiser and it was on this wisdom that we were able to flourish intermittently. We were never permitted to use the beautiful marbled bathroom since girls were seen as 'unclean' to my aunt's husband but had to make our crude outdoor bathing facilities as beautiful and sanitised as we could. I simply don't know how Audrey could smile so ungrudgingly because in view of what I know now, her heart inside was breaking. Not surprising, I awoke one morning and Audrey was gone; like an owl, she had flown away under the cover of darkness and I never saw her again. It was about twenty years later I was given her telephone number in New York and she and I talked for a very long time, but never once did we mention that wretched house. Audrey fled to a safe haven and left me in unreserved hell. I missed her more than anything and my work load got heavier and heavier, for my aunt, though fierce to those outside, was redundant and ineffective in her home against the might of her conniving and objectionable husband.

I remember them eating the choicest cuts of meat and fish when they thought I was sleeping. I was routinely given 'prison food,' what is commonly known a 'turn cornmeal,' the meal that very poor people eat to stay alive but is a favourite for the dogs of many well-off families. I am not a dog and so, I refused to eat it and would wait an opportune moment to hurl it out the window to the waiting dogs when I was certain no one was watching. I never complained and remained hopeful of real change in the foreseeable future. The politics in families can be as divisive as those in parliament. Although my grandma lived in my mother's home just a stroll away, I can only remember one occasion where I was permitted to spend a day with her - this wasn't because I was missing her terribly but simply because they needed to off-load me for that day.

The purpose of my grandma living in my mother's house was to take care of my three brothers. There was my older brother, Stevie who was fourteen and fairly strong-willed and independent and Fitzgerald who had spent a majority of his life in diabetic coma. Finally there was Wayne - he was the baby and although only two years old when my mother left and sixteen when he first saw her, in a number of ways he was more fortunate that the rest of us since he did not know her and simply had nothing to compare. Furthermore, he was loved and protected unreservedly. There was the difficult issue of the three orphans my grandma had adopted, since her ability to provide for them was debatable but her love for them remained unquestionable. My grandma Valcy was a beautiful woman, both inside and out. She naturally had made a number of errors in the early part of her life but I simply did not care for what she had done. My aunt in particular, was her greatest critic and held grudges and doubts, on a scale as grand as her estate. I can never understand why people become embittered instead of learning to forgive and I accept that if my own mother was deemed unwell and was unable to take care of me, then a few decades later adopted three children and lavished untold love and attention onto them, perhaps my reaction would be similar to my aunt's. Who Knows? I believe my mother and aunt first met their mother, [my grand-mother], when they were seven and nine respectively. Regardless of all this ancient family politics and histrionics, to me grandma was lovely and kind and I was delighted to have her beside me in the space left vacant by my mother. Children don't actually want the world; they just want the time and attention of those whose love they depend on for support and encouragement. Grandma was more than reassurance; she was the one source of light and goodness from which I could hope and this hope was intensified, each time I touched her hands or her face.

Touching her made a light shone brightly inside me, so bright in fact, that it outsourced the midday sun. I simply cannot explain this phenomenon to a mere observer and grandma was exceptional since, she was one of the few people who permitted me to touch her to my hearts' content. As a child, many saw it as a comforting act on my part, as an adult, a major irritation on theirs. I would touch family, friends and even strangers. My friends would dare me and I would dare myself. I simply had to touch everyone in whom I could sense a genuine level of goodness and kindness and my touching was affirmation of those perceived qualities. I knew when I touched them any goodness present would increase the light within me and if I was mistaken, though rare, my light would fade briefly but never went out. But of course touching grandma surpassed them all.

There were times as a child my need to touch another 'good' human being was so overwhelming, I would simply extract myself in a non-communicative position, such was my need to touch. Seeing my distress, my poor brothers and sister would permit me to touch their hands or face until I was full of joy and lost in deep slumber. Naturally, as an adult, hurtled in a strange culture, touching was not permissible. What a strange way of living! If you wanted to touch another human being you simply must pay; in the massage parlours, the brothels and every place where an inherently priceless gift that affirmed the essences of humanity had now become a cheap and uncharacteristic thrill.

Naturally, not everyone in my culture has a fixation with touching others but at least the years have granted me more wisdom. Admittedly, two of the most significant places of comfort and healing in my life have come by way of Caribbean women and European men; although it's not been that simple! I only touch women who are fully aware in advance, those who know me well; family and extremely close friends and the men I had a need to touch, I also had a desire to marry. Touching a man would tell me of his dexterity and where his priorities and focuses were. As a child, touching was my comfort through every painful and indeterminate moment and as an adult remains my most vulnerable but unequalled and satisfying peculiarity.

There were occasions where my aunt was tender with me but tenderness was not her greatest strength. Her husband on the other hand, is not a man any wise person would ever choose to touch. He appeared a pillar of righteousness to those outside but was in fact, a devious and scheming man; essentially, a Scribe and Pharisee at heart. I remember the number of malicious actions he undertook against the neighbours, even his own niece whose puppy he poisoned because it had wrecked a small area of the garden. I remember distinctly the promised ball I never got to attend but was simply ordered to remove my beautiful handmade dress five minutes before they left, because there was no room in the car for me. Cinderella was home alone and there would be no prince to the rescue, only an intruder attempting to break in as I guarded it all alone in the dark. I ran to the place I knew my uncle kept his guns and picking up the shotgun that almost dwarfed my size and shouted in my boldest voice, "I have a gun and I will shoot," he must have seen this child with a shot gun twice her size and decided not to trespass any further and fled.

I was trembling as I relayed the story to my aunt when she returned later that evening and for once, she was proud of me. Wisdom is a very strange attribute that seemed to escape me whenever I have tried to apprehend it in the past but when I did not seek it came of its own accord. I know that if I had dared fire that shot gun I would have been killed with the intensity. I believe that was why she was proud of me; I saved her a lot of potential embarrassment.

There was at least one other occasion I believe my aunt was proud of me and that was the occasion I did my first recital at church, winning first prize - she was delighted with me then. Whether she was proud of me or not I refused to stop hoping and praying and I am so aware that anyone can kill the dreamer but they can never kill the dream. I remember the house being directly over the flight path. Each time I spotted a plane going over, I was mesmerized, I simply could not believe the stories I had been told of people eating, sleeping and doing normal things inside those strange metal tubes. The more I saw them pass over, the more intense was my appetite for freedom. I knew that it would take a miracle for me to be granted the right to eat, sleep, drink and do normal things in one - carrying me, on my first flight to autonomy and change. I knew that the people around me were not supporters of my dreams only destroyers and it was in this acknowledgement I that I suddenly realised that God was also above me and he never passes over since, the preacher said unequivocally, that he stays with us and secures all our dreams. This affirmation was the turning point in my life and so, each time hence, that I saw an aeroplane passing over, I would beg God to let me have a seat on one, just one small seat to Manchester to join my mother and father and I would never ask him for another thing again. I was always told that God hears the prayers of children in preference to those of adults and because of this, have made it my duty and commitment all my life to pray just like a child before him. My grandma was the 'angel' my aunt was the 'demon' for without my knowledge she had been badgering my mother on a regular basic to send a ticket for me as a matter of urgency. Then my turn came, a ticket arrived one morning. Even though it was not supposed to be my turn, for God had given a long awaited gift with one hand, but death had taken it back with the other.

Someone said that no sooner something is given that something else is immediately sanctioned. This ticket was not for me, it was for my diabetic brother but it arrived much too late for him and not early enough for me. Four days before he died he came to my aunt's house, looking very ill and emaciated, weeping and afraid. He showed me the marks on his legs where he had been injecting his insulin, not very successfully. He told me, he had no further wish to live, because the diabetes had ravaged body. This was to be my final encounter with him and a few days later he descended into a coma and was rushed miles away to the hospital most capable of helping him. There was no one with him, not a single member of the family and he died destitute, afraid and alone in a strange place.

This is the one thing in my life that holds me permanently in fear and one that I simply cannot reconcile since, no child should have to die alone when there were so many members of his family around; aunts, uncles, and numerous others. He was simply discarded like an expired object. I wept for him, I wept for myself. I wept for the foolish and selfish decisions my parents had taken in the hope of giving us all a better life but one by one we began to perish. In the pursuit for economic improvement everyone left behind was hurting and diminishing and although I was pleased when the ticket was changed in my favour, I knew instinctively that all my life I would have to accept that someone whom I had loved very much had to die in order to secure a permanent freedom for himself and a temporary one for me. The only way in which I could show sufficient gratitude was to become determined in my approach to life and to make the utmost of every opportunity that was available to me. I had to live worthy of someone whose death had given me the freedom to a new life from where I could become all the things that was not possible for him. This was the first time that I recognised the true cost of freedom, its pricelessness, its unlimited orientations and its very nature of being always associated with sorrow and pain.

The day of my leaving had come and it was a strange feeling, for on one hand I was overjoyed, yet on the other sorrowful. I looked at my grandma and recognised her advancing years and knew in my heart that it was highly unlikely that I would ever see or touch her again. I never did see her again for one day she curled up on the veranda with my youngest brother Wayne in her arms and died in her sleep. She was found sometime later clinging to him, the post mortem was inconclusive. We believed she died of what is termed; 'a broken heart'. In Joel 2:25, the Lord promises to; "I will repay you for the years the locust have eaten-the great locust and the young locust, the other locusts and the locust swarm-my great army that I sent among you." I believe in the words of God for two very simple reasons; the words of God are true and faithful and secondly, they are the only words with the power to bring transformation and healing. The majority of humans can neither be believed nor trusted, they seldom trust themselves in the responsibilities they have, so how can they inspire others to trust in them? I remember sitting where the stewardesses could keep a watchful eye on me on that BA flight from Montego Bay to Manchester. I was quiet outside but excited on the inside. I was given a little tray of unusual things to eat, some of which I had never seen before and I was perplexed, so much so, that I even attempted to eat the little wet wipe, the one used to clean up afterwards. I soon realised it was not food and spat it out but I tasted chocolate for the very first time and it delighted all my senses and created new ones!

Naturally, British Airways remains my preferred airline since; they were the ones who brought me to Manchester, giving me the chance of a new life. I asked God as a child for only one seat and to think he has multiplied that a hundred times over. I have travelled to over one hundred and fifty destinations around the world, visiting every continent and have gone back to some places a dozen or more times. If I had kept all my boarding passes I would need an over-sized cabinet to fit them all in. I cannot recall all the leading hotels, motels, river boats and cruise boats, the suites and balconies that provided panoramic, city, river, ocean and garden views.

I never asked God for anything more than I have ever needed but could not believe how much he has bestowed upon me. In my act of surrendering to him he has remained faithful. I trust him implicitly. I know that this is the reason for my continued love and worship for him, because the only thing in my life that has made any sense over the years has been suffering and it's made so much clearer when I consider the passage in Isaiah 53:3-4; "He was despised and rejected by mankind, a man of suffering, and familiar with pain. Like one from whom people hide their faces he was despised, and we held him in low esteem. Surely he took up our pain and bore our suffering, yet we considered him punished by God, stricken by him, and afflicted." I thank God that he suffered so much pain and humiliation on my behalf; so who am I to bemoan my lot? If I never had difficulties in my life I would never know that God could solve them and if I never showed my weaknesses, he would never have been able to show me how to be strong. If I had never learned to forgive those who caused me the greatest pain in my life, he too would not have forgiven me and thus, my life would have remained captive to the past. I thank him however, for whoever Christ sets free, becomes truly free, not freedom in flight but freedom through faith.

I finally found the courage to face Miss Linda thirty years later. I had been faithfully praying all through the years that God would grant me one final day before her, since I had one question I needed answering; my one question imperative and so, my sister Carol accompanied me for moral support one sunny afternoon. She invited us onto the veranda and while they chatted, I merely observed. After a while I got her attention and looked straight into her eyes and asked her my one permitted question; "Miss Linda, why did you hurt me all those years ago? She was barely able to raise her eyelids but said very softly under her breath, "You have grown into a lovely woman and your hair, it's looking beautiful, and I am very pleased about your hair. Do you remember how I used to braid it when you were small? That was it; she had nothing further to say to me, I was confused. "What does braiding my hair as a child got to do with the question I just asked," I thought to myself? There was no hope of any further meaningful discourse since, she was now looking past us into a distant place we could not go with her. It was during this pause that we noticed she was holding a pot to her side and her dress was becoming soaked with blood. Upon closer examination we realised there was a wound to her abdomen, created from her advancing bowel cancer. We had no idea she was terminally ill, this was all too surreal. We both got to work, cleaning her up and getting her a change of clothes.

Sadly, all her children were busy with their own lives and although reasonable efforts were made to employ the support of a nurse, her demanding and irascible nature, halted all their attempts. Naturally, we were not in possession of the facts at the time but were made fully aware of them sometime later. Gordon was married and getting on with his own life so were the others. Roy had died many years previously and a few months before our visit, Bev had wandered out of her bed in the middle of the night and was killed instantly by a freight truck at front of their house. God in His wisdom knew that Miss Linda's life was almost over and that Bev would have no one to love and care for her and as tragic as it seems, it was his compassion at work and not his wrath. We said goodbye and I left much bolder than when I first arrived and was certain, the past to some extent, had been released.

I arrived back in Manchester a few weeks later with a few answers and one less question. Sadly, less than a month after getting home Miss Linda died and was buried alongside her husband and two children. I was so grateful that God had kept his promise and allowed me to come face to face with her one final time. During the weeks which followed, I did a lot of soul searching and tried to find meaning to the one thing she said but which had made little sense at the time; braiding my hair. I instinctively knew that the answer I had sought for thirty years was partly to be found here. After much wrangling and debating, I finally knew the answer and even though it was not the one I had sought, it would become the catalyst to my freedom from the past. My mother always hated the texture of my hair, it was stubborn and difficult and she was never able to braid it without cursing its texture. The brief spell I was living with Miss Linda, she was at her best with my hair; she loved it, nurtured it, prayed over it and for the very first time it started to grow, to thrive and I was transformed. This was her at her best and her best far exceeded my mother's worst; naturally. She simply wished for me to remember her at her best and not her lowest, her worst. If love is at the very beginning, it will also be at the end. I don't expect that I will understand everything during my life but I will try my utmost to appreciate some things. In this appreciation, I can begin to change my attitude and turn from fear to hope, darkness to light and from apathy to action. In this state of transformation I was compelled to forgive and in so doing have moved from fault and blame to a credible aspiration. I forgave her, just as I had forgiven a number of other people in my life; even my mother for leaving me.

Unlike Miss Linda, my aunt died unexpectedly at the age of fifty-seven from breast cancer. Although I loved her with all my heart, I have chosen to erase her almost completely from my memory. She was my mother's only sister and should have loved, supported and encouraged me as she did her with own children. It seemed that her main purpose was to extinguish the tiny flicker of hope present within me. I am confident she would pour inflammable fuel over her own children in a hope they would outshine us all. The difference between a good man and woman who is overtaken by evil is that they fight against it; they repel it and try to find a way back to a morally right path. My aunt's malevolent attitude and selfish aspirations overtook her and sadly, her life was halted when it should have excelled.

For those people who arrive at a particular junction in their life and gaze backwards, I wonder what in fact will be either pursuing them, or gently guiding them on. "An evil man continues moving along looking over his shoulders either because of his enemies or his conscience." Thomas Aquinas. The idea of being propelled along uncharacteristically due to past errors is burdensome. It is for this very reason that effort and determination must be provoked in order to alter the corrosive path behind us, for it is only when this occurs that we become exonerated from fault and blame. Although I have been disappointed with a number of malicious individuals who, either inserted themselves in my life or who, were unfortunately attached to my life, I continue to believe in the goodness of humanity. Admittedly, just when things are on the verge of change, another struggle ensues as a reminder of the sheer size of the fracture that interleaves the human family.

As a child, it was an unspoken rule that the utmost respect should be shown at all times to a number of people within the community. The oldest naturally, were treated with the highest regard; beginning with a person's own family and then those of other families. Next, were those people who had positions of influence; mothers, fathers, uncles, aunts, policemen and women, but above all these, religious men and women were held in the highest esteem. Respect is something that I have never taken lightly. I believe that when respect is shown to others, there is an acknowledgement of one's own sense of place and purpose. While I advocate good manners and discipline on almost every level, I would vehemently refuse to grant respect to another person who was woefully lacking in morals and values – I firmly believe that respect is a mutual undertaking and hold all parties equally accountable. The nature of accountability becomes more acute, when those demeaning my boundaries are in fact, the very men and women I was taught to respect above all others. Each person is supposedly, an autonomous being but I beg to differ. Although I am a Born-Again Christian, born again because, I made an informed choice to seek God, to love him and spend my life in service to him. Yet, in some ways, I don't believe I had a choice. My convictions were affirmed from a very young age and although I understood the basics of Christianity, it was not until I became an adult that I could adequately discern the appropriate direction for my own life. It is for this reason that I firmly believed the original choice was made for me and not one that I had spent hours debating in absence of knowledge. As a Christian, the autonomy would become more visible as I interleaved with all types of different people, especially other Christians. It was during this period of exhaustive search that I enrolled in a Christian institute to acquire a stronger footing for my belief. The other people in the school were from a variety of backgrounds but by and large the majority of them were a lot younger than me. Nonetheless, I felt that for the first time in years, I was inserted amongst 'family,' a Christian family.

Of course I retain serious doubts surrounding the integrity of families; I have often found them a place of disharmony and retribution. My perceptions of Christian families however, were different since, I viewed a majority of Christians as Christ-like and not Pharisee-like in their attitudes and beliefs, where like Christ, their integrity should always remain transparent to all. Sadly for me, I began a series of discoveries which dismantled my observations of many Christians who like everyone else, can be judgemental, objectionable, pretentious and the most uncompassionate people imaginable. I simply do not believe a vast number have any real depth of understanding the, 'Christ' in Christianity. I believed I was kind and gracious to all at the institute and showed respect whenever I was met with the same and because of this sense of wanting to fit in; I was oblivious to the fact that there was a devious mission to undermine and dismantle my character. There were numerous confrontations where other students were openly encouraged to goad me into heated debates; admittedly, this is my greatest strength even though it would seem unfair to an observer when there was often twenty against one. I traversed back and forth during my time with them seeking answers from the ruling Scribes and Pharisees, sadly to no avail. The most alarming thing of all, was the fact that I was often first to take a stand for others but there was never another person who chose to stand with me on matters of principles.

Of course I was counting the days to the end of this programme and remarkably, they were doing the same. In anticipation of the end, a comment sheet for each departing student was placed in a public area to be endorsed by all their fellow students. Naturally, all the sheets belonging to other students were overflowing with comments, so much so that others sheets had to be added. Altogether, they remained on the wall about a month. In that time, my sheet was the only one that had only two comments that was so illegible, I could neither read them nor determine who had written them. In my disgust, I met with the 'high priest', notably the principal and aired my disdain at the lack of inclusiveness and regard towards me. The following day, another four or five comments appeared on the sheet which at this point was neither worth reading or acknowledging. The day it was taken down and handed to me, I received it, graciously and brought it home, burying it in the darkest place that I could find. I did this for two reasons; dark intentions belong in dark places and since, so little regard and care was given to me, neither does it deserve any from me and so, it will stay in that place until I become less apathetic towards it and one day hurl it into a deep abyss where it belongs.

I have found Christ on numerous occasions in my life but rarely in Christians. I have found him at the well rescuing the woman caught in the act of adultery, in the kindness of a stranger who wrapped me in his coat to keep me warm from the cold. I have found him in the streets when I needed a hand with a heavy load and again when I had lost my way. Christ was when a stranger came alongside me and did not simply point me in the right direction but made the journey with me. I have found Christ in the nurse's hand when I was lonely and afraid. Jesus was particularly ardent for everyone to first examine their own faults before looking with hostility into the lives of others. In Matthew 7:3 we read, "Why do you look at the spec of sawdust in your brother's eye and pay no attention to the plank in your own eye? I believe I was judged, tried and condemned, yet those doing all of the aforementioned acts, were themselves seriously lacking in morals and goodness. My intention of going to school was to become a better person; sadly there was no one there capable of teaching me this simple quality. I was only too please to beat a hasty retreat in order to protect any fragment of individuality still present with in me. I have often deliberated on the idea of perfection but have failed to arrest its qualities in a majority of people.

I have no illusions of attaining perfection but I continue to strive towards it, for even though I may never reach a point that resembles a 'perfect place,' I will at least have done my utmost to underscore my life with those things that are commended in Scripture. I have no intention to compromise, nor will I hasten to accommodate the wishes or intentions of another person; this simply enslaves and does not bring about the peace and freedom that I continue to pursue. When I consider my faults and the ways in which I have chosen to live so that I may harness ways in which to eradicate every known and hidden liability; I cannot help ascertaining the fact that the faults that others have attached to me are in fact, the perfection they seek in themselves – my faults, their perfection.

My Faults – Their Perfection

What if my faults were other people's perfection? I may begin to accept and believe the bias from where a number of views originate; from culture, from ignorance and the stereotypical images they have drawn of me, drawn of my life. The things others believe I value in my life but in fear, I would simply enter my home, lock all my windows and doors to stop the proliferation of the skewed ideals from those wishing to contaminate my cherished world. From the moment I allow the world in; newspapers, internet and television, I see headlines that are in the centre of the lives of those in wars, despair, suffering and every type of emotional and psychological struggle, highlighting the disappointments common to human beings; but I am not there. There appears to be both corporate and personal suffering, in unity and in solitary confinements;

but again, I am not there. As I flick through the pages of every tabloid paper, every glossy magazine, every tawdry and second rate publication, I find stories of paupers, of princes, teachers, lawyers, doctors, sportsmen and women, those who govern the nation and those who entertain for vast financial rewards but alas I am not there. I seldom find anyone whose face reminds me of my own and whose dreams are not suspended between probability and real possibility. I perceive what initially looks like soft brown velvet skin but not from birth, those acquired from salons and spray tans and wishing to emulate but not bearing the burden of my fate. I see 'faultless' bodies perfected by the surgeon's knife and the over sanctioned Botox technique, that makes me look outrageous, almost like a 'freak'.

The 'nip' and 'tuck' generation whose buttocks are enlarged, noses reduced, breast implanted, all beyond 'perfection,' God's perfection. My lips full and tender, perfected in their surrender and my hips swaying from side to side as I glide effortlessly in attires of colour as one would imagine fine silks woven from a rainbow. Alas, my faults too daring, to bold to conceal, the reality that has shaped me, are the faults that some have chosen to mock in me. My faults, my defects from birth and my cultural identity are the perfection it seems that is beyond the material possessions that some may pursue. No one seriously wishes to be like me since, they would have to disarm completely and step inside my shoes but this is too precarious, too demeaning and much too indeterminate to wish to become someone who is not valued as having 'measurable influence' and so, is often bypassed through ignorance. And so, every day I witness the faces that look like me, though not me, in a cursory apologetic tone. This is the first time I find someone who resembles me but is a criminal, a drug dealer, an asylum seeker, a rogue trader, a knife wielding rioter, all being convicted of the most hideous crimes against humanity and are incarcerated for the protection of the 'saints'.

There is a brief apology for the ones who look like me, as they are sent to institutions to assess their humanity. One by one they are eradicated from history and in the place where they should stand; another assumes it and they become the forgotten ones. This same motif is played over and over again in the upper rooms and corridors of the rich and powerful and in the alleyways of the poor and un-influential. Apologising complete, to satisfaction and in those same colourful magazines stuffed with high European ideals, the glamour models plying their wares scarcely leave enough room to depict the dreadful aid campaigns. The image of the little dark child who looks like me, starving and asking for help to improve the poverty that holds him or her a prisoner of circumstance. Everywhere I look there are images apologising for my humanity, apologising for my right to be gifted with life, as though life was a 'right' for some and not a privilege for all. Every image I see in the world tells me that I am not there and everywhere I seek to find me or anyone who looks like me, I realise I have been erased and another has assumed my place and my brown face has been permanently replaced with some other who, at a brief glance, looks like me but once more, highly unlikely to be me.

I see many enjoying indescribable wealth and resources beyond the imaginings of those who cannot grasp their sense of self and their wretched state of poverty through no fault or blame of their own. And during the brief pause in which so many seek to applaud themselves and their allies, it's time again to apologise for me and anyone who resembles me. For those like me whose faults are the perfection of those who cannot abide my existence, who night after dreadful night are able to lie in sumptuous beds covered with the finest linens and cottons from afar and made by the same poverty stricken hands that looks like mine, but is not me.

Those privileged minority remain curiously unmoved and are neither provoked by conscience nor by guilt since they are blameless and pure and my faults venerate and grant them their desired 'perfection'. And so, I will keep my doors and windows locked both day and night in my home and I will photograph my face hundreds of times to remind me what I look like when the world uphold lies and distortion of who they have defined as 'me,' but this thought of manipulation can be further dismantled in Galatians 2:20; "I have been crucified with Christ and I no longer live, but Christ lives in me" and all the faults present within me are the perfecting agents which propels me further into the fullness of God's amazing and compelling identity.

And so, whether I am acknowledged or not, I am here in the world, God's world and I wish to be no place else in the short-term. I believe I have everything I need since; I have God who is able to change and transform my life in the direction of his choosing. There is my family, who continue to love, encourage and support me in every difficult and challenging situation, and I have me, in whom apart from God, I have the greatest trust and confidence. A faithful reminder, that whether a hopeful move from fault to perfection, that assurance of victory is unquestionable in every number greater than one.

And that this one is neither starving, neither is she a thief nor a liar, but would sooner give than take from another. She requires neither aid nor pity and no amount of erasing her existence will halt her journey of triumph. In my quest for truth concerning the way people ought to live, I am confident that nothing can diminish hope, overtake God, outrun time, nor can anyone but Christ claim to have died and return back to life. I am grateful to be perforated with every type of fault since, they are God's perfection.

When God encircles the life of a human being, all their previous faults are consumed by his grace and mercy and those debilitating sarsens that once gripped them, becomes the very defence towards their perfection. In this act of defence I am permitted to become open and it's an openness that I have not previously experienced. This vulnerability is the first step towards the exasperating disciplines that leads to specific areas of awareness. As I lose more and more of myself in God, I begin to find more of him, of his divine nature, his passion, his love for the truth and the exact purpose to which he has called my life. I simply could never have found this out by merely stumbling upon a 'situation vacant' and applying within, for with God, one must pursue him in order to gain understanding, as this allows the idea of perfection to have a measure of reality. In my painstaking and continuous analysis of myself through the years, I remain grateful for the wretchedness I have found time and time again, for in this astute discovery, I have been privileged to work on the construction of a 'new' person whose hopes are centred upon the perfection of God. It is in this unearthing that I became fully aware of the specified path towards perfection and it is from here that I can finally begin to acknowledge those things I have 'lost' in the world. The usual marks of distinction from where a majority of perspectives are drawn, although I am confident I have gained a great deal more in Christ.

It is for this reason that I ceased to be concerned about those things I have lost; instead, I gratefully accepts what remains. Naturally, I cannot compare myself with God's flawless perfection but I remain appreciative that he does not reject me because of my faults but accepts me in spite of them. It is imperative I remain patient of the things that I am not and move triumphantly towards the things that I can be; humble, obedient and possessing enough courage for myself and compassion for those who suffers on the peripheries of life;-

Whilst I am deeply flawed, He is flawless

In me there is still a hint of darkness

But in Him only goodness and light

For when my day concedes to night,

He is my piercing ever present light.

We all aspire to be our best

Yet my God cannot improve an ounce

He is both the beginning and the end

I am neither, only just the present.

His heart is flesh when mine's a stone

He is a king in heaven upon His throne

But I am just a pauper, seated on earth's lowly floor.

He chase the storm clouds across the sea and shore

His is the voice of comfort I seek to hear more and more.

His name is Alpha, Omega too

He is king of all the nations but especially the Jews.

He is God and saviour to every tribe and tongue,

He is the heartbeat of the universe;

The great I am.

So to the God of Jacob I dedicate this song

For when others see just a hopeless end

I rejoice in the endless hope of Christ my friend

For He is worthy of praise to the last setting sun

And I wait to hear His voice saying; "Good and faithful servant, well done".

If I am to connect with the uninterrupted hope from God, my attempts at perfection must be from a place of uprightness and where my values about right and wrong, become unquestionably uncompromised. My morals must encompass an infinite understanding of good and evil, while I endeavour to shun evil and walk towards the 'good path.' It is only from here that my judgements of myself and others become less severe as I adopt an increased level of acceptance of my own faults and become less critical of others. I must allow the persistent nature of my conscience to inform me continuously, otherwise any attempts to understand the righteousness of God will be lost in my own misguided assaults on those with whom I share my common humanity. If I am to stand any chance before God, I must first limit my hostilities with myself and others. This is my first act of humility since, it is at this point where difference is acknowledged, upheld and celebrated and ultimately, leading to increase moments of perfection in God.

The perfection of one's faith, of one's nature and attitude to God and towards others, need to be raised from our broken floors and basements to unbelievable heights. Sadly, as a brutal and unforgiving people, as illustrated in 2 Timothy 3-5; "People will be lovers of themselves, lovers of money, boastful, proud, abusive, disobedient to their parents, ungrateful, unholy, without love, unforgiving, slanderous, without self-control, brutal, not lovers of good, treacherous, rash, conceited, lovers of pleasure rather than lovers of God-having a form of godliness but denying its power. Have nothing to do with such people."

I am thankful that God assist me whenever I permit him because, without him my struggles would infinitely surpass my insufficient faith. When I became totally dependent on the Holy Spirit's qualifying power I was strengthened to relinquish all my previous hypotheses and develop a single-minded willingness. I was then instructed and directed by God in whose truth I am empowered to bring a roundabout turn within my life and the lives of those outside the peripheries of belief, wherever permitted to do so. If I was drowning due to my poor swimming skills, I would refuse emphatically to surrender my hold onto a make shift raft until something more substantial appeared.

A majority of people seem to prefer to cling to relics and haphazard visible objects rather than surrender to a powerful invisible source. Humans believe in what they see but there are moments when faith must take precedence over all fears and allow a, 'letting-go' in order that a person may flourish and grow. This propagation has become substantial as I move fearlessly from one known orientation to another. For me, the worst thing is being inactive because, nothing changes in this unproductive period of barrenness. I like changes, regardless of whether they are astronomical or microscopic. While I could never advocate that all change is beneficial, it is nevertheless a better option than to remain stagnant. Admittedly, I may never devise plans and schemes to excavate deep inside the arctic tundra, unearthing its many mysteries. I also accept that I may not be able to fuel scholarly debates for centuries to come. I am certain however, that there is one bridge to real human freedom and it is only by way of the bridge of humility.

CHAPTER SEVEN

Humility: The Bridge to Freedom

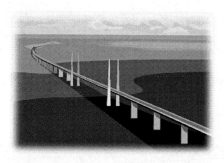

Imagine a world devoid of love, compassion, and hope? Imagine no longer, because we are only a matter of years away. Again, imagine your friends and neighbours contacting you for the sole purpose of boasting about the extraordinary circumstances within their own lives and not caring in the least that you had just been shattered by overwhelming circumstances? Unfortunately, this is a daily occurrence for a large number of people. Finally, imagine that, in the place of humility there was pride and all other virtues that promoted human cooperation had been replaced with unpalatable vices; sadly, an advancing reality. This lack of humility is evident in a large number of people, those in particular, whose main purpose in life is to achieve everything at any cost. I am uncertain as to the exact size of the earth but aware of its vast number of inhabitants who rely, not only upon crops and produce generated through various means but there is also an unparalleled duty of care towards each another. This regard for others is inextricably linked to the guardianship of the earth, as each person becomes dutifully engaged in the preservation of its natural resources. My one question imperative is, "If human beings continue to destroy each other at the current rate, then who will inhabit the planet when all are dead? I am not a genius but this does not need the aid of maths or physics to figure out the calculations and logic. If it is our aim to save the planet and eradicate humans then, there is absolutely nothing to explicate the rationale behind such an infertile action. While I may not wish to share every aspect of my life with my 'neighbours,' I certainly do not wish to harm them. Human conflict is indelibly etched on the minds of millions; we simply cannot escape wars and rumours of war. This sadly, has become more evident in the world as we become time and space travellers from the comfort of our own sitting rooms.

The technological advance over the last fifty years has seen the evolution of every type of communication tools imaginable, where in an instant; we can be transported to the other side of the world. In this transportation, we are able to exceed borders, religion, race and every acknowledged difference that would have disabled a number of people centuries earlier. Yet, with all this information available to us, our knowledge of ourselves and others appears to be swiftly diminishing. I simply could not imagine a world where my neighbour was hurting and I remained unaffected since, it is the first instinct of humans to respond to a variety of needs; first individually, then universally. For those who remain the centre of their own worlds in every instance, there is a deep pride that appears to either disable or restrict their move towards truth and freedom. In all such cases, there are echoes of noncompliance and selfishness and it is only when all affectations are discarded that there is a credible hope of being propelled towards genuine humility.

In almost every instance of my life thus far, I have sought tirelessly to take an optimistic view over an incapacitating and pessimistic one. In my attempts to remain empowered rather than become disabled by overwhelming circumstances, I have nearly always found refuge in the acknowledgement of life's uncompromised freedoms. I have also learned to accept that not all battles will be won, neither will every situation have a favourable outcome, nevertheless, on many occasions humility remains the presiding factor. I am aware humility is not an attainment that comes by way of efforts and 'good' works but has nevertheless, empowered me to accept failure graciously, be courageous when I am weak, to show compassion unremittingly and to praise a number of people more highly than myself. Humility is one of life's defining virtues that does not come by way of singular actions but can only become a reality through the exhaustive disciplines of faith and obedience. Since it is believed to be the pathway to a virtuous life, all other virtues must interleaves through its microscopic perforations from where a person's character is fully absorbed by its presence. It is only through this process that pride, will undoubtedly fall.

Pride is the grave misfortune of the arrogant. It is the vehicle in which they travel but will invariably halt with a mighty crash. Sadly, pride remains the pre-cursor to every fall. In Genesis, the reality of the fall validates the beginning of the end of human freedoms. It is unimaginable the number of people who willingly remain captive to pride. This captivity obscures the perimeter of all known truths since; nothing that opposes the values of a conceited person is permitted to impact their perceptions, especially those pertaining to others. In this constant drive to promote selfish needs, all other values are eradicated. The danger of only believing and living within the narrow fields of our own corrosive values is, we become so absorbed with our own importance and needs that, in our pursuit to outshine, out-perform and even out-live each other, we fail to see the signs of disaster approaching.

A number of years ago I returned home for a brief holiday and to spend time with my family. During my visit, I was disgruntled with one family member in particular, [my late aunt's eldest son] who, having made a reasonable success of his life was constantly making disparaging comments about the lives of others. He was one of the most obnoxious human beings one could wish to encounter; nevertheless, I smiled with him, not because I wanted to but because I had to show willingness, though begrudgingly. A few days into my holiday a very close family member died and arrangements began for the burial. I remember a group of young men who had volunteered to dig the grave and as they were digging, this man came by to chat and see how things were progressing. As he came over and looked at the grave, his remarks were equally as repugnant as he was, "This is as much of my time that I will give and I will not be attending the funeral, because I am too busy." Needless to say, we were all deeply upset by his comments since; in my culture it is customary for everyone in the community to attend every funeral. Funerals are seen as a joyous celebration of the life that has passed and families always endeavour to make each one an uplifting occasion for all to remember. I recall the sense of disbelief on the faces of everyone at the grave but the sadness felt, was not entirely to do with his unforgiving comments but the one for whom the grave was being dug. Two days after this encounter with my cousin, as he was in town doing his shopping, he collapsed and died suddenly. This was unbelievable. He had no known illnesses and was in the prime of his life at the age of fifty five. His self-fulfilling prophecy is remembered by all who stood by the grave and listened to his arrogant denunciation of another human life. The post-mortem to establish the cause of his death was inconclusive and by the time his funeral took place I was back in Manchester.

I have a strong belief which continues to affirm and reinforces my values every step of my life; if I have nothing good to say concerning the lives of others, I simply say nothing. Since the minute I begin to prophesy and condemn, I immediately condemn myself. I have arrived at the place in my life where I now understand the power of words, the intensity and venom that can be before or behind them. I am a firm believer in destiny. My cousin was not permitted to live beyond his allotted time. This moment at the grave was his final opportunity to make reparations for the years he had maligned others but sadly, his arrogance simply could not be overcome. The opportunity was lost in his failure to demonstrate one final act of compassion by disarming and stepping alongside others in their suffering; by simply, filling the space left vacant by their sides. His relinquishing of pride may have created an alternative picture of him but sadly, only confirmed his character by adding further blemishes to an already tainted man. This was the first time I can recall where someone I had known all my life died and my only concern was to keep digging. While digging, I was working out the laws of the universe and exhuming a number of tensions present within men and women but through it all, I was no wiser at the end, than I was at the inception.

When pride was my most auspicious garment, uncertainty and frustration remained my closest allies. In my recent attempts to become separated from everything which opposes my path to genuine freedom, I have had to leave a number of additional things behind. It is no longer a question of how heavy my load and responsibilities; but how light the weight of my acceptance? From the moment I was able to accept the things that I could not determine, I gained a substantial grip onto a number of meaningful realities. These realities inform my decisions each day in my determinations to succeed and to continue along the path of my destiny, in a direction of my choosing and to accept anyone who wants to walk beside me as an advantage and not an interruption. Nowadays, I am more likely to accept the support of those who insert themselves by my side, in the space which is no longer visibly empty, for in this display of support, my humanity and dignity are perpetually reaffirmed. If the space beside us remains empty, pride is often at fault and in this vacancy; there is simply no voice of conscience or indeed encouragement. If in our perilous quest for freedom, no one made the journey to safety, there would simply be no voices to articulate the tales of cooperation that led to our accomplishments and defeats and the elevation of another's dignity, even in their suffering.

Dignity in Suffering

Humility is a continuing theme in both the Old and New Testament and is considered, one of the most preeminent virtues that have become justifiably linked with dignity. This has been especially true in recent times, as dignity has become a by-word in a number of people oriented services. The care system in particular, advocates a variety of procedures that demands rigorous application in its attempt to safeguard the dignity of a number of vulnerable individuals. The most alarming aspect of this for me however is, why local authorities have to implement such stringent measures in the first place. I cannot understand how one human being would have to be compelled with threats of criminal convictions in order that he or she may show respect to others for whom they care and to uphold their dignity at all times. There are many different types of instructions regarding the way we treat others; whether lesser or greater than ourselves. It is for this reason that I would like to consider briefly what it is that satisfies the life of another human being: sense of importance and achievement, family values, strong principles that will be wholeheartedly defended. It could be as simple as acknowledging that each person is of equal value and should be treated with the equivalent respect and dignity. I must reiterate once more, the simple manner in which I approach a number of issues in my own life.

I have witnessed over the years how effective children are at gaining the right answers from adults around them and regardless of whether they understand what they hear in essence, they nevertheless get a response. I remember my friend's four year old son asking her why my skin was brown and not knowing exactly how she would respond to his enquiry, I waited eagerly. I was nevertheless, surprised and pleased at her dignified response. She had to explain something to him that he could at least understand in part. She simply informed him that I was originally from a very hot country where my skin had to be brown; otherwise the sun would hurt me. He was absolutely fine with that and although I am not sure exactly what parts he understood, I nevertheless commended her wisdom. I duly approach a variety of matters in my life in much the same way; simplicity and honesty since, situations only become complex because we are afraid to ask difficult questions. Of course, the problem with this approach is that, not everyone is prepared to have difficult questions directed at them and subsequently become defensive. I have learned over a lengthy period that people in general prefer an honest attitude, as long as their dignity always remains the utmost priority.

Safeguarding the dignity of a person promotes their individuality, it also affirm their values, although the ambiguous nature of what is currently prised, can create a number of ethical impasses. It is a very disabling position when a person refuses to compromise and often, what are defended fiercely are not necessarily matters of principles but the compulsion to maintain the inflexible positions of superiority and pride.

A number of years ago I attend a seminary affiliated to Christian values and principles. Although these were actively promoted in a number of verbal communications, they were woefully absent in the lives of my fellow students and teachers. In Luke 10:18 we read of Satan being hurled from heaven to earth and for the first time I discovered his whereabouts; in the heart of this institution. For some reason, I was simply not accepted. Every day I faced challenges of indifference, exclusion and criticism from those around me. Whenever I am faced with challenges, I automatically upsurge my determination by becoming more focussed and my strength and wisdom increases threefold. In the end I simply accepted that they scorned me because I did not look like them and highly unlikely that I would ever wish to be like them. I am completely my own person and one who makes decisions independently of any other. For some reason, a number of people prefer those who yield effortlessly to their doctrines and although I was seeking new revelations in my life, I was by no means prepared to forfeit an ounce of my values or dignity.

It was a brutal morning. I arrived for class, knowing my mother had died thousands of miles away during the night. What do I do? Stay at home and fall into sadness, or go in as usual with a hope that this may impel them into an outpouring of care and compassion. Before the commencement of class, I shared this news with the speaker in private and he asked my permission to convey this to the other students. Prayers were said and the lesson commenced. At the end, I believed a number of students would show regard and compassion but was astonished since, not a single person approached me; in fact, a number of them, went out of their way to avoid me. I left the classroom and made my way across the car park and as I was about to enter the library, a Greek girl came over to me and hugged me with a genuineness that surpassed them all. I was humbled and recognised that sometimes the only thing that is necessary to align us back on track is one other since; there is always assurance of victory in every number greater than one.

I thanked her and continued on my way. As I sat alone in the library deliberating on the events, I could not help imagining that if the speaker had communicated that one of the likeable faces dog had died, the whole school would probably close for the rest of the day. It is often in moments like this where the essence of my humanity is reaffirmed since, there are so many who profess to have unlimited compassion in their polished speeches written by others from the pulpits of deception but when there is a real need to prove beyond doubt, they failed miserably. The following morning I sat in the library going over the events meticulously. My unquestionable humanity was questioned and they drew their own answers regarding my worth and dignity. The further we distance ourselves from objectionable individuals, the more our freedoms increase. Admittedly, this was the worst place I have ever been but the lessons I learned have become the most life affirming. In almost every chapter of Psalms, David is pleading to God to advocate justice on his behalf. He prayed fervently that God would destroy those who attacked and deliberately accused him. Unlike David, I refuse to seek retribution of any kind since, for me the greatest justice imaginable, would be to see my adversaries live long enough to witness the increased dignity and integrity in my life, the very things they maliciously withheld and denied me. That day, I began to write.

A Place like That; For a People like This

In the place of compassion, I found apathy

In the place of humility, I found pride

In the place of forgiveness, I found harmful judgements

Pointing fingers to others instead of to themself

Instead of learning from the pupils

I was reminded they were the teacher in the room

And instead of celebrating life's diversity

They created a refuge in out-dated rhetoric, which loomed;

Loomed larger than a grotesque ailing Jurassic beast-

A brute wishing to lead the herd astray

To pastures where they will perish for lack of wisdom

A time therefore, to call back the 'good shepherd' with prayers of repentance

So every heart can respond to the Gospel's truth

And where it's no longer presented to mirror the youth;

The malicious ones who bear no shame,

Because the word 'sin' was dressed up in a different claim

Claims of inequality, justice and truth

Are mere contextualised images, borne from aggressive cancerous fruits?

And in the place of all men being created equal;

I saw inequalities which breathe separateness.

And in the place of the love of God and neighbour above all things

I saw profanity and shameless acts of sin; the type only hate can bring

And in the place of acceptance;

Exclusion made me ONE.

In the bleakness of the night, a familiar voice called

You are never alone; I am Jesus

I died for all.

So place me above yourself and all life's trials

And when I am your truth

There can be no denial.

For the stranger wrapped in poverty and creed

And whose difference does not outweigh his spiritual needs

Always see beyond the veil of skin

By doing so, you let the Lord your Saviour in.

For if your hopes of eternal things

Is only proclaimed when you sing;

Your vision of me is all but lost

So too is the Holy sacrificial cross.

So remember that I am the Lamb

And was only too pleased to serve

By being the greatest amongst you

Your dying God and servant of earth.

Now in the place of death, there will be life

And all judgements of others and self will cease

When the human heart is more than willing

To have eyes that see what Christ always sees.

To become flesh through humility, from the greatest to the least

And in the place of humanity's profoundly ugly things
The true love of God will unfold each part,
And will lighten the darkness which surrounds,
The veiled and mysterious, repenting heart.
So in the place of separation through a lack of knowledge
The stranger will be made more welcomed
To your work, your home, your school and college
For every heart is guilty of sin
But a life of victory is ours to win
Through the selfless act of a dying God
Whose blood is a prove currency of love?
For each person must play their part;
By mirroring Christ in actions and deed-
A perfect harvest-grown from holy seed
So we scatter them with the fullest of measure
In our chapels, our homes and around our hidden treasures
So the love we scatter upon us return
In places of height and depth to help us learn
That a place like that; for a people like this-
Whose friends are encouraged to excel beyond
The meagre goals for ourselves we had planned
The joys we then are everyday given,
Go on to bless the lives of our children's children.

Rarely have I encountered genuine kindness yet, I refuse unequivocally to believe that the majority of people are malicious, I was simply looking for good people in bad places. It is mainly for this reason that I object when others attempt to define my life since, God gave me a free-will so I may choose the direction it should take. There is absolutely no one qualified, except God and me to either direct or impact me since, in view of what I have learned over a number of years, if I had allowed the influence of others to breach my defences; I would have lost my entire sense of purpose and identity. Of course a number of insalubrious individuals came alongside me and this was nothing to do with weakness on my part but on theirs.

In my continuous observations of a number of people, I am aware that those who are often the strongest are usually the most confident. It is those who are naturally weak who apprehend the strongest, latching onto any observed areas of weaknesses to secure a seamless, rather than a forced entry. Unfortunately, my weakness remains my love for people. I have to be prepared that the same ones I routinely embrace are the very ones who will morph into toxic substances in the shortest time. Admittedly, this has happened less and less in recent years since, I now take a comprehensive appraisal of those permitted to get close to me and this has become my formidable tower of strength. I nevertheless, celebrate the courage of those who came alongside me with no other intention than to add value to my life. The men and women who, for no discernable reason, chose to insert themselves in the space, evidently vacant by my side.

I can never forget Dick Wilkins, the English gentleman I met on a trip to South Africa a number of years ago. It was late in the evening and we were travelling to our lodge in Kruger National Park. The weather was rather peculiar, so much so that, our plane had to abort landing after three disastrous attempts on the tiny landing strip in the bush due to poor visibility. It was for this reason we had to make the journey by road after an alternative airport was chosen since; it had the necessary equipment to bring our flight in safely. As we continued our over-extended journey, the weather became increasingly cold. Naturally, I was not prepared for this and found myself shivering uncomfortably. I had not met anyone in this group previously but was humbled when Dick removed his warm flee and put it around me. It was another first; someone chose to care for me and wished nothing in return. Needless to say, the entire safari was spent in the company of this man. My companion and I continued to be impacted by his warmth and regard long after our holiday had ended. I was so comfortable with the fleece that I kept it for the entire period of our stay. On the last day before we left, I began searching for him to return his fleece but he was nowhere to be found. In the end, I had to leave it at the reception desk accompanied with a thank you note. Although I always return everything loaned to me, this was one occasion I really wished that I had kept this fleece. As we was about to be transferred by jeep to the landing strip, I was met by one of the managers of the lodge who informed me that Dick was with a television crew filming in the bush. It was only at this point that I finally realised who this man was; Dick was in fact, the head of one of the largest publishing houses in South Africa; 'Sunbird Publishing,' suddenly, a lot of things began to make sense.

The early morning drives he took before breakfast, the late dinners and a number of telling signs I failed to notice at the beginning; he had come to Mala Mala to promote his latest project. It was fortunate that Dick had in fact exchanged contact details with us previously and had made us promise faithfully to visit him at his home in Port Elizabeth on our returning trip. This was a time in my life when I simply could not recognise the 'angels' from the 'demons' and so, would have to allow time to reveal the real person in him.

We stayed in touch after returning home and Dick surprised me with his thoughtfulness and generosity every step of the way. The book he was promoting during our stay, was dispatched to us by FedEx; 'Tuli Land of Giants,' and each time he was in London, there were a number of phone calls, apprising us of a number of things in his life. There were two things in Dick's life that were the most prominent; his impending wedding to the woman he simply adored and the further investigations into his throat cancer. Although he had been clear a number of years he kept regular appointments as precautionary measures. Some months later, he was travelling to Paris via London to be married and we spoke at length about a number of things.

A few months had passed and I began to notice the timeframe for his contact had been exceeded and so made a decision to contact him via email. I was not prepared for the email I received from his wife who informed me that Dick had died as a result of secondary cancer in his lungs. I simply did not want this news. A good man had died and so soon after his wedding. My sadness was unbelievable, yet, I was so grateful that he allowed me into his private space, the one that was partly vacant by his side. I can never forget kindness; neither can I ignore pain and sadness in those around me. Since, the moment I choose to forget, I am diminishing my most basic humanity. A number of people have entered my life over a number of years and while some have been lessons, others have been tremendous blessings, I remain grateful that Dick was both. "It is pride that changed angels into devils; it is humility that makes men as angels." Saint Augustine. (354-430).

Humility is the pre-cursor to the Christian life, where there should be a visible number of qualifying actions. Understandably, Christ was the most humble person who has ever lived and although it is impossible to be fully like him, every effort should be made to exemplify, if not exceed his actions; "Very truly I tell you, whoever believes in me will do the works I have been doing, and they will do even greater things than these, because I am going to my Father." John 14:12. He was undoubtedly, a caring and compassionate man who demonstrated on every level, unconditional regard for the poor, the alien, the stranger and those suffering under every type of oppression and scrutiny, thus highlighting, the need for all people who follow him, as church and believers, incorporate into their doctrine Christ's impassioned pleas for love and acceptance of all. This statement should support my idea of what constitutes, 'Church';-

"The 'true church' is God's people in the world doing effective ministry with the absolute and uncompromised love of God within them and as they allow the Holy Spirit to mirror back to believers and non-believers the power of God's saving grace and compassionate nature, they are re-affirming God's on-going, un-surpassed compassion and humility. There should never be the need for overzealous superiority, self-praising and a lack of encouragement, or a loving hand or correction over those whom we serve. A 'king' can never be a king without subjects. Likewise, a leader can never lead without those behind him who has a desire to be led. It is worth being reminded that Christ, who having made himself of no reputation in order that humankind, [you and me], would be exalted beyond our perverse and sinful nature and that we, who crucified him; and his only 'fault?' He bore a truth that no one wished to hear, since the moment it was heard, one immediately recognised that the dreadful sinners, hypocrites and Pharisees Christ spoke of, was, in fact, you and me. And so for this very reason many wished the Lord Jesus to remain in heaven for fear that He would assert His Kingship, Lordship and authority over all. The exclusivity of our social hierarchies, framed within the grand spectacular of churches and fine cathedrals, are utterly worthless and meaningless and all such grand designs are far more suited for 'saints' in heaven than sinners on earth! It is only when the love of God in Christ is unambiguously manifested in a honest and transparent way and when the dark shrouds of every diverse human complexity are no longer the burden of unfounded perceptions, of integrity and where, an individual action is grounded in the first principle of the love of God above all things; this indeed is the duty of all; servants, priests, leaders and kings. In the absence of love, hate occupies, for love remains the one true enabler. The true definer of 'church' is that unique place where all who have met with Christ have died to self; died to sinfulness and in faith, are meeting daily and graciously in the centre of God's divine purpose."

I have witnessed the church 'falling' in with the world and have subsequently fallen out, first with God and then the world; since the world view it as, not worldly enough and God view it as, not Godly enough. I cannot imagine being in a place with two drastically opposing realities where neither can be fully apprehended. It would be similar to one of those inexplicable nightmares, where there is an acknowledged level of consciousness but objects cannot be apprehended and movement is unquestionably constricted as you become increasingly paralysed by forces unknown to you. This is one of the most frightening and disadvantageous positions. It is like watching a truck approaching you at speed and knowing you will definitely be crushed since you are incapable of removing yourself to safety. Equally, there are many people who are trapped in the past to a number of paralysing factors but who are powerless to defeat such forces. This period is like the aforementioned nightmare from where there is absolutely no means of escape.

Admittedly, a number of people trust what they know, rather than the apparatus of change but while change is beneficial on the whole, not all aspects are to be embraced. My simple philosophy concerning change has worked reasonably well in recent years; "change nothing significant, until I have changed significantly," since, I would neither recognise them nor be prepared to live them. As I have gradually progress and changed during the course of my life, I have become more flexible in my approach to those seemingly unalterable elements where, under normal circumstances, would have kept me a prisoner to a number of indiscernible fears.

I have observed a number of things throughout my life and recognise when I moved from imprecision to discipline, pride to humility and from ensuing darkness to a visible light. The vacant space beside me for much of my life has proved a powerful tool, for while it has largely remained vacant, I have been impelled to fill it with my own faith and conscience. Admittedly, it would have been beneficial if during a number of difficult periods to have the trust of another person on whom I could ultimately depend. It is for this reason my faith is paramount and in addition to this, my decision taken a number of years ago to record my life in words and pictures so that, some day when I finally look back, I can unquestionably affirm when that space was empty and when it was completely filled. As part of my on-going pursuit for freedom, I have developed a passion for photography. I have no interest in its professional status in terms of competitions and prizes, since it is merely another way of identifying new freedoms; sheer delight of capturing aspects of my life, infinite. One thing that has come to my attention recently, is the way each picture conveys my life as it fluctuates. Having amassed over one hundred and fifty thousand images, I can see the times of confinement and liberty, times of triumphs, humiliation and defeats. There are images bearing frowns and smiles. I am dancing and laughing, in my uncertainties and convictions. Overall, this vast library, chronicling my life's journey – whether free or in chains, never fail to keep me inebriated with hope. Words and pictures are my preferred medium and although I have chronicled my life daily for twenty-five years, the pictures are the most telling by far.

My diaries are precise, recording both minor and major events, whether; virtuous or unprincipled. The most remarkable observation however, is the visible transformation throughout. In one image, my eyes are sparkling and filled with life and in another; they are empty and full of uncertainties. Would I have known this had I not kept my life in pictures and words? I doubt it! A number of us will go through changes without even recognising the process of transition and it is for this reason that those we select to walk alongside us, are able to reflect back those changes to us.

In my continuous assessment of my life and the things that are of value to me, I would be no wiser today if I had allowed my principles to become tainted with the views of others. Of course not everyone would choose to chronicle their life in this way but in view of the fact that so many who came alongside me and made me felt inexcusably undervalued, I simply had to affect a number of changes. While I find no intrinsic value in self-praise and love, I have nevertheless come to accept that, in order to be the autonomous being I was created to become, I had to recover all the power that had been prised away from me. I understand a number of key issues in the world, from where many values are drawn for a number of people. I understand what are of value to some people and what are meaningless to others but over and above all, I understand the things I value most. I simply could not believe in the laws of the universe if I could not apprehend its values and freedoms since, it is from these ancient rules that I have found the true meaning of liberty.

Furthermore, the longer I am able to maintain my flexible approach to truth, the unyielding nature of my character will remain firm against every potential untruth. I have learned not so much from those around me since, I have met so few people who possessed right morals and values but I have learned from my Christian values and belief that humility is the strongest bridge to freedom and victory.

"Humility is the most overtly evident proof of the most desired of all known Christian virtues; since without it we retain all our faults, which are merely covered over by pride in order that we may conceal them from others, but especially from ourselves." Francois de la Rochefoucauld (1613-1680).

The freedom I seek is inexplicable since, I could not easily define it to an observer. Many may be wondering why I feel I am a prisoner but it is a far-reaching complexity and way beyond a simple nuance. Freedom for me is no longer the desire to be accepted by others but a freedom that defines and pushes the boundaries of all known equivalences. The erosion of these formidable boundaries begins with the vestment of humility. While I may have no precise measurements to assess what freedom means to others, I will define briefly, what it means to me.

Freedom is my human right to affirm my place in society and not be continuously overlooked because of my notable difference. It is the right to choose my destiny and to articulate my opinions with the power and conviction of a worthy human being. Freedom is also the right to be included on merit and not to be excluded on the beliefs, values and principles I hold. Indeed, if I am being judged on these virtues then let me be judged by another whose moralities and ethics outweigh those of all others. Freedom is a where my difference is acknowledged, without the obliteration of potential unities. It is having autonomy to change my life from one orientation to another without the accompanying doubts and cynicism of others. Freedom was where my life began, five days of labour and intense agony, granting me the privilege of life. I simply cannot imagine being held captive to the needs, hopes, fears or visions of those around me and it is for this for reason that I have sought interminably to cut the umbilicus of each element that would inevitably, suffocate my entire being. I always take a measured, yet realistic approach to everything in my life and this has often proved a helpful means of realignment.

Although I have fallen through a number of wilful acts by others, I have nevertheless recoiled and reasserted my values. Of course, everyone prefers to be accepted rather than to be excluded but if I am excluded on matters of ethics, then so be it. I would sooner be alone on an impoverished island than in a thriving city with people who I cannot stand beside. I imagine a life that is perfect in a number of ways and even though I have failed to apprehend this perfection, I can at least shelter in the quest of this far-reaching aspiration. Unlike all my pointless material acquisitions over the years, humility is simply not an acquisition, nor is it an outer garment that I can effortlessly inter-change at will. It cannot be used as adornment as my moods and situation changes from one moment to the other. Humility is the inner garment, the one woven into the folds and creases of the entire person, allowing for the emergence of a unique freedom. Some people however, try and learn humility by becoming wholly preoccupied with their faults which can be seen as minor annoyances and stumbling blocks to liberty.

I am thankful for every crossroad I encountered since; they gave me a space to pause and reflect on the things which are essential to me and to reassess the direction I should take. It is also a time to re-evaluate my voyage thus far and to examine what is still of value to me. I accept I find no intrinsic worth in positions of 'power' and 'influence' since, the greatest power and influence begins with God and will end at the conclusion of my earthly life. I have never held an executive position, nor have I ever had an overbearing desire to become besmirched in the seats of power. My life can never be defined by those common attributes to which so many fruitlessly aspire. If 'success' was to be defined by what I had gained from life in terms of status, money, power and recognition, then I have failed dreadfully. If however, it was to be defined by what I have sacrificed, given, cared about or loved; I should measure up reasonably well against a number of others. The fragile human nature, the deep seats of despair which are created by a number of people in their own lives and those that are deliberately created in the lives of others, are the routes that inevitably leads perilously close to falling in with the world and falling out permanently with God. In my pride, I saw only myself but in my fall, I saw a million pair of eyes piercing me, judging and condemning me, yet it was in this moment that I was reminded of his pardon, his love and his amazing grace; what else?

Amazing Grace: What Else?

It is at this point where I wish to briefly examine the life of Paul, the Apostle to the Gentiles and explore exactly what love and humility permitted him to do. If pride was the thorn in his flesh, then humility was the crown in his life. It is conceivable that anyone can change from one alignment to another, or from an embedded set of views to liberal and open-mindedness. Paul's views, although highly demagogic and divisive yet, he was nevertheless transformed by God's grace and pardon. He was effectively, a man on a mission but the power of God made that mission, downright impossible. Imagine a man with such contempt for others and whose sole intent was to inflict hurt and suffering on those who held conflicting beliefs to his own. As a sinner persecuting the Jews in the Graeco Roman world, Paul was never ashamed of God's grace and pardon but he was very ashamed of the man he once were; reminiscent of thousands of people, both past and present. Paul was chosen in spite of his tarnished character, since; it was by virtue of his lack of conscience that he became a formidable opponent against the same state that had previously sanctioned his actions. Paul became aware of his faults the moment he met with Christ. (Acts 9:1-7).

It was in this cathartic encounter, as he journeyed to persecute innocent men and women, that he was blinded by the revelation and sight of God. Although blinded, this was in fact, the very first time where Paul could see; his errors, his weaknesses, his diminished view of others and his cold and calculating heart. The empty space beside Paul, would at last be filled; not with resentment and anger but with righteousness, instead of righteous indignation and humility instead of pride.

Paul's past life and actions was no longer a matter up for discussion; for God's compassion and mercy had dealt with them on the road to Damascus; the road that would not only lead him to freedom but would become a highway of liberty for thousands of pilgrims, centuries to come. Every time I hear the hymn; 'Amazing Grace,' by John Newton and consider the way he was living, his exploits as a slave trader and his lack of regard for those he sold in chains, when I consider the transformation that followed the final course of his life, I simply marvel at the continuance of God's grace and love. In moments such as these, I think of dozens of others just like me, wrestling with God, family, friends and with truth, until a final revelation transports me to the beginning of freedom and I immediately realise that I am no longer expulsed from the Garden of Eden but that I am in fact, being realigned with the commencement of my destiny. I have found nothing lacking in God's grace and pardon.

A number of observers may be wondering where exactly I am going with this appraisal of Paul's conversion but in order for me to fully appreciate just how far I have come on my own journey, I believe it is essential to highlight the things that have been a lasting placement in my life. Of course there are a number of things that I have deliberately omitted since, highlighting every minor detail would not be beneficial and so, I have included only those which has allowed me to move through every aspect of my life and where a noticeable improvement was unmistakable. The idea of humility and a number of elusive virtues are not what I am professing to be but what I am in fact attempting to achieve is, a complete embodiment of everything which is permitted to influence my world. Regardless of the fact of whether I have been a humble or proud person, this is simply not the journey I embarked on at the inception but that, freedom through humility would be the artery from where I could navigate securely to a 'new' fundamental beginning.

I do not believe for one moment that the story of my life is unique but what I do in fact believe is that I am unique since, there is no other person like me, nor would they wish to be like me. In spite of the difficulties I have encountered during my life, I have never complained, neither have I sought retribution from anyone who has caused me pain. I have simply viewed those periods as difficult mountains, winding roads, cascading waterfalls, dark foreboding abysses or simply, another lesson to improve the person I was created to be. The contrast with Paul is merely an illustration to highlight the power of one who is unquestionably greater, more loving and wiser than any other. It was always in my failures that God was the light in the dark places and even though I was blind, I am grateful that his redemption has brought sight and renewal to my life. I continue reiterating throughout, along the same number of themes; forgiveness, love, humility and acceptance. I have never been afraid of the darkness 'outside,' only 'inside' since, the darkness inside is impenetrable but the one outside is confident of a number of interruptions to breach its defences. I have never been a victim, neither of life nor of circumstances, what I am in fact, is a resilient and optimist woman who believes the changes she pursues always comes from within. I maintain my position from the outset that I would rather continue being excluded from everything than to be brought into a derisible 'nothing.'

I deem it highly pugnacious of those who have questioned my integrity since, we admittedly gain knowledge by questioning the unknown but when we question in arrogance with the intention to condemn, we simply become fools instead of becoming visibly enlightened. Naturally, I have seldom chosen my 'friends' but they have in fact chosen me. While I have no quarrel with individuals who possessed warped interpretations of right and wrong, good and evil, I know that I possess an unquestionably sense of fairness.

My mother used to say to me; "Those who know better should do better." So, I will not diverge from the core of my individuality since, I can never become corporate responsibility. I came into the world alone, I stood alone amidst some of my greatest fears and challenges throughout my life and it is for this reason any affiliation with any establishment would suffocate me sooner that being immersed in deep waters; in fact, the latter would be my preferred option. More recently, my focus has shifted dramatically onto others and away from myself, looking at one's self is an exhausting exercise and wholly unproductive. I believe there is simply nothing further to be gained by traversing back and forth, grinding each capricious path to rubble in my quest to find the answers that are already present within me.

My one question rule has also changed since; I have begun to find a number of people so apathetic, those who do not appoint their minds before opening their mouths. There have been so many occasions where I have been asked the most obvious questions; at least they are obvious to me, when in fact, if a few seconds consideration were given, it would be noted that the answer was in fact, in the question itself. So, if all the answers are in the questions, then I will endeavour to ask more of myself, more of others until I am satisfied and if, what I seek is continuously denied, I will offer it in return.

Fill the space left vacant

If you feel desperately unloved
Learn to give love
If you were never told you are beautiful
Learn to appreciate beauty in all you see
If they treat you with contempt;
Saying you're neither academic nor bright
Encourage others around you to sparkle
Like the stars that light the sky at night
If you try to show initiative and they name you proud
When you stand alongside them, curious to join in
And they cruelly exclude you, like an abhorrent, dreadful sin
Each time you give an opinion and they stop you dead
Your voice will grow fainter as the years roll on ahead
But while they were judging with rebuke, reproach and hate
You will silently draw strength from the wisdom gained;
For all who had emptied you
Was now looking to be filled
This cursed broken vessel; becoming the abusers' bitter pill
They had to swallow their pride, their guilt and shame

As they turned towards you sadly,

A forgotten 'worthless' name

The one whose tears remained unseen

But lovingly offered up to God

For the more you give, the less you'll cry

And the less you cried the more clearly you will see

That low self-esteem is not inherently 'me'

For it is neither who you are nor who you will remain

It's just the world's way of dealing,

With their burden of guilt and blame

Endowed in new strength, time to dismantle

Every bar every chain that hemmed you within

Now mighty steps towards the truth

As you gain your voice and you're no longer mute

And you lay down your arms and no longer fight

Assured you are loved, highly favoured;

This is a human right

Alas! Not quite there – but really close

Really close;

To confidence over fear

Inclusion over exclusion

Love over hate

Humility over pride

Success over failure;

Far too much failure

New hope in tomorrow

Joy over sorrow; from a weakened thread

To God's signet ring

Living over dying;

Far less fears and a little less crying

Really close; I must not boast

For alas! I am just half way there.

I can in particular instances get irritated by the weaknesses and flaws I see in others but I have been more than exasperated with them in my own life! I am determined however, to conqueror them daily through the power and grace which God has bestowed upon me. I abhor the wrong and wish only to pursue the right and whether I find the 'right' often or seldom, I continue along this unalterable path. I accept that absolute humility is a high ideal found in the remotest and most unexpected of places and rightly so; for how many would believe that their attainment of this virtue merited them equality with God? But since no ordinary human being has ever died in absolute humility, except the one enduring image of the Lord Jesus; beaten, rejected and pierced for the transgressions of all human beings and struggling for his last breath asked; "Father, forgive them they don't know what they do." This was Christ epitomising humility and compassion but since he did not attempt to remove himself from his suffering, he also exemplified complete obedience to God.

The Bible is not silent on the matter of humility and throughout its many passages, from Genesis through to Revelations; we can count time and time again where human beings were either in disputes with each other, or with God because of their pride and disobedience. From careful evaluation of the Bible's various Books and Chapters we can see patterns gradually emerging to the reader where humility is inextricably linked to obedience. Since God has so graciously bestowed upon all human beings a free-will in order that they may chose every direction they wish. Although many pursue morally right paths; still, a great number, through pride and disobedience will perpetually make unscrupulous choices. In Philippians 2:5-8; "Christ so graciously and obediently not demanding equality with God, but, making himself of no reputation." The humility of Christ is poignantly illustrated in John 13:12-17, of the Lord Christ, humbly washing the feet of His apostles. Humility cannot be self-supporting, it requires the rigors and demands of an inner and absolute transformation, it needs to be fully supplemented by both internal and external factors, that when combined will cause ripples and flows wherever it is seen. "Do you wish to rise? Begin by descending.

You plan a tower that will pierce the clouds? Lay first the foundation of humility." Saint Augustine. One main factor highlighting the pursuit of humility in this illustration by Augustine is honesty. Honesty with self and with others since, the seeds of humility remains dormant in the hearts of everyone but it depends upon the actions taken by individuals which allow the seeds to be transmissible. Augustine is merely reiterating Christ in Mark 9:35; Sitting down, Jesus called the twelve and said, "Anyone who wants to be first must be the very last, and servant of all." One may well ask; "How can serving many make one great"? But of course I continue to be convinced that, there is always assurance of victory, in every number greater than one.

The concept of greatness in particular cultures will vary enormously; westernised culture place much emphasis upon individual achievements, whilst others, eastern cultures in particular, are steeped in a tradition of cooperate and community achievements. A simple question that I always ask and of course I know the answer is in the question; "Is every human being of equal value"? A resounding yes since, this simply realigns the 'man' in my humanity and those who may wish to oppose my final assertion, may need to re-evaluate their integrities. The Bible is as much against pride as it is against immorality, for much of the sins visible have their origin in pride; "When pride comes, then comes disgrace, but with humility comes wisdom". Proverbs11. 2. Many people seem to 'wear' pride as a garment suited to kings and nobility without understanding the merits of a humble disposition. Through pride, I have witnessed divisions and conflicts throughout the ages; in families, between neighbours, states and nations. With the ending of mankind's oppressive rule, the transformation of the earth and all its inhabitants will become a visible reality for all. God will transform everything, from shoreline to skyline, from heads to hearts. God, the foremost inexhaustible agent of change will breathe a newness of life into all those who dare to believe in his power of change and restoration. It is God who authors the universe and the lives of believers. His words remain true and faithful; he will make all things new.

"I am Making Everything New"

Imagine being given the opportunity to begin your life all over again and the chance to avert every single place where you had previously suffered unbearable pain? Imagine that, the people who despised you were now at your side, filling the empty space that was created because of their pride? Finally, imagine a 'new' world that was perfect, one where men and women were always seeking the good of others above themselves and where all selfish ambitions and goals were swallowed up in what used to be? Then, imagine no more for in the promises of God, this is exactly what will take place; "And I heard a loud voice from the throne saying, 'Look! God's dwelling place is now among the people, and he will be dwell with them. They will be his people, and God himself will be with them and be their God. 'He will wipe every tear from their eyes. There will be no more death' or mourning or crying or pain, for the old order of things has passed away." He who was seated on the throne said, "I am making everything new!" Then he said, "Write this down, for these words are trustworthy and true." Revelation 21:3-5.

The Bible is the infallible word of God; it stands alone without support, for it is sufficient in and by itself. From Genesis through to Revelation, we have allusions of God, sometimes distant and at other times in serious confrontations with, kings, priests, prophets and his chosen people, Israel. But one remarkable observation which cannot and should not be ignored is that God is a loving and forgiving Father whose integrity remains above questioning. There are so many who wish their friends, lovers, addictions and numerous encumbrances could permanently fill the vacant space beside them but never God. I cannot understand why so many people continue to refuse to be conformed to the likeness of God yet, they imitate a vast array of unhealthy and pagan idols. In Genesis 1:27, we read; "So God created mankind in his own image, in the image of God he created them; male and female he created them." In Genesis we come face to face with the creativity of God, who in his power and wisdom brought humans from the earth and lovingly and miraculously brought man to life by breathing his living spirit into the nostrils of Adam, then Eve. It was at this point, where they became autonomous, living and creative beings. Many generations of the past have witnessed the unmistakable presence of God and whether or not one chose to believe in God or the creation reality, a lack of belief does not in any way diminish God's authority, nor does it negate his presence in the universe.

The universe simply is not sustaining in and by itself, for within every minuscule spectrum of life there is an even greater veracity and a higher authority. Although God remains invisible, those who choose to disparage or deny him, does not in the slightest way affect his position as creator and Lord. Of course this invisibility is only within human realms and perceptions or admittedly, within their lack of meaningful discernments. Understandably, the angels and all the heavenly hosts, consistently sees God face to face. The vision of humans is vastly opposing to the reality of heaven since, angelic beings are way above the wisdom and knowledge of humankind. For believers, this is the undeniable reality of God as creator, one who created everything from nothing - angels, mankind and even that demon, the devil, at the beginning and will do so again in the end – except on this occasion, the devil will be conspicuous by his long overdue absence! God does not occupy himself by skilfully creating with his 'hands' for this is what humans do; God remains in every way above those whom he have created, thus showing pre-eminence, power and sovereignty. In Genesis 1:3; And God said, "Let there be light and there was light," a God whose words brought forth life and transformation, as this narrative demonstrates the extraordinary power of God, not only in his creation of the universe but the creativity and power that he allows to penetrate the lives of men and women.

God is a God of new beginnings, a God who willingly and graciously forgives all the errors of my humanity. God is only too aware of my failings and shortcomings and it is for this reason that Christ has equipped me to be radical within my own life and far-reaching within the lives of others; whenever and wherever they permit me. I believe I should respond positively to change, be it immense or microscopic and embrace new beginnings; a sound theory but one that is not achievable in practice until I am prepared to forego off all my pre-suppositions and enter a crucial place of acceptance. There have been monumental changes where I was simply swept along and there were also subtle ones that have been equally impressive in the results they produce. Nothing is a foregone conclusion and there is a definite call on my part, for a willingness to allow myself to be guided by positive influences that facilitate change and to refuse those that limit my transformation and growth.

It was Paul the Apostle who said; "I can do all things through him who gives me strength." Philippians 4:13. An affirmation based wholly upon his faith in God since, Paul was confident that God would see him through every difficulty he encountered. The Bible speaks confidently about fear since; fear is often the power that enslaves many lives to the past, to failures, to brokenness and to addictions. The newness that has been promised in God will be the force that abolishes all the dominations from where there was no other means of escape. Fear is the opposing spectrum of faith because, the two can never co-exist; one has to supersede the other in every way. It was President Roosevelt who said; "The only thing we need to fear, is fear itself." Fear is the one thing that keeps us rigid within the same margins during the most fruitless and negative periods within our lives. People have a way of becoming perpetually incapacitated by those things they most fear. The inescapable phantoms that refuse to relinquish their hold over our fragile states and where every effort is made to break their stronghold, thus, releasing each person to move into areas of increased confidence. I recall my youngest sister Natalie at age five being attacked by a dog one morning on her way to primary school, which was in fact, an ordeal for one so young. Natalie was to become a prisoner to her fears since, the impact of her assault by the dog meant, she could barely leave the house unaccompanied and this curtailed her freedom for many years. I am uncertain as to the exact point she came to realise that not all dogs are 'biters' but wisdom and maturity were key factors in her confidence and growth.

The idea of freedom and change can produce paralysis in many individuals because, many prefer the monotony of daily tried and tested routines. God on the other hand, though he never changes, changes everything sporadically in his creation; the rain has to fall and replenish the earth, the sun has to rise and set again and the seasons must continue their cycle of change as they have always done. Within the processes of change are to be seen, the dynamics that are constantly at work, bringing together and separating as each specific function engages with its processing along definitive contours. Admittedly, if the seasons failed to change, there would be a degree of chaos within nature for what was the norm previously, would now lose its position within its own allotted place.

This can be better illustrated by the way in which airports work for the arrival and landing of aircrafts. Should a particular plane be late for its appointed slot, it would lose its priority and would have to wait until all the others that were ahead in the queue, have landed or taken off. Much the same principles apply in creation; if all the seasons were to merge into a mass, they would simply not be recognised and their distinctiveness and functioning would interleave, creating a blend of peripheral anomalies. While many people have an optimistic view of change, a large number still hold a very pessimistic view of it on many different levels.

Recently a young couple won the unbelievable sum of forty-five million pounds on the Euro Lottery and as I observed the media frenzy to interview the 'lucky' couple whose lives had changed irrevocably, I was almost deafened by the underlying cynicism that accompanied their interest. I read criticisms and unkind rumours pertaining to the couple's past and cynical views regarding that amount of money being given to two so young. Many observers described such unearned wealth as, 'obscene', [simply because it was not them that had won it], advocating how this would buy them new enemies and lose them old friends. There were further comments about their wealth opening old wounds and invariably, buying them a fast track ticket from past mistakes and struggles.

The one positive comment was the fact that this much wealth would give them the chance of a completely 'new beginning' and if managed correctly would grant them financial freedom for years to come. One of the most astonishing thing that transpired from this frenzy of having wealth beyond ones wildest dreams was the fact that, some weeks down the line the couple had swapped their former two-bedroomed home for a two hundred and fifty thousand pound detached house, apparently sandwiched between a busy main road and a housing estate.

There was a sense of incredulity in the journalists tone but I was not in the least amazed, for people however young or old, are often frightened of changes, afraid of new situations that they may view as 'too grand' for their own particular situation. There has to be willingness on the part of such individuals if they stand any chance in the future of making a successful transition to any place worth going. One simply cannot hold onto the past since, while there is much to be learnt from particular ways in which set patterns were formed and how behaviours and attitudes impact attitudes, these are transferable and can easily meet every future change. As long as there is willingness on the part of those who find themselves hurled into new situations to become more adaptable and malleable, they are better prepared for both successes and failures. This incident reminded me of Puncy, the little calf I had as a child, tied along a path at the back of the house; always with the same rope which allowed her to feed up to a point. This calf was forever pulling along the rope to get to the tasty young shoots in the neighbours garden, but the rope was secure and she could only get as far as it permitted. One day, in devilment, I decided to untie the rope just to see how far she would go. Naturally, the poor beast did not realise she was temporarily free and made no attempts whatsoever to get those tender shoots in my neighbours garden. Freedom is so much more than a principle or allusion; it is an undefined reality proving that, if one had never been a prisoner, they simply would never recognise the motifs of freedom. Freedom may simply be where one is actively engaged in life choices and where everything is no longer down to mere 'luck' or chance, [like winning the lottery] but where the freedom granted, came by way of one's humanity and that there was simply nothing that had to be accomplished to be worthy of it. Just try and recall the number of times where you placed deliberate obstacles in your way in order not to have to address your fears? "I can't go to that place, everyone will hate me," or "I won't fit in because I am different from the others." There are many times where the human mind place invisible obstacles in its own pathway to combat advancement, change, rejection, or fear and admittedly, this defence mechanism is in direct conflict with the opportunities that grants liberty.

What if an albatross always had to be reminded it was equipped with the most outstanding pair of wings, made to soar high and free above oceans, hills, valleys and mountains? Naturally, this magnificent bird would become the envy of all those fledglings that possessed inferior wings but how demoralising that, due to lack of confidence and conviction, this bird would need the approval of others every time it opened its wings to soar. I have to interject at this point and ask; "Does freedom begin in the mind or is it an illusion that can neither be grasped nor apprehended?" Some time ago whilst on safari in Kruger National Park I observed an eagle soaring high, lofty and effortlessly and I stood mesmerised, gazing up into the distance until it was no longer visible. I thought quietly to myself, "It is not wild, it is free," for the very briefest of moments, I wish I knew the type of freedom that bird was experiencing and I could not help wondering if what seemed like freedom to me, was indeed freedom to him. What questions would he pose about my life if he was able to intellectually debate the ideas of freedom and confinement? There is still much to celebrate when we become effective in relinquishing past fears and embrace new beginnings but we must have the confidence in the value and priority we place upon freedom; a true acknowledgement of the complexities and yearnings of our true and enduring humanity.

It was for this reason I chose to challenge the obstacles that were in front of me; visible or invisible, the ones that had often caused me to stumble. In fact, many of those seemingly difficult sarsens ahead were occasionally ones of my own making and since I was so akin to behaving in a particular way, I seldom recognised when they were present. As I began to grow spiritually, my enriched discernment allowed me to work through my blind optimism by finding ways either through or around those awkward areas and in so doing, brought an immense sense of peace and acceptance to all my endeavours. Admittedly, I would spend a great deal of time processing the benefits of everything and ensuring that duplicity never manipulates its way into the place of humility. Without the power of the Holy Spirit who allows me to relinquish all my previous inferences, even being in the centre of God's gracious will, watching humbly, in every situation and learning in willingness and patience, I would by no means be able to understand what God was trying to do. I would certainly not be in any position to allow God to include me in every process of change which would ultimately impact my life beyond recognition.

Christ was brought from a small town to an enormous platform from where all people would hear his 'voice.' He was able to impact each person who touched his garment, his hands, his heart and those who acted upon his words. In the revelation of the new things that

Christ came to the world to both fulfil and complete, he was the complete embodiment of all such revelations and refused to stand on ceremony to please his accusers but in defence of his authority and divinity, stood unwaveringly on all matters of truth and principle.

Standing, because of Him

In Ephesians 6:13-15; we see encouragement being given for all to stand, "Therefore put on the full armour of God, so that when the day of evil comes, you may be able to stand your ground, and after you have done everything, to stand. Stand firm then, with the belt of truth buckled around your waist, with the breastplate of righteousness in place, and with your feet fitted with the readiness that comes from the gospel of peace." We are all encouraged to stand, whatever else we fail to do, we should stand and this of course is only possible when we are armoured with faith which is a gracious gift through the in-dwelling of the Holy Spirit. There is something commendable about standing in the face of adversity, danger and disappointment; one of my favourite idioms; "The more it hurts the stronger I become." Of course it is better when life runs smoothly without the wounds and bandages, the postponed dreams and far-reaching hopes. It is often those people with the strongest voices who are most silent, sitting instead of standing, until the moment where real courage is demanded from them. There is a notable shift in their behaviour and immediately one is aware of who is amongst them. For those who refuse to stand up for anything; they are usually the very people who spend a majority of their lives falling down. Imagine a tree that was unable to mature to its full potential and had to be supported by reinforced sticks and twigs in order that it may stand but in actual fact, the twigs and sticks that are largely disregarded by the gardener are doing a far better job that the tree! It would become such a frustrating enterprise that eventually the gardener would chop it down completely since he got tired of helping it to stand. This is excruciatingly disappointing. True courage in the face of adversity is not about having all the right answers but finding appropriate solutions; solutions that invariably reinforce a weakened position and secure all known breaches.

Some years ago I was travelling around the UAE with my companion in a Toyota Land Cruiser and having arrived at a half-way point in the middle of the Hatta desert, decided to take a much needed comfort break. This was at a time when foreign women had to be completely covered up; naturally, it is their country and their rules, so respect yourself and them, do it. We stopped and were met by a group of young men who directed my companion to an area some distance round the back of the tent like structure and I was directed to the little stalls inside selling all kinds of novelties and souvenirs. Without noticing immediately, I was deliberately escorted to the very back of the tent and I suddenly realised that the only way out was the same way I had entered; only now there were six young Muslim men standing defiantly in my way and they began advancing menacingly towards me. I seldom panic in difficult and tense situations but for a brief moment began feeling annoyed and a little concerned and so, I kept moving back until I had ran out of space to move any further. I realised that the two men who had escorted my companion to the back of the tent, must be delaying his return and it began to feel like he had walked back to Bur Dubai leaving me to fend off these scoundrels alone.

I remember feeling hot and angry by this deliberate 'entrapment' but I also realised that I had to turn the situation around to my advantage since, this was the only way I would regain my composure and sense of safety. I knew the only way out was to march straight at them with confidence and strength and without a moment to draw my breath, I began my advance against them as though I was being shunted by a giant arm. Although a little nervous, I looked neither to the left nor right and kept marching straight ahead until I reached the exit and was reunited a few minutes later with my companion who had no idea of the predicament I had left immediately behind me.

Throughout that briefest of walk to safety, I kept reminding myself of that documentary I had watched a number of years ago where the Black Panther held his ground against an unruly mob of Baboons; "It's not the size of the animal but the spirit of the beast." There are occasions when it is almost acceptable to feel vulnerable or threatened but I refuse to allow anyone who has caused me to feel this way, to ever know that for a brief moment they truly had shaken the ground around me but as long as there is still a fraction of earth beneath me I will keep walking; to safety, to freedom, to truth and to wherever my call of faith takes me, I will stand.

I suspect that those men were not wicked, for if they were, I would not have stood a realistic chance against six of them; they simply pushed the boundaries as far as they could but when it remained inflexible, they retreated. This is the way a number of people function in the world; they are always testing boundaries, seeing what is permissible before the inevitable halt signs appear. The determination of human beings allows many to forge their characters and resolve during failure or a potential fall. Many will seek to underscore those things that empower them into new and fiercely challenging situations where they had previously failed. As I have matured in wisdom, I have become more astute concerning right and wrong and more able to discern real danger from fictitious inventions created in my mind or by others.

I believe that humans possess only two known fears; fear of failure in self and the fear of success in others; many wishing to extinguish another persons' light before they are given the opportunity to shine. It was Johann Wolfgang Von Goethe [1749 - 1832], who said; "Treat people as they were what they ought to be and you will help them become what they are capable of becoming." This is a very astute assertion by Wolfgang, for indeed, if a different principle was to be applied to all living beings; a tree for example, that did not receive an equal amount of sunshine and rain, would simply not reach its full potential but if one were to tend it lovingly, giving it all that was needed to facilitate growth and strength to maturity, that tree would proudly affirm its position alongside all other trees of its kind and would not be conspicuous in its appearance. The inescapable human nature that inclines towards malevolent acts remains undiminished as I continue to witness the impact that the actions of a minority creates in the lives of others.

Although I refrain from making harsh judgements against many of the perpetrators of immoral actions in the world, it is very difficult to remain silent on such a deafening planet. Of course there are those people who refuse to surrender to the insecurities of others and whether they are granted approval or not, will pursue the life they believe is right for them. I simply cannot find anywhere in the Bible where God speaks of the human life as a vehicle of glory for another. For when it comes to glory, all human beings are limping blindly in the shadows of the almighty God through whose power and design the world and everything in it was made. This is clear from the very outset; "In the beginning God created the heavens and the earth," not some unknown culture, amoeba, or 'big bang' theory but a divine and powerful God whose authority and wisdom knows neither beginning nor end. There is neither beginning nor end to God for he is a Contiuum occupying a timeless, ageless and space less spiritual dimension that connects directly in the hearts and minds of men and women. From this spiritual attachment God has direct access to the thoughts, intentions, desires and hopes of every human being. A reassurance for those who love and obey his words but a stumbling block to those who are far from his will and purposes. God is more than outstanding and greater than the highest excellence, a God who knows every wrong-doing that goes out from the hearts of men and women into the universe. In John 1:2; "In the beginning was the word, and the word was with God, and the word was God. He was with God in the beginning." If God is effectively 'the word,' making perfectly good sense and those same words word were expressed over creation, bringing everything to life, the Bible is effectively God since, he is inextricably linked to his words.

God is as faithful as he is reliable; nothing stands unless they are rooted within the cornerstones of his words. This suggests that since he pays so much attention to words, he will bring all to judgement for the words they should or should not have spoken but especially the deeds a person should or should not have done. So many individuals bend so easily in weakness that it would be no surprise in the future to see a majority of men and women walking bent over in permanently stooped positions. So many enable their wishbones instead of their backbones, especially concerning fear and exclusion, hence many follow the crowds everywhere, without the least pause to question the integrity of the one leading the 'herd.'

I remember many years ago being told a story of a poor donkey who had been thrown into a pit and left to die. All who passed by was equally cruel, for instead of rescuing the poor beast, they hurled stones into the pit hitting the donkey; this is human nature at its absolute worst and those things we fail to understand become the focus of our derision and hostilities. I have found an inconsistent pattern of behaviour in human beings, some have proved worthy of many virtues, while others, if they possess any, for me such qualities simply could not be apprehended. This lack of goodness and integrity spans the boundaries of culture, race, religion and gender. I simply have no preference over man or woman; men have been demons and women have allowed them a free reign and have been complicit in the suffering of their children. I cannot denounce a person over their religion since, there is only one God and if I witness devotion and willingness to serve him then I cannot criticise. I have no preference over race, for there is but one; the human race and in all of these sub-families there are good and evil men and women.

I married white men because they happened to be the men I loved and trusted the most at that time. My heart seems more inclined to the persuasion of European men, not because they possess hidden depths which merits my attention but because they are like fortified rooms, locked securely day and night but in an instant, I can bypass this nonsensical posturing and find an array of little books; open, amusing and predictable.   I believe I have been loved but not nearly enough, for those who declared they 'loved' me, was in fact the very ones who caused the greatest pain within my life. I am confident I have been loved sincerely by one man in my whole life and he possesses sufficient goodness and integrity to withstand many of the struggles we encounter day by day. Every night he is by my side and whether awake or sleeping, he continues to safeguard as many of my future dreams as he is capable of capturing.

I firmly believe in the sanctity of marriage and enjoy the companionship and commitment of this institution more than any other. This is God's gift revealed and I will do my utmost to honour God and my husband in my fortitude and to appreciate the joys as well as the sorrows, in the sharing of everything with this exceptional man. I have been married all of my adult life and has a deep sense of duty and loyalty within its boundaries and of course one error of poor judgement almost destroyed the one thing in my life I most value and has brought me the most stability and the greatest joy. But I thank God that he is both loving and forgiving and he always suspends his judgement of me when others choose to sentence me to 'death' or banish me to purgatory in absence of a judge and jury. A majority of people are at their most animated when witnessing the public 'execution' of another person. I am always grateful of the one enduring fact however, that there is always assurance of victory in every number greater than one, for God plus one is always a majority!

I may not be 'dressed' in excessive titles awarded by the queen and her subjects to bring me renown but my preferred garments are strength, dignity and integrity. My lips may not be perfumed and as necessary as fine wines and exquisite champagnes but they speak only the truth. I have no aspiration to associate myself with men whose only wish is to satisfy their sensual desires, for I believe that destiny is far greater than any amount of appeasing a person's physical appetite. I honour the mouths of men, not because they may yearn to be kissed by me or any other but I honour them for speaking truth over lies and advocating justice for the poor, the marginalised and also those oppressed. I do not concern myself with popularity or the opinions of those who knows nothing of my life and I have no desire to be remembered for being 'popular' but would sooner be appreciated for fulfilling my destiny. For me, it is far more productive to be with a few people who are seriously committed than to be with an army of reckless and selfish individuals.

There have men who have followed me for as long as I can remember; at sixteen I was followed from the bus every morning to college, at eighteen it was the Irish man from the newsagent. This was a time in my life that could have been disturbing but as always, I retained a sense of humour throughout it all. At twenty two; hallelujah! I passed my driving test and I began to feel safe for a brief spell until I started being followed in my car and would have to take detours miles away from home until the pursuant got bored and abandoned his 'chase.' There have been some extremely brave souls who have followed me into shops and restaurants and asked for my telephone number but when the inevitable halt sign appeared, they invited me to their church instead. How strange that in a fraction of a second a man wanted me to become his 'lover' and when I declined, he beseeched me to become his 'sister.' The idea of incestuous relationships is both repugnant and inexcusable to me and the church appears to cover over a multitude of known sins? I remember my mother's admonishments to me as a young girl against becoming ensnared in a life of promiscuity; the type she had witnessed in young women in newspapers, television and generally in the communities around her; "dem jus like clothes peg, queese dem head, dem foot open," effectively she was telling me a promiscuous woman was like a clothes peg; squeeze her head and her legs open.

Whether this was another scaremongering tactic on my mother's part is beside the point, for to me, she was always the 'last word.' I am so grateful mama taught me that it was not necessary for any woman to be loved effortlessly, completely and passionately more than once in her life, for when this happens, everything else becomes tarnished, unimpressive and wholly uninspiring. I could not imagine anything worse than to spend the remainder of my life making unfavourable comparisons about the one I had most loved, cherished and admired. This is the first time that I am fully able to step cautiously alongside my 'namesake,' Sophia Loren, in my own shoes and stand in full agreement on the matter of loving another after the greatest love of her life; a complete impossibility for the foreseeable future. Whenever I was faced with a potential suitor in the past, I would make him jump through hoops as high as heaven, I would make him fly in contest with the angels and I would ask him to walk backwards through the Antarctic with no shoes. I would tell him I found him dismal and unimpressive, I would ask him to count the stars and then bring them into my lap, one by one. Did I say I really asked all that of another fragile human being just like myself? No not me. If any man was foolish enough and wished to have my heart; all I would ask of him is that he first circumcised his mind and his body and after all his internal purging and cleansing "If he still wanted my heart, he must first give his to the Lord."

I am never inspired or impressed by the external appearance of anything or anyone and I care neither for wealth, status nor the position an individual holds but I am especially concerned with those essential values to which they cling and 'worship.' I am a firm believer that whatever 'god' a man or woman worships they will eventually become; if one worships alcohol, they usually become an alcoholic, or if its drugs, they invariably becomes a drug addict. If they worship money and power, the dark unreachable vacuum that is created within them becomes unsustainable and unquenchable and it is for this very reason, whenever they cross my pathway, I must always excavate deeper, much deeper until I finally reach the depth of the man, from where I can begin the rapturous work of recovery that leads to fascinating avenues and endless discoveries. If I find traces of humility, this is a ground-breaking revelation, if there were aspects of integrity there is much hope for a man such as this. But greater than all of these is an undeniable sense of identity in Christ; a man like this is already on the road to greatness but his humility prevents him from becoming preoccupied with this notion of accomplishment. I am grateful I have never been on the perpetual treadmill of relationships and while there have been few fairy-tale endings, I am optimistic that much of the delightful dynamics between two people are equally present and vibrant at the very beginning and throughout the most promising happenstance. So, with such poor understanding of what constitutes a 'happy ending' since, I am continuously in pursuit of new beginnings, I nevertheless remain extremely grateful that I was incredibly gifted at finding resolutions to almost every challenge I faced and was often able to turn many to an advantageous position.

The donkey in my earlier depiction was no dumb ass neither, for he recognised that the very stones meant to injury him was in fact the same ones that would allow him to climb up slowly and escape to freedom. There have been so many individuals during my life who have opposed me on almost every level imaginable and who believed it their right to become 'taskmasters' over me. This was not because they saw me as weak and inconsequential but because they possess a hideous notion that I am neither worthy nor good enough to stand beside them or alongside others; whether in their joy or in their sorrows and preferred in essence, that the empty space beside those hurting was better left vacant, than for me to be inserted there. This unwarranted impunity levelled against me was naturally another way to further damage my self-esteem and identity. Logically, distress and repression changes the focus of any one suffering under intense scrutiny and encumbrance. Obviously, my inner strength and resolve allowed me to find a way and thus, chronicling those periods as the most productive and triumphant of my life.

Those individuals like me, who possess an indomitable human spirit accompanied by an unbreakable will, do in fact increase our strength under the banner of oppression. In Exodus 1:12 we can see a clear illustration of this thought where the Children of Israel began to multiply under the torment of Pharaoh in Egypt. In spite of years of torture and suffering the Israelites displayed a complete lack of regard for their Egyptian slave masters whose attempts to destroy their identity and break their spirit proved both retributive and momentous against their oppressors. When Christ said in Matthew 5:39; "But I tell you, do not resist an evil person. If anyone slaps you on the right cheek, turn to them the other cheek also." This admonishment is almost unbearable and my one question to God in response to this remains unchanged; "If I don't stand up against hostility and indifference, who will stand up for me?" Paul explained the answer very eloquently in Romans 8: 31; "What then shall we say in response to these things? If God is for us, who can be against us?" And so, I simply allowed everyone to treat me as they wished; because God continues to be my defence in the same way he has defended all those who have suffered rejection, those despised, afflicted, brutalised and judged throughout the ages. In Psalm 94:16 we can see where the psalmist David is affirming this very promise of God; "Who will rise up for me against the wicked? Who will take a stand for me against evildoers?" From this passage of Scripture I am assured that the position that God asserts on my behalf is one of 'standing' and in this action, I am confident that through all the challenges of life, like Christ, I too will stand.

I know the love and consolation that God imparts to believers is as important as life itself and no one can harm anyone who remains completely in his care. And even though I have gone through some challenging situations, God has remained in control throughout them all. Moses, [a typical example of God's ultimate power at work] was downhearted to have missed out on the 'promised land' but this teaches me optimism over pessimism and triumph over what may initially appear as defeat. For many who believe they have failed because they missed out on what they thought was the 'big plan,' are to be reminded like myself, that God is in control of all things; for although Moses did not set foot into that special place he nevertheless gained access to a place greater and higher than that of his people; he was ushered straight in the centre of God's eternal promise; the man who did not get the land, but got the promise instead! This is God at his best and humanity at its worst, for we always focus upon the material and perceptible elements, where God's focus bypasses all of these transitory entrapments.

God knows where all our focuses are for it is by him that our thoughts are given form, life and direction and it is God who ultimately decides on the outcome of everything concerning those whom he have created. God is good, he exemplifies goodness and he is also the one who prevents us from becoming consumed by every type of evil. This thought can be better supported in Isaiah 54:16; "See, it is I who created the blacksmith who fans the coals into flame and forges a weapon fit for its work. And it is I who have created the destroyer to wreak havoc." This is a clear demonstration by Isaiah that God is in control of all things; upholding good and crushing evil. Of course we are further reminded in the continuation of that passage that "No weapons forged against us will prevail." God continue to protect the lives and destiny of all those who have surrendered to his will. We can further understand God's love and power from Psalm 94:18-19; when I said, "My foot is slipping," your unfailing love, LORD, supported me. When anxiety was great within me, your consolation brought me joy."

I understand from the Bible that all suffering borne by humans is nothing to do with the absurd pagan notion that God willingly inflicts punishment on mankind. This is wholly contrary to the plan of a suffering God who was nailed to a cross in order to halt the unbearable eternal anguish of every life that he himself had created from mystery and wisdom. Suffering sadly, is an inherent part of the human condition which is inescapable and is only permitted in order that every human being can choose authoritatively and unquestionably the righteous paths, leading straight to God's purpose and promise. I am encouraged and strengthened daily as Christ walks alongside me in light of his glorious resurrection and exaltation and so, I remain empowered in the fact that "Greater is he that is in me than he that is in the world," 1 John 4:4. Christ chose long before I was born to assume my place and to walk in my shoes, inserting himself in the empty space by my side and subsequently, absorbing all my sin and guilt. Because of this knowledge I have longed surrender all my insecurities, faults and failures to him in complete humility, which has allowed me to accept the image he graciously reflects back to me daily as a true, untarnished and unbroken vessel fit for purpose. For when God proclaimed that this is undeniably who I am in him, no one can supersede his final valuation of me.

Naturally, this image I knew and trusted from time to time became ambiguous under a number of difficult circumstances and created moments where I had to outthink a number of my adversaries. While it was never my intention to gather all the stones thrown at me over the years into a pile and wait for an opportune moment to hurl them back into the path of each offender; it seemed to make perfectly good sense when I have been heartlessly and maliciously judged by so many who knows nothing of my life and character. Admittedly, I have lost my direction on a number of occasions but this has proved an invaluable part of my progression to freedom because; "Sometimes we must lose our direction in order to find our way." Whenever I am now faced with new challenges I immediately recognise them as strategies to offset my course towards my destiny and so, from this point I began to appreciate the complexity of each situation and processes within my life. For no sooner that I became complacent I found I was faced with something new with the potential to overwhelm me once more but with persistence and courage, I am now able to avert or manoeuvre around every difficult junction or obstruction ahead. In the past decade I have begun to rejoice and celebrate when certain things disappears from my life and instead of weeping for what has been lost, I celebrate what remains.

I have lost many battles in my life but have won the important wars; the war from poverty, the war from physical, emotional and psychological abuse, the war from a lack of knowledge to wisdom, the war from insecurity to safety, the war from exclusion to inclusion; though only in part and the acceptance of a once broken image restored back to me. My life has been one of victory; victory over adversity, laughter instead of tears and standing firmly once more after I was pushed down against the hostile and unyielding ground. I recall my father saying; "nuh bady neva kick a ded dawg," meaning, no one kicks a dead dog; effectively saying, an aspiring person is always subjected to criticism. I am now more willing to acknowledge all my limitations and for this reason have never wished to compare my life to the lives of others; I would not like it nor could I live it! I have simply gathered these stones together to make the strongest connection possible in order that I too may scale a wall to liberty; from purgatory to self-worth, bondage to autonomy and hate to love and complete my journey of triumph and freedom, across the bridge of dignity and humility.

If I should be judged further, especially in view of the brief walk in my shoes then, I shall let you the jurors decide. So whoever is without fault, let them step forward and throw yet another stone, initiating ripples on the past, overwhelming the present and eradicating the future; – innocent or guilty? You are the adjudicator. Remember however, there is always a unanimous victory in every number greater than one. Soli Deo Gloria!

Postscript I

Knowledge Speaks; Wisdom Listens

There is something that pride does to the human mind; it makes it impoverished it makes it blind.

If you are going to cause the earth to tremble under the feet of others, make sure it is because you are blazing a path behind you, and creating a multi-lane highway ahead for those who will follow after you.

Concern yourselves with likeminded individuals who hold your interest in the highest regard, and whose commitments to others far outweigh their commitments to themself.

God in His relationship with humankind watches meticulously with wisdom and will only intervene when a 'man' is in desperate need of a little lift up; or a big put down.

The burden of fame, the quest for riches, the unfaithful friends, the genuine enemies; are all paths which causes humans to stumble.

What you don't want your enemies to know, don't tell your friends

The only person that one should control, is the self

A powerful head and a gentle heart; a perfect combination

God gave us His best when we deserved His worst; yet we continue to give Him our worst when he deserves our best.

Perfect silence is a haunting, a stirring deep within the vacuous mind of man, a flowing, tilting, sliding in a rhythmic pulse. Yet nothing is rousing, other than faith and hope, as one is realigned with nature, with the creation of all things. A timely recognition of the last great mystery in the universe, in this rare enchantment, the soul begins a dance of life, as it illuminates the answer, which is; the very reason to which 'man' is born.

As long as you have not given up; the battle is not yet lost.

Life - the more I surrender to God, the greater my joys the lesser my fears.

It's not demons I'm afraid of, its mankind, for even demons fear the name of God. But mankind possess only two know fears, they are; the fear of failure in themselves and the fear of success in others.

The world is a devastating battlefield where all its peoples are destined to be wounded in degrees; a few will be mildly wounded, others severely wounded, with the majority predestined to be fatally wounded.

There are no errors in the truth - just in lies.

If the Lord God is so big and so mighty that he fills both heaven and earth: how is it possible therefore, that having created the heaven, earth, constellations and unknown spheres and galaxies; that he still fits into heaven and earth? A God who is big enough to fill both heaven and earth but 'small' and wise enough to fill and fit right into my heart. Awesome God!

Some people cannot bury the past because they have such little depth to

them

If you seek elevation from a lowly position; ask God. It's a fact that a majority of people find it entertaining and empowering to look down on others. So few are sufficiently gifted with humility to allow another to rise above them; they simply have never learned that all the greatest men and women look up, not down.

A majority of men simply do not know the difference between a boardroom and a bedroom; one is for resolving a majority of pressing difficulties, the other is for pressing oneself deeper into them.

I am not outstanding because I have a pair of legs; but standing out because of my outstanding faith in God.

Too many people; too little purpose

My convictions will never change, for the day that I stop believing what I believe in; is the day I stop living, stop breathing

If all else fails; at least I have tried to succeed and in the trying have managed to beat all attempts of the enemy who tried to convince me success was about awards and prizes; another vile untruth- for if I am not sufficient without man-made awards and prizes, I will never be enough with them.

In me they are merely words; but when my heavenly Father comes alongside me, they are words full of healing, conviction and power.

Seek courage when you are afraid, source a little flicker of natural light when darkness surround your pathway, and always show humility whenever you are triumphant.

If you do not have the truth present within you; you have no means of defence when faced with devastating and crushing lies.

Allow God into the 'frame'; and don't let him be just a name.

Real love is your footsteps before they hit the ground

When you open your eyes to self you open them to all

If you want to be distressed look inside, to be defeated look back, to be distracted look around, but if you wish to be delivered look up.

Whatever you wish to see at 'play' in the world, work hard at it yourself. If you wish to see love, then give love, and kindness, and compassion and so on.

Strength: Suffering builds character, character, perseverance, perseverance, hope. With hope comes identity, identity reinforces strength.

How can you tell how much a person really loves themself? Observe how tenderly they hold others in their suffering.

The longest thing I have ever known; Time. The shortest thing I have ever seen, Time. The sweetest memories from my storehouse; Time. The bitterest thing I have tasted; Time.

Every night you hold my dreams aloft and whisper ever so softly that I must continue to reach for the stars for you are hiding amongst them.

If I can kneel before a mighty and merciful God; I can stand before any number of sinful men.

Gentle people are not weak; just clever

Acknowledgements

I wish to thank all the members of my caring and supportive family, especially my sister and best friend Carol Davis whose strive for continuing excellence throughout her life has been the thing which I most admire. I also wish to thank my brother Wayne, who is a great friend and confidant. I wish to express a heartfelt thank you to my 'adoptive family' at my local gym, with particular attention to my friend Carol who for so many years has expressed her struggle to have the 'perfect' body, but comes week after week armed with so much encouragement for others. I celebrate her generosity of spirit and thoughtfulness.

There are so many men and women who remain unacknowledged simply because they do not have friends in what might be described as 'high places', which in fact is another vile untruth, for everyone who has God at the centre of his or her world, has the greatest and most influential friend in the highest of positions. I much prefer nowadays to have 'high' friends in low places, than 'low' friends in high places. My God exemplifies this, for he shows interest and concern for the humble and those suffering, the broken and despised. In psalm 18:16; "He reached down from on high and took hold of me; he drew me out of deep waters." The incredible power and love of God who, despite his high and lofty position, reaches down to the seats of pain, misery and suffering and draw each person unto himself; God's best always meets humanity's worst and this is the beginning of every spiritual human revolution and transformation of mind, soul and destiny.

I would also to thank Dorothy Thompson, 'auntie' Pet, Richard Mason, Tommy and Noel Anderson for the kindness and courtesy they have shown to me week after week. I see so much of myself in them and in many ways they resemble me; for they understand my silent struggles, my pursuit for a place in the world because much of their dreams are also temporarily suspended between probability and real possibility. They are never afraid to correct me if I appear to falter and will do so only from a place of gentleness and compassion. I would like to thank God for the man he has placed at the centre my life, Christopher; the one who shares every joy, sorrow and adventure. I have met interesting people, kind and thoughtful people, people who profess to have unyielding faith in God but I have yet to meet a kinder and more generous heart. Whilst Christopher may have no particular claims to a Christian life as such, he has by far outweighed many of the feeble excuses for Christians that I have encountered during my life.

And finally, to my wonderful sons, Daniel and Thomas; I give you my heart and my love, absolutely and unconditionally. I genuinely wish to express to you the drive for excellence you both observe in the world and to highlight the fact that this ideology is not driven by men and women who are themselves exemplifiers of excellence; it is often a façade created around them, obscuring both truth and meaning, and it is only those who dare to look deeper into fundamentals, ethics and real values who will excavate the real fragile, suffering souls, masquerading under the semblance of distinction in order to keep themselves aloft. I therefore, implore you both to be the very best that you can be, marked only by those benchmarks that you create for yourselves, for no sooner you begin to run the race with the masses, you fall victim at the first hurdle. If you are tired, rest, if you are confused, ask the right person the right questions and if you have reason to doubt, stand back and reconsider. Just remember to continue trusting God throughout your lives.

Finally and most importantly, to the God and Father of our Lord Jesus Christ; who walked into my life when the world walked out and who has strengthened, restored and endowed me with wisdom and every blessing to be the woman he has called me to become. I believe this call concerns being faithful in matters of principle and to speak my truth with love and with the conviction of the Holy Spirit; the exemplified facilitator, and finally and most importantly, to Love Him [God], above all else, as stated in the 'Greatest Commandment' in Matthew 22:37-39 and to love my neighbour as myself. As demanding and as agonizing as it can be to love those who are often the ones who has caused the greatest pain within my life; the neighbour who is un-neighbourly, unforgiving, proud and self-seeking, yet I know I will have failed miserably as a human being, if I simply cannot love my neighbour as much as I love myself.

I asked for riches that I may be happy; I was given poverty of experience and the soul that I might be wise. I asked for all things that I may enjoy life, I was given life that I may enjoy all things. I was given nothing that I had asked for but everything that I had hoped for.   (Author Unknown).

ABOUT THE AUTHOR

Sheryl Sophia Sleigh – BA (Hons) Theology, Dip. Couns

Sheryl spends much of her time supporting people faced with extreme difficulties in their lives and also those she believes society has simply overlooked. Whilst she does not advocate to any particular organisation she possesses a deep sense of social justice and intervenes wherever she finds a vacant space and is permitted to do so. She has travelled extensively around the world and believes that it is from her many journeys that much of her inspiration has been drawn. She enjoys playing the saxophone, poetry, teaching and public speaking. She is a fighter, wife, mother and a Born-Again Christian.

To contact the Author, visit www.time4reflection.com